STUDIES IN HISTORY, ECONOMICS AND PUBLIC LAW

Edited by the
FACULTY OF POLITICAL SCIENCE
OF COLUMBIA UNIVERSITY

Number 155

THE REVIEW OF AMERICAN COLONIAL LEGISLATION BY THE KING IN COUNCIL

BY

ELMER BEECHER RUSSELL

THE REVIEW OF AMERICAN COLONIAL LEGISLATION BY THE KING IN COUNCIL

BY

ELMER BEECHER RUSSELL

OCTAGON BOOKS

A DIVISION OF FARRAR, STRAUS AND GIROUX

New York   1976

Reprinted 1976
by special arrangement with Columbia University Press

OCTAGON BOOKS
A DIVISION OF FARRAR, STRAUS & GIROUX, INC.
19 Union Square West
New York, N.Y. 10003

Library of Congress Cataloging in Publication Data

Russell, Elmer Beecher, 1885-
 The review of American colonial legislation by the King in
council.

 Reprint of the ed. published by Columbia University, New York,
which was issued as v. 64, no. 2, whole no. 155 of Studies in
history, economics, and public law.

 Originally presented as the author's thesis, Columbia University.

 1. Law—United States. 2. Law—West Indies. 3. Great Britain
—Privy Council. 4. Law—Great Britain—Colonies. 5. United
States—Politics and government—Colonial period, ca. 1600-
1775. I. Title. II. Series: Columbia studies in the social sci-
ences; no. 155.

KF361.R88 1976   340'.0973   76-14457
ISBN 0-374-96994-9

Manufactured by Braun-Brumfield, Inc.
Ann Arbor, Michigan
Printed in the United States of America

PREFACE

THE power exercised by the English Privy Council, of annulling the enactments of the royal colonies, afforded the home government an important instrument of administrative control. It constituted a necessary check upon the only branch of the colonial governments which was responsive to popular sentiment, and gave the English executive a final word in regard to the minutest details of local administration in the dominions. Its importance both to the mother country and to the colonies, together with the fact that no detailed study of its operation has heretofore appeared, constitute the justification for this work.

The author realizes keenly the limitations of this monograph. It is primarily a study of the action taken upon colonial legislation by the English government; and only incidentally does it consider the purpose and contents of the enactments which met with favor at the Privy Council, or which provoked the royal veto. In its preparation the writer has confined himself very largely to the use of materials which present the English point of view in regard to colonial administration. A careful and systematic examination of the colonial laws, together with a study of the legislative journals and other sources which reflect the aims of the assemblies, and reveal some of the forces at work therein, would shed additional light upon the whole subject, and might modify to a considerable degree the conclusions reached as to the effectiveness of the Council's work of review. This study, as its title indicates, is also confined largely to the continental colonies which afterward became part of the American union. A well-rounded treatment of the government's attitude toward all the colonial assemblies and its action upon their legislation would necessitate an examination of extensive manuscript material relating to the island colonies which the author lacked the time to undertake. A study thus broadened in scope would probably afford little additional light upon either the procedure or the policy of the government in legislative review. But it is essential to any just and definitive conclusion as to the results and effectiveness with which that policy was pursued.

This work is based primarily upon manuscript material in the Public Record Office, London. Some eighty-odd volumes of the *Board of Trade Journal* give a fairly detailed account of the Board's participation in colonial administration prior to 1776. This has been supplemented by the *Original Papers* and the *Entry Books* which are listed at the Record Office and referred to in this volume under the call number "*CO/5*". The former include papers addressed to the Board by governors and other colonial officials, law reports and copies of orders in council. The latter comprise letters from the Board to the governors, commissions and instructions, Board " Representations " and other papers which were copied for convenient reference by the clerks of the Board into large folios. Extensive use has also been made of the printed material in the *Acts of the Privy Council, Colonial Series*, and the volumes of the *Calendar of State Papers, Colonial Series*, which relate to America and the West Indies.

The kindness and courtesy of the officials and attendants at the Record Office is gratefully acknowledged. This work was undertaken at the suggestion of Professor Herbert L. Osgood, of Columbia University, and has been carried to completion under his guidance and helpful criticism. To him the author's most sincere thanks are due.

ELMER B. RUSSELL.

NEW YORK CITY, FEBRUARY 19, 1915.

TABLE OF CONTENTS

CHAPTER I

INTRODUCTORY—THE REVIEW OF COLONIAL LEGISLATION PRIOR TO 1696

CHAPTER II

The Procedure of the English Government in Legislative Review

CHAPTER III

The Procedure of the Government in Legislative Review (Continued)

CHAPTER IV

THE POLICY OF THE GOVERNMENT IN LEGISLATIVE REVIEW—TRADE
SHIPPING AND FINANCE

CHAPTER V

THE POLICY OF THE BRITISH GOVERNMENT IN LEGISLATIVE REVIEW : INSISTENCE UPON CONFORMITY TO THE LAW OF ENGLAND

CHAPTER VI

THE POLICY OF THE BRITISH GOVERNMENT IN LEGISLATIVE REVIEW : ATTITUDE TOWARD ENCROACHMENTS UPON THE PREROGATIVE

CHAPTER VII

THE POLICY OF THE BRITISH GOVERNMENT IN LEGISLATIVE REVIEW: ATTITUDE TOWARD LAWS DEEMED INEXPEDIENT

CHAPTER VIII

THE RESULTS OF LEGISLATIVE REVIEW

CHAPTER I

INTRODUCTORY; THE REVIEW OF COLONIAL LEGISLATION PRIOR TO 1696

THE English government in its royal colonies exercised what was virtually a double check upon the activities and enactments of the colonial legislatures. By instructions to the governor it insured the veto of anticipated legislation of objectionable character, and more or less effectively curbed his conduct as a constituent part of the law-making body. And furthermore it required that all enactments be transmitted to England, where they were subject to examination by the Privy Council and its subordinate bodies, and if deemed objectionable to a summary disallowance. The exercise of this power imposed upon a government, far removed and much occupied with larger concerns, a necessity of grappling with numerous problems, which although of domestic import, were nevertheless of immediate and far-reaching importance to the colonial inhabitants. Moreover, it often confronted the English authorities with the delicate and dangerous necessity of finding a basis of conciliation between the political ideas and economic interests of the Empire, and the apparently diverging ideas and interests of the several colonies which were struggling separately towards a political self-consciousness. It is, therefore, significant that when the Continental Congress came to cast about for grievances which would justify the impending separation from the mother country, they made the alleged abuse of this control over the colonial assemblies the basis of eight counts in the indictment summoning their tyrannical sovereign to the bar of a candid world.

It is the purpose of this study to trace from its beginnings the exercise of the government's power of reviewing colonial legislation; to examine the administrative bodies of the English government engaged in the task, their composition, manner of procedure, and attitude toward colonial problems; to find, if possible, what the government sought to accomplish by the confirmation or disallowance of laws; to form some estimate of its success or failure in achieving these aims; to consider whether the restrictions imposed by this system of legislative review were in any real sense a hardship and a grievance to the colonists; and, finally, to inquire whether it may be said to have prepared the way for the judicial annulment of laws subsequently practised under the constitutions of the several states and of the United States.

No regular and systematic review of colonial legislation was undertaken by the Privy Council or Parliament, or by their committees, prior to the Restoration of 1660. Nor does it appear that any colonial law was confirmed or disallowed during this period. The Virginia charter of 1606 assumed that " Laws, Ordinances and Instructions " should originate in the crown and pass under the privy seal of England; while that of 1609 conferred upon a council the power to make " all Manner of Orders, Directions, Instructions, Forms and Ceremonies of Government and Magistracy," and imposed no restriction upon the exercise of it.[1] Beginning with the third Virginia charter of 1612, however, grants conferring the law-making power invariably stipulated that acts should be not contrary nor repugnant to the laws and statutes of England. This document im-

---

[1] Macdonald, *Select Charters*, pp. 5, 14.

powered the treasurer and the company in the four general assemblies held each year, " to ordain and make such Laws and Ordinances, for the good and welfare of the said Plantation, as to them from time to time, shall be thought requisite and meet: So always, as the same be not contrary to the Laws and Statutes of this our Realm of England." [1] A similar proviso appears in the patent of the Council of New England, issued in 1620, and in the first charter of Massachusetts, issued in 1628-9.[2] The Maryland charter of 1632, which provided for a colonial assembly, stipulated not only that laws should be not repugnant and that they be "(so far as conveniently may be) agreeable " to those of England, but also that they be "consonant to reason," [3] —a restriction which appears in many subsequent grants of importance.[4] The Privy Council decided in 1629 that laws " ordained " by the " grand assembly " of Virginia " must be temporary and changeable at the King's pleasure," and in 1638 they agreed that Virginia laws should be " correspondent to the lawes of England and but Probationers onely untill confirmed here." [5] Despite its inaction, therefore, the British government assumed from the first that colonial laws should be as nearly as possible in conformity with those of England, and that the enactments of a royal colony

---

[1] Macdonald, *Select Charters*, p. 19.

[2] *Ibid.*, pp. 27, 41.

[3] *Ibid.*, 56, 57.

[4] The proviso that laws be " consonant" or " reasonable" appears in the first Carolina charter of 1662-3, the New Jersey " Concessions" of 1664-5, the Pennsylvania charter of 1680-1 and the Georgia grant of 1732. Macdonald, *op. cit.*, pp. 120, 141, 186, 241. It was, however, omitted from the patent of the Providence Plantations in 1643, the Connecticut charter of 1662, the Rhode Island charter of 1663 and the grant to the Duke of York. Macdonald, *op. cit.*, pp. 91, 116, 125, 138.

[5] *Calendar of State Papers, Colonial Series*, 1574-1660, p. 100. *Acts of the Privy Council, Colonial Series*, vol. i, p. 239.

were subject to review and confirmation, and even to revision, at home.

By insisting, later, upon the submission of legislation, the crown was but adopting a precedent of the proprietary governments, of which it was, in some cases, the successor. Thus, the Virginia company in sanctioning the establishment of an assembly there, had provided that " no Law or Ordinance . . . should . . . continue in Force or Validity unless the same . . . be solemnly ratified and confirmed in a General Quarter Court in England, and . . . returned to them under our Seal." And in like manner the New Jersey *Concessions and Agreement* of February, 1665, granted the power of making laws which should be presented to the Lords Proprietors for ratification within one year of their enactment.[1]

Moreover, during the thirty years subsequent to the Restoration there was a considerable economic development in the colonies, and a corresponding increase in the number and prestige of their assemblies. At the same time there occurred in England a revival of royal power, and the consequent development of a fairly comprehensive colonial policy. Under such circumstances it was inevitable that the home government sooner or later should come to realize the necessity of reviewing colonial enactments. Otherwise the assemblies themselves became sole judges of what was consonant to reason and conformable to the laws of England, as well as the final arbiters whenever their economic interests in regard to quit-rents, fees, trade, or the establishment of revenue came into conflict with those of the crown.

It was all but inevitable, also, that the task of review

[1] Macdonald, *op. cit.*, pp. 34-36, 143. The laws of Maryland, the Carolinas and the Bahamas were also subject to a proprietary disallowance.

should be assumed by the Privy Council. Except during the Commonwealth, the crown had always been the branch of the English government most actively concerned with the settlement and control of plantations; and England was now in the midst of a reaction from parliamentary to royal government. Nor were the administrative tasks incident to a closer supervision of the colonies suitable to perform-ance by a legislative body.

On July 4, 1660, there was appointed by order in council a Committee of the Privy Council, to meet Mondays and Thursdays for the consideration of " petitions, proposi-tions, memorials, and other addresses . . . respecting the Plantations." Most of its members were great officers of state. Its functions were deliberative and advisory.[1] But the importance of this standing committee was eclipsed, for a time, by the appointment of separate and subordinate councils of trade and plantations.

A council for foreign plantations, consisting of " six noblemen and forty two other noblemen and gentlemen," of whom any five were to constitute a quorum, was com-missioned on December 1, 1660. A larger body than the committee, its membership comprised not only Clarendon and the "Great Officers of State "—the latter being at the same time members of the Privy Council and its commit-tees—but also a second group of administrators and men actively identified with colonial enterprise. These colonial experts constituted the usual working quorum, the coöper-ation of the councilors being sought in matters of special importance. This body was instructed to give an account

---

[1] Beer, G. L., *Old Colonial System*, vol. i, p. 228. *Acts of the Privy Council*, vol. i, Introd., p. xiii. *New York Colonial Documents*, vol. iii, Introd., p. xiii. Special committees of the Council, also, were ap-pointed occasionally for specific purposes,—one on the state of Jamaica in October, 1660, for example, and a committee for New England in 1661. *A. P. C.*, vol. i, Introd., p. xiv.

of the laws and government of each colony " in what modell and frame they move and are disposed." [1] There is no evidence that it examined the colonial laws in any comprehensive or systematic fashion; although it does appear that, from this time on, the royal colonies sent their acts to England with fair promptitude and regularity.[2] After a period of considerable activity this council came to an end in 1665, leaving the control of colonial affairs once more with the Privy Council and its committees.

In 1670 the combined oversight of trade and foreign plantations was again intrusted to a subordinate council—a smaller group with salaried members, who advised with the noblemen and great officers upon special occasions. With its committees this body proved an effective instrument of colonial control. It carefully scrutinized legislation " to see if it were not detrimental to English or imperial interest." [3] But this was among the least of its manifold activities during a career, the briefness of which necessarily precluded the development of a consistent policy regarding colonial legislation. Various causes, among which were a lack of executive power and a consequent dependence upon the Privy Council, together with a widespread demand for economy and retrenchment in administration, led to the revocation of its commission in December, 1674.[4] In 1665,

---

[1] *N. Y. Col. Docs.*, vol. iii, p. 35.

[2] One hundred and thirty-eight Virginia acts are mentioned in March 1662. Others follow in December 1662, September 1663 and September 1664. *C. S. P.*, 1661-8, pp. 82, 115, 162, 235. Barbadoes acts appear regularly after 1650 and Jamaica acts after 1661.

[3] Beer, *op. cit.*, vol. i, p. 247. Evelyn "was on the Committee with Sir Humphrey Winch, the Chairman, to examine the Laws of His Majesty's several Plantations and Colonies in the West Indies." Evelyn's *Diary*, November 8, 1672. Quoted by Beer, note 2.

[4] Beer, *op. cit.*, vol. i, pp. 253, 254. *N. Y. Col. Docs.*, vol. iii, Introd., p. xiv. Andrews, "Committees, Commissions and Councils" in the *J. H. U. Studies*, vol. xxvi, pp. 97, 103.

during the brief interval between the tenure of subordinate councils, the committee of the Privy Council considered seven laws from the Island Colonies and recommended their confirmation. The committee objected, however, to a proviso exempting certain lands in a Barbadoes impost act, and this clause the Council "disallowed and made void," although the act itself they confirmed.[1]

By an order in council of March 12, 1675, all matters "left loose and at large" by the dissolution of the council of trade and plantations, reverted to the committee of the Privy Council. The committee, officially styled "the Right Honorable, the Lords of the Committee for Trade and Plantations," which thus resumed entire control of colonial affairs, consisted at this time of twenty-one councilors, who met at least once a week, reporting to the Council from time to time.[2] Although subject to occasional changes in organization and membership, and subordinate always to the Privy Council, it remained the administrative center of the plantations from 1675 until the establishment of the Board of Trade in 1696. Save, perhaps, for a period of apathy and procrastination extending from 1681 until the Revolution of 1688, its review of colonial legislation was far more systematic and effective than that of its predecessor.

Prior to 1685 the royal colonies, whose acts alone were

---

[1] *C. S. P.*, 1661-8, pp. 162, 189, 293. *A. P. C.*, vol. i, p. 396.

[2] William Blathwayt, who had spent "some time in this service," was appointed "to continue always as an assistant to the Clerk of the Council at 150 pounds per year." *A. P. C.*, vol. i, p. 665. In November 1677, the Council raised Blathwayt's salary to 250 pounds, "for his great pains and application to your Majesty's Service in the Business of Trade and Plantations." *A. P. C.*, vol. i, p. 743. Nine members were designated to have immediate care of matters in regard to which they had been formerly conversant, any five to be a quorum. *A. P. C.*, vol. i, p. 619. *N. Y. Col. Docs.*, vol. iii, Introd., p. xiv.

subject to review in England, were: Jamaica, Barbadoes, the Leeward Islands and, on the continent, Virginia. New Hampshire, it is true, became a royal colony in 1680, but it submitted no laws until after the year named. During an important period, therefore, when precedents were in the making, and policy in process of rapid formation, the action of the Privy Council upon colonial legislation was confined very largely to the Island Colonies.

In 1679 the attention of the committee was directed to several Barbadoes laws, passed between 1660 and 1672, by a complaint lodged against the revenue acts of 1675 and 1678 by the farmers of the provincial revenue.[1] The governor's instructions had authorized his assent only to laws of two years' duration, which should be transmitted "with all convenient speed" for his majesty's allowance. When, therefore, the committee found that the more important of these acts were limited in duration to four, five and six months, and that excepting revenue acts, " never any one was ever yet sent over," they expressed disapproval of the governor's conduct and agreed that subsequent legislation should be " indefinite and without limitation of time," and be transmitted " within three months or sooner." [2] Their decision received formal embodiment in Governor Dutton's commission issued in 1680. This provided that laws should continue in force until disallowed by his majesty, and that upon pain of the forfeiture of one year's salary the governor should transmit them under seal within three months, sending duplicates by the next conveyance.[3]

[1] *Board of Trade Journal*, vol. iii, p. 30.

[2] *B. T. J.*, vol. iii, pp. 30, 34, 35. *C. S. P.*, 1677-8, p. 388. *A. P. C.*, vol. i, p. 857.

[3] *B. T. J.*, vol. iii, p. 183. Similar instructions were issued to John Cutt, President of the Council in New Hampshire, in 1680, and to Governor Cranfield in 1681. *N. H. Prov. Papers*, vol. i, p. 379. *Entry Books*, in the Public Record Office, London, *CO/5-940*, p. 39.

Later, when the committee received a militia act limited to three months, the governor was directed more explicitly to pass no law concerning the government " which hath not a temporary end in any other terms than such as should render the same indefinite." [1] By the adoption of these provisions, which became thenceforth a part of the customary form for instructions to governors, the English government reversed its early policy of insisting that colonial laws be of limited duration.

During its consideration of these Barbadoes acts the committee sought from " the Judges " legal advice upon four questions, the scope and penetration of which reveal how thoroughly the powers of the crown in regard to colonial legislation were considered. They inquired: "(1) Whether the laws of Barbadoes remain perpetually in force without the King's confirmation. (2) If the King confirm [a law], may the Governor, Council and Assembly repeal it without [his] consent? (3) Can laws sent to England be amended or must they be [wholly] allowed or rejected? (4) May the King at any time declare dissent to laws which he has not confirmed, and do such become void immediately." [2] Apparently these questions received no authoritative answer at this time, although, judging from the terms of Governor Dutton's commission, the committee seem to have decided the first and the fourth in the affirmative. [3]

In 1676 the committee " took in hand " certain acts of Jamaica, " all bound up in a particular book." Their lordships expressed themselves as not pleased with certain fea-

---

[1] *B. T. J.*, vol. iv, p. 247. *B. T. J.*, vol. v, p. 137.

[2] *C. S. P.*, 1677-80, p. 569. *B. T. J.*, vol. iii, p. 180; 10 July 1680.

[3] In practice the crown ultimately answered the second and third in the negative, although the possibility of a partial confirmation or disallowance was considered at the Council as late as 1760. *A. P. C.*, vol. iv, p. 440.

tures of these laws and proposed sundry amendments, agreeing that their alterations might be " approved of by the Governor, Council and Assembly, without reënacting them, and sending them back for His Majesty's approbation again." [1]   But the willingness of the committee thus to expedite matters was of no avail, for the assembly never conceded that its laws could be amended in England. Some months later the committee noted that the term of two years during which these acts were to continue in force was almost expired, and again undertook their consideration. " Upon the whole matter," their lordships decided to refer them to the attorney general for his opinion " how far they are fit to be allowed by His Majesty."   They also desired him to prepare a bill, like Poyning's Law in Ireland— which authorized the Irish Parliament to pass only such bills as were submitted to it by the crown and the English Privy Council—directing the manner of enacting, transmitting and " amending the laws of Jamaica by His Majesty here in England." [2]   In other words, the committee not only assumed power to amend the laws of Jamaica, but also determined that for the future none should be enacted there save such as were drafted in England and transmitted to the colony for ratification.

Because of delay upon the part of the attorney general, no further action was taken until September, 1677, when the committee received additional acts from Jamaica. Upon examination, these were found " prejudicial to His Majesty's Prerogative and authority," and after debate it was reaffirmed " that noe Law be assented unto by the Governor untill it bee first approved by the King."   " The Governor to present to His Majesty a scheme of such Laws

[1] *C. S. P.*, 1675-6, p. 394.   *B. T. J.*, vol. i, pp. 118, 120, 121, 127.

[2] Beer, *Old Col. System*, vol. i, p. 210.   *C. S. P.*, 1677-80, pp. 65, 67. *B. T. J.*, vol. ii, pp. 26, 42.

as hee shall think fit and necessary according to the . . . exegencies of affairs, that His Majesty may take [them] into consideration and return them in the forme wherein he shall be pleased to have them enacted." [1] These acts likewise were dispatched to the attorney general, not only to be examined, but also to be " framed " and " modeled " according to their lordships' intent.[2] Four days later the committee resolved more definitely " to frame a body of Laws such as are fit for the Earl of Carlisle (the new Governor) to settle on his arrival at Jamaica." [3] They also questioned the attorney general whether a revenue act of 1672 might not be revived and made perpetual; and when he replied, that by the terms of the governor's commission such a proceeding would require the consent of the assembly, some of the members urged that a former governor had made laws without an assembly. But the committee contented itself with carefully framing a permanent revenue act with the assistance and approval of the lord treasurer and the commissioners of the customs.[4] At length, in December, 1677, the attorney rendered his long-deferred report, presenting such a body of laws as he conceived fit to be passed by the assembly. In this form they received the approval of the committee, the sanction of the Privy Council and the stamp of the great seal.[5]

The Jamaica assembly, however, refused to endorse the laws thus carefully drafted. They complained that the

---

[1] *B. T. J.*, vol. ii, pp. 67, 110, 111, 112.

[2] *B. T. J.*, vol. ii, p. 114.

[3] *B. T. J.*, vol. ii, 115.

[4] *B. T. J.*, vol. ii, 195. Beer, *op. cit.*, vol. i, p. 210.

[5] Thirty-seven laws were approved on February 15, 1678. The committee were in doubt whether they should be confirmed by Order in Council, or passed under the great seal, and the Council decided for the latter procedure. *A. P. C.*, vol. i, pp. 761, 763. *B. T. J.*, vol. ii, 172, 195. *C. S. P.*, 1677-80, p. 601.

committee's revenue bill was perpetual and the revenue liable to be diverted; that distance rendered this manner of passing laws wholly impracticable; and that the plan deprived them of all deliberative power.[1] The committee, in their report upon this remonstrance, mentioned the advantages which would accrue to the colony from an established body of law. The late power of making temporary acts— a mere expedient, resorted to only until " wholesome laws founded on many years' Experience should be agreed on by the people and finally enacted by Your Majesty "—had been abandoned because of " irregular, violent and unwarrantable proceedings " on the part of the assembly. They suggested, also, that if the assembly persisted in their obstinate course, the governor might be given power to ignore them and to govern according to the laws of England with the advice of the council.[2]

Meanwhile the Jamaica assembly had twice rejected the permanent revenue bill sent over for their ratification, and had passed another conceived " according to their own will and humor," which granted a revenue for one year only and contained an obnoxious clause exempting Jamaica ships from all manner of impositions.[3] Consideration of this act led to renewed discussion as " to how far English laws and methods of government ought to take place in Jamaica." Four questions as to the royal power of making laws there were referred to the attorney and solicitor general.[4] Their content is not given, but they were probably identical with the four questions propounded on this subject in connection with the Barbadoes acts.[5] The attorney general found them

[1] *A. P. C.*, vol. i, p. 828.

[2] *C. S. P.*, 1677-80, pp. 367-369. *A. P. C.*, vol. i, p. 833.

[3] *B. T. J.*, vol. iii, pp. 94, 110.

[4] *A. P. C.*, vol. ii, p. 6.

[5] *C. S. P.*, 1677-80, p. 569, *supra*, p. 23.

"of such difficulty and moment" as to require the opinion
of the judges, and a conference between the judges and
the attorney was held, apparently in the presence of the
committee.[1]　The result was a definitive opinion from the
attorney general that the colony should be governed " by
such laws [only] as are made there and established by His
Majesty's authority." [2]　Reluctantly the committee now re-
ceded from their untenable position.　With the assistance
of Chief Justice North, an agreement was effected between
their lordships and certain gentlemen of Jamaica, whereby
the assembly was to pass a perpetual revenue bill, together
with a bill for the payment of contingencies to continue
seven years—the proceeds from quit-rents and the tax on
wine licences to be appropriated solely to the support of
the government.　On the other hand, the power to make
laws which should continue in force until disallowed — a
privilege already enjoyed by Barbadoes—was conceded to
the assembly of Jamaica.[3]　In accordance with the terms of
this agreement, the Earl of Carlisle was instructed to call
an assembly, which was empowered to make laws " with
the advice and consent of the Governor and Council."　Carlisle was to "endeavor to procure" the passing of a revenue
bill according to a draft sent over by him, and to permit no
material variations from it.[4]　These instructions mark the
victory of the Jamaica assembly in the constitutional
struggle which decided once for all that colonial laws should
be passed not by the Privy Council, with the consent of the
governor, council and assembly, but by the governor, council
and assembly with the consent of the Privy Council.

[1] *B. T. J.*, vol. iii, p. 167.

[2] *B. T. J.*, vol. iii, p. 167 ; 27 April 1680.

[3] *B. T. J.*, vol. iii, pp. 214, 220, 221.　*C. S. P.*, 1677-80, p. 621.　Beer,
op. cit., vol. i, p. 211.

[4] *C. S. P.*, 1677-80, pp. 623, 624; 3 November 1680.

On receiving information, a year later, that the assembly had passed several laws without establishing the desired revenue, the Privy Council issued a warrant declaring these laws void if no revenue bill were passed before the arrival of Lynch, the succeeding governor.[1]   This is the only case recorded in which laws were disallowed conditionally before being submitted to the Council.

With difficulty the governor (Morgan) secured a revenue act within the prescribed time.   But it was for seven years only, and objectionable also because it provided that the governor should account to the assembly for expenditures each year, thus rendering an annual assembly obligatory. Furthermore, it was to be void if the other laws " tacked to it" were "altered or diminished "—an unjustifiable effort to oblige the king to confirm all the other laws in perpetuity.[2]   The Council insisted that until the assembly should amend this, no action would be taken upon any of the Jamaica laws.   It was further suggested that the laws of England, by no means excluding the duty of tonnage and poundage and tax upon wines, would be enforced there.[3] In the following year Governor Lynch secured a revenue act which repealed its predecessor and satisfied the exactions of the home authorities.   This, also, was limited to seven years, and the Council in confirming most of the other Jamaica laws did so for a like period.   Of the remaining acts, one was disallowed and several were returned with suggested amendments.[4]

[1] *A. P. C.*, vol. ii, pp. 25, 26; October 1681.

[2] *C. S. P.*, 1681-5, p. 316.

[3] *B. T. J.*, vol. iv, 74.   Beer, *op. cit.*, vol. i, p. 218.

[4] *A. P. C.*, vol. ii, p. 833.   *B. T. J.*, vol. iv, pp. 109, 110, 111.   The journal notes " His Majesty's great Grace and condescension * in confirming the laws * for seven years whereby he puts it out of his power to vacate them within that time if he should think fit."   This

Governor Lynch subsequently secured an extension of the revenue for twenty-one years, and the Council re-confirmed the Jamaica laws, with one exception, for the same period.[1] These constitute the only cases in which the Privy Council confirmed colonial acts for a limited time.

The action of the Council upon Virginia legislation during this period follows a cycle similar to that pursued in the case of Jamaica, except that the government was more conservative in its exactions while the assembly proved more complaisant. In 1677 the committee examined certain laws passed since Bacon's Rebellion, and sought the opinion of the attorney general and of the royal commissioners to Virginia upon them.[2] The committee reported after consideration that three of these acts for the punishment of participants in the late rebellion conflicted with the terms of his majesty's proclamation of amnesty, and exceeded the legislative powers of the Virginia government. Their lordships recommended, therefore, that they be " Disannulled and abrogated," and that other laws "more agreeable to His Majesty's justice and honour be prepared and sent to Virginia." [3]

A few months later two packets of "Orders and Acts of the Assembly " were received, together with a complaint

was done despite a clause in the governor's commission providing that laws should be in force "until our pleasure be signified to the contrary." *A. P. C.*, vol. ii, pp. 46, 47. Twenty-eight acts were confirmed, many of which were modeled upon those sent over in 1678 and rejected by the assembly.

[1] *B. T. J.*, vol. iv, p. 263. Beer, *op. cit.*, vol. i, p. 219.

[2] *C. S. P.*, 1677-80, p. 139. *B. T. J.*, vol. ii, p. 174.

[3] *B. T. J.*, vol. ii, pp. 180, 181. *A. P. C.*, vol. i, pp. 757-760; 18 January 1678. *CO/5-1355*, pp. 222, 227. These laws, passed at Green Spring in February 1676 were entitled (1) "Indemnity," (2) "Attainder" and (3) "Inflicting Paines, Penalties and Fines upon Great Offenders." Their repeal was again recommended by the committee in April 1679. *B. T. J.*, vol. ii, p. 327.

that his majesty's commissioners had forced from the clerk of the assembly the original journals. Observing unsympathetically that the assembly should be brought to a "due sense of their duty and submission," the Council ordered the committee to prepare " such a Scheme of Laws and Orders as they shall thinke fitt to be approved and transmitted unto Virginia." [1]   The committee acquiesced and resolved to send over a body of laws under the great seal of England, to be confirmed by the assembly.[2]   But this plan had to be abandoned because there was not sufficient time to complete the proposed revision before the departure of Governor Culpeper for the colony, and because many of the existing laws had never been transmitted.[3]   It is by no means impossible, also, that intimations of the recalcitrant attitude of the Jamaica assembly had already reached the English authorities.   It was agreed, therefore, that Culpeper, after his arrival, should consider and compile, with the assistance of his council, all the Virginia laws and send them to England, " that we may take them into consideration and return them in the form we shall think fit they be enacted in." [4]   Meanwhile the revenue act and such others as were absolutely necessary were to be amended as proposed and sent over by the new governor.   Three acts, for " Naturalization," for a "General Pardon and Oblivion," and for " Raising a Public Revenue " were accordingly drafted and entrusted to Lord Culpeper, together with a

[1] *A. P. C.*, vol. i, pp. 789, 790.

[2] Also * " wherein all defects in the stile may be amended and all forfeitures granted to the King only, Particularly wherein several clauses in the act raising two shillings per Hgs. on tobacco exported * may be explained and amended, and several frauds hindered." *CO*/5-1355, p. 238.

[3] *CO*/5-1355, p. 258, Marginal note.

[4] *CO*/5-1355, p. 313.

warrant for his giving assent when they should be passed in Virginia.[1]

The assembly " thankfully embraced " the act of pardon, and passed with some reluctance those of naturalization and revenue.   But when the latter was examined in committee, it was found to contain a clause exempting Virginia owned or built ships from the taxes imposed.[2]   Their lordships, desiring to save the grant of revenue, but loath to accept the obnoxious proviso, which " Lord Culpeper had no power or direction to add," cited as a precedent the Barbadoes revenue act and suggested that the law be confirmed and the objectionable exemption disallowed.   This was done by an order in council of October 14,1680, dated three weeks prior to Carlisle's instructions, which embodied the government's compromise in the Jamaica controversy. The partial disallowance of this act was hardly a violation of the powers conferred upon the assembly by Culpeper's immediate instructions.   But that the committee nevertheless felt the weakness of their position is shown by the care with which they cited the Barbadoes act as a precedent.[3]

During the period under consideration, the number of royal provinces was increased by four.   New Hampshire obtained a separate legislature in 1680 and New York its first established assembly in 1691.   The Massachusetts charter of the same year required the submission of her laws, while the Maryland proprietor gave way to a royal governor in 1692.

The commission of John Cutt, the first president of the

---

[1] *CO*/5-1355, p. 258.   *C. S. P.*, 1677-80, pp. 450, 452.   *A. P. C.*, vol. i, p. 818.

[2] *C. S. P.*, 1677-80, pp. 558, 612.   This act granted to the crown in perpetuity the revenue from the two shillings per hogshead on tobacco exported, from tonnage dues of one-third penny per ton, and from a pole tax of six pence on every immigrant.   Beer, *op. cit.*, pp. 205-207.

[3] *B. T. J.*, vol. iii, p. 210.

council in New Hampshire, provided that laws passed by the president, council and assembly should be in force pending confirmation or disallowance in England.[1] After considering the first laws sent from there, the committee pronounced them " unequal, incongruous and absurd," and the methods of the council and assembly in establishing them "disagreeable and repugnant to the terms of Your Majesty's Commission." They recommended that all these acts be rejected and a suitable person commissioned as governor.[2] This drastic action was due probably not so much to inherent defects in the laws, as to the fact that the assembly had presumed to take part in local land controversies and to confirm certain disputed township grants. Other acts, subsequently passed, met with a more favorable reception; but the assembly was so prone to indulge in unfruitful disputes with the governor that comparatively few laws were passed prior to 1696.

The first assembly of New York was called by Governor Dongan in 1683. Acts agreed to by the governor and assembly were to be in force until the Duke of York should signify his "dislike of & refusall to passe them."[3] Thirteen acts were assented to by the Duke on October 4, 1684. One of the laws transmitted, entitled the "Charter of Liberties and privileges," which was at once a bill of rights and a frame of government, was compared unfavorably by the committee with the "Commissions by which the government of other Colonies is settled," and was disallowed, in view, it was alleged, of the intended consolidation of New York with New England.[4] Indeed James, now King,

---

[1] *C. S. P.*, 1677-80, pp. 390, 391. *N. H. Prov. Papers*, vol. i, p. 379.

[2] *C. S. P.*, 1681-5, pp. 174, 182. *CO/5-940*, pp. 58, 59.

[3] *Col. Laws of New York*, vol. i, p. 110. *Col. Docs.*, vol. iii, p. 332.

[4] *N. Y. Col. Laws*, vol. i, p. 111. *CO/5-1111*, p. 61. *CO/5-1112*, p. 53. *B. T. J.*, vol. v, pp. 91, 100. *C. S. P.*, 1685-8, p. 7. *N. Y. Col. Docs.*, vol. iii, pp. 357-359.

not only annulled the "Charter," but revoked his grant of an assembly as well. Consequently, until the assembly called by Slaughter in 1691, the acts of New York were drafted, as before, by the governor and council. After 1691, New York laws were transmitted regularly to England; but owing to the laxity of the committee at this period, their consideration was deferred, for the most part, until after the formation of the Board of Trade.

Copley, the first royal governor of Maryland, was commanded to revise the laws in force, and to send over a complete body of them for approbation or disallowance. But the committee took definite action upon only four laws prior to 1696. A tonnage act was disallowed at the instigation of Lord Baltimore; while two acts for the " Establishment of a Protestant Religion " and an act for " Erecting Free Schools," all subjects of contention within the colony, met a like fate in January, 1696.[1]

In 1676, during a debate as to the status of New England in reference to royal control, the committee questioned whether Massachusetts laws " should not have like approbation from His Majesty as in other Plantations." [2] As a result of complaints from Edward Randolph, the Council ordered the Massachusetts agents to attend Solicitor General Winnington with copies of their charter and laws.[3] The attorney and solicitor each rendered a report citing many acts which were repugnant to the laws of England, and consequently contrary to the terms of the charter.[4] In

[1] CO/5-713, p. 101. CO/5-724, p. 20. C. S. P., 1693-6, pp. 31, 636.

[2] C. S. P., 1675-6, p. 350.

[3] B. T. J., vol. ii, p. 61. A. P. C., vol. i, pp. 725, 726; 20 July 1677.

[4] The Massachusetts charter granted the common privileges of a corporation, with the reserving clause that laws be not repugnant to the laws of England. C. S. P., 1677-80, p. 140.

Regarding these laws the attorney general remarked somewhat naively that the agents of the colony were themselves " in a manner ashamed

order to preserve their privileges, the Massachusetts authorities agreed to several conditions, one being that the objectionable acts should be annulled by the colony and due care
taken that no more such be made in the future.[1] From time
to time during the next few years the committee scrutinized
and even amended the laws of New England with a view
to their suitability after the proposed annulment of the
charter.[2]

In considering the draft of a new charter, the committee
insisted that Massachusetts acts be subject to disallowance
by the Privy Council. It was suggested at first that they
should be transmitted within one year and be void if disallowed within a like period after they were received.[3]
Later it was proposed that they be transmitted " at the
first opportunity," to become void if disallowed at any time
thereafter. But the agents for Massachusetts objected
strongly to the latter proposal, urging that the period during which acts might be disallowed be eighteen months.
The final draft of the charter fixed this period at three
years, and stipulated definitely that unless declared void
within that time after presentation, laws should "continue
in force until the Expiration thereof or until Repealed by
the General Assembly." [4]

of them, only as regards that concerning the observation of the Lord's
Day they seemed somewhat tenacious." The criticisms of the law
officers were set forth at some length " as a guide that the Massachusetts may proceed according to their patent," and the agents were
called in and consulted as to improvements. *C. S. P.*, 1677-80, pp. 139-141.

[1] Proposals from the Agents. *C. S. P.*, 1677-80, p. 366; 23 May 1679.
An account of what had been done by the Colony, from Joseph
Dudley and John Richards, *B. T. J.*, vol. iv, 47; 24 August 1682.

[2] *C. S. P.*, 1681-5, pp. 415, 752, 762, 764. *B. T. J.*, vol. v, pp. 57, 78.
B. T. J., vol. vi, p. 81.

[3] *CO/5-856*, p. 511.

[4] *C. S. P.*, 1689-92, pp. 470, 511. Goodell, *Acts and Resolves*, vol. i,
p. 17. *B. T. J.*, vol. vii, p. 32.

Fifty acts of 1692, the first passed under the new charter, were duly submitted to the Privy Council, and referred to the committee, who, despite an elaborate criticism of them submitted anonymously by a resident of the colony, took no action thereon until March, 1695.[1] At several meetings held during the spring of 1695 they were taken up and carefully considered. On June 4th the committee agreed to recommend the confirmation of thirty-eight acts. Eight they found objectionable and urged for repeal, while three acts of a general nature—" Punishing Capital Offenders, " Establishing Courts," and " Securing the Liberty of the Subject "—they criticized without definite recommendations as to confirmation or disallowance. The Council confirmed thirty-five acts and disallowed fifteen—seven more than the committee had recommended—a fact which shows that the latter's weakness and indecision, at this time, was to some extent offset by the exercise of discretion upon the part of the Privy Council.[2]

The laws of 1693-4 were also presented to the Council, and by them referred to the committee. Two acts concerning commerce and navigation the latter body sent at once to the lords and commissioners of the treasury; the remainder, as usual, to the attorney general.[3] The commissioners of customs consulted a revenue collector for New England who chanced to be in England, and reported objections against the two acts referred to the treasury. The committee recommended that they be disallowed, and the Privy Council complied by an order in council of the same date.[4]

[1] *C. S. P.*, 1689-92, p. 730.

[2] *B. T. J.*, vol. viii, pp. 10, 16, 23, 26, 29. *CO*/5-906, pp. 187, 194. *C. S. P.*, 1693-6, pp. 497, 498.

[3] *B. T. J.*, vol. viii, pp. 52, 125.

[4] 26 December 1695; *C. S. P.*, 1693-6, p. 633. *CO*/5-906, pp. 206, 209. (1) " Coasting Vessels within the Province " and (2) " To Restrain the Export of Raw Hides."

The report of the committee upon the remainder of these acts was made in February, 1696, and in accordance with its recommendations several of them were disallowed by the council in the following December. After noting a discrepancy between an act for establishing courts and a former law of the colony upon the same subject, the report continues: "Agree to represent the matter especially in Council." This, again, would indicate deliberation in the Council meetings, as well as a tendency upon the committee's part to defer the solution of difficult problems to their superior body.[1]

The grants to the proprietors of Carolina and Maryland empowered them to make laws with the consent of the freemen, stipulating that such legislation should be consonant to reason and not repugnant to the laws of England.[2] Nothing was said regarding submission to the Privy Council. By virtue of their control over the governor and his veto, therefore, the proprietors possessed virtually a double check upon the legislation of their colonies, while the king in council had none. In response to general inquiries regarding the state of his province, Charles Lord Baltimore responded in 1678: "The Laws are generally temporary, and continue only for three years. Where the exigencies of the Province do not force any particular laws to be made, no other laws are used than those of England." Copies of Maryland acts were sent to the Privy Council more or less regularly, but no action was taken upon laws from this colony until it became a royal province in 1692. One act of Carolina, however, for " Restraining Privateers and Pirates " was drafted by the committee and passed by the assembly at its request.[3]

[1] Report, *CO/5-859*, p. 11.

[2] Macdonald, *Select Charters*, pp. 53, 120.

[3] *B. T. J.*, vol. iv, p. 272.   *C. S. P.*, 1685-8, p. 338.

The preliminary draft of Penn's charter, based upon that of Maryland, granted legislative powers under like conditions except that, in time of emergency, the proprietor alone could issue ordinances. When this draft was submitted to Lord Chief Justice North, he observed: "There wants a clause to enable the King within [blank] years to repeal the laws and ordinances of either sort." [1] The final draft of the Pennsylvania charter, accordingly, provided that a duplicate of laws should be delivered to the Privy Council within five years after their passing. Acts disallowed within six months of their presentation were to become void; otherwise to remain in force unless they expired of their own limitation or were repealed by the assembly. [2] Thus, by virtue of a charter granted just as the general drift toward the royal province was setting in, Pennsylvania became the only proprietary government whose laws were subject to review by the Privy Council. Because of the disparity between the time allowed the colony for the presentation of its laws and the short term within which they had to be examined, this arrangement proved far from satisfactory to the English government.

Despite the proprietor's instructions to the governor that the laws be collected and " sent over in a stitcht book," [3] some two hundred acts passed during the first eleven years of the colony's existence had never been transmitted when Fletcher assumed the governorship by royal appointment in 1693. He declared them invalid because they had never been submitted for approval, and because he conceived Penn's charter to have been contrary to the laws of England, and consequently invalid. [4] The assembly afterwards

[1] *C. S. P.*, 1677-80, pp. 629, 632; November 1680.

[2] Pa. *Charters and Laws*, vol. i, of the *Statutes at Large*, p. 84.

[3] Instructions to Blackwell, *Pa. Records*, vol. i, p. 318, 1689.

[4] *Pa. Stats. at Large*, vol. i, appendix, pp. 547, 548.

presented to the governor a " Petition of Right," citing the
terms of the former charter and asking that the administration of justice be agreeable, for the time being, to eighty-
six of the rejected laws therein enumerated. To this Governor Fletcher agreed. Many of these acts were subsequently re-enacted and considered by the Board of Trade,
after 1696.[1]

Thirty acts passed by Fletcher in May, 1693, were duly
transmitted, and were referred to the attorney general, with
the request that he report upon them in order that they
might be considered by the committee, together with a petition from Penn asking reinstatement to the proprietorship.
The attorney general rendered a formal report, taking exception to three of the laws.[2] On August 9, 1694, after
consultation between the committee, Penn and the attorney
general, the former reported favorably upon Penn's petition. It was recommended also that twenty of the acts be
confirmed, two repealed, and that six be returned to the
assembly for further consideration. Penn, as Proprietor,
agreed that the latter should be in force until altered or revoked by the assembly. This arrangement was sanctioned
by an order in council on August 9, 1694.[3]

Perhaps the most important addition to the machinery of
legislative review made during this period was the custom
of referring colonial legislation to the legal advisers of the
crown, for an opinion as to its fitness " in point of law."
In the first recorded instance several Jamaica laws were
dispatched to the attorney general, together with the obser-

---

[1] *Pa. Stats. at Large*, vol. i, pp. 188-190, 220.

[2] There is attached a postscript by Penn stating his objections to still
another. He probably consulted with the attorney before the latter
rendered his report. *CO/5-1236*, p. 49; 25 July 1694.

[3] *CO/5-1114*, p. 134. *B. T. J.*, vol. vii, p. 309. *CO/5-1236*, pp. 48, 60.

vations of the committee upon them.[1]   This constitutes the
only instance in which a number of laws were referred after
having been considered at length by the committee.   Subsequently it became customary for the committee to refer
acts to the law officer at once, and to consider them later in
the light of his recommendations.

Two months later the attorney and solicitor general rendered each a separate report as to the conformity of certain
Massachusetts laws with the terms of the charter.   Although
these acts had been referred only to the solicitor, both officials rendered a report, and it was the attorney who appeared
in person before the committee when the matter was under
discussion there.[2]   In 1679 the acts of Barbadoes were referred to Mr. Serjeant Baldwin, " one of His Majesty's
Councill Learned in the Law." [3]   Why they were sent to
him rather than to the attorney or solicitor general does
not appear.   A few months later the committee ordered a
private act of Barbadoes "to Mr. Attorney for his opinion,
as is usual in like cases." [4]   Thenceforth until 1696 laws
were sent, in the ordinary course of events, to the attorney
general; while matters of unusual difficulty or importance
were referred jointly to the attorney and solicitor generals.[5]
Thus, the attorney and solicitor reported jointly regarding
the extent of Penn's rights under the Pennsylvania charter,

---

[1] *Supra*, p. 24.

[2] *A. P. C.*, vol. i, p. 725; 20 July 1677.   *B. T. J.*, vol. ii, p. 101.

[3] *A. P. C.*, vol. i, p. 857.   *C. S. P.*, 1677-80, p. 401.   *B. T. J.*, vol. iii,
p. 174.

[4] *B. T. J.*, vol. iii, p. 88; 6 November 1679.

[5] For example, a question as to the royal power of making laws for
Jamaica, and whether the disallowance of a law by order in council
revived a former law repealed by the act disallowed. The solicitor
alone rendered one report, concerning a dispute between Lord Baltimore and the Maryland assembly, over a duty on tobacco. *A. P. C.*,
vol. ii, pp. 6, 142, 246.

while at the same time the attorney alone reported upon the
Pennsylvania laws.[1] During this period the attorney not
only rendered a written report upon laws, but also appeared
in person before the committee when they came up for consideration there. Subsequently this practice was discontinued, the Board of Trade contenting itself, in most cases,
with a written report.

Upon special matters, the committee often obtained advice and assistance of other officials. The lord chief justice helped to work out a compromise in the controversy
with the Jamaica assembly, and reported upon the draft of
Penn's patent for Pennsylvania.[2] The lord chancellor and
the lord treasurer were asked to assist at the committee in
connection with the Jamaica laws; and certain acts passed
under the old charter of Massachusetts were referred to
the lord chancellor alone.[3] Revenue acts for Jamaica and
Virginia were drafted by the commissioners of customs;
and laws concerning trade, manufacture or shipping were
generally referred to them through the lords commissioners
of the treasury.[4] A memorial from the Lord Bishop of
London was considered in connection with the drafting of
a Jamaica act for the " Maintenance of the Ministry," but
the participation of that office in the review of colonial
legislation was of little consequence prior to 1696.

The governor's commissions and instructions—the near-

---

[1] C. S. P., 1693-6, pp. 310, 313; July 1694.

[2] B. T. J., vol. iii, p. 215. C. S. P., 1677-80, p. 632.

[3] C. S. P., 1677-80, p. 65. B. T. J., vol. vi, p. 82.

[4] C. S. P., 1681-5, pp. 157, 529. The report of the customs upon acts
of Virginia for establishing " Ports & Towns " and " Reviving an act
for Manufactures " was endorsed by the commissioners of the treasury, and when the assembly refused to amend them as the committee
recommended, the whole matter was re-referred to the treasury. C. S. P.,
1689-92, p. 611. CO/5-1358, p. 162. B. T. J., vol. vii, pp. 104, 328;
29 June 1692.

est approach to a fundamental law in the royal colonies—
empowered the governor, council and assembly, under vary-
ing restrictions, to make laws which should be subject to
royal disallowance.   The subsequent demand of the English authorities that the Jamaica assembly adopt unaltered
acts drafted in England, constituted a violation of a previous concession which rendered the government's position
politically, if not legally, untenable.   Other acts of the king
in council prior to 1696 were contrary to the fair implications of this grant, if not precluded by its express terms.
Such, for example, were the disallowance of clauses in the
revenue acts of Barbadoes and Virginia, and the insertion,
in a private act of Barbadoes for the sale of lands, of a
clause safeguarding the rights, both of the crown and of
certain heirs to the property affected.[1]   Under Charles II,
Lord Howard of Effingham, when governor of Virginia,
was instructed to repeal three acts "when convenient," and
acordingly the laws were declared void by a proclamation
of the governor, without the customary order in council.
Some three years later the assembly complained of this
proceeding as "unwarrantable," and asked that the proclamation repealing an act regarding attorneys be revoked.[2]
When the matter was referred to the attorney and solicitor
generals, they simply assumed the legality of the proclamation, and rendered an opinion that it revived a previous law

[1] This act was for "Enabling John Kirton to Sell certain Lands
for the Payment of his Debts." The committee probably knew that
the parties interested had no objection. A. P. C., vol. ii, 265. C. S. P.,
1693-6, pp. 219, 247, 276; 8 February 1694.

[2] These acts had to do with (1) the export of iron, (2) the manufacture of linen, and (3) attornies. Early in 1678 Lord Howard wrote
to the committee: the assembly "boldly dispute the King's authority
in the repealing of laws by proclamation." The animus of the assembly's objection seems, however, not so much the fact of their having
been repealed by proclamation, as the loss of popular laws. CO/5-1356,
p. 268. CO/5-1357, p. 125. A. P. C., vol. ii, p. 142.

which the assembly had repealed in the act thus disallowed; while the committee suggested that the objectionable act thus revived " might be repealed by a like proclamation." [1] The Privy Council, however, made little, if any, further use of this method of disallowance.

In the case of several Virginia laws the council refused to take definite action, and simply decreed that their execution should be wholly or partially " suspended." Thus it was ordered that an act " to enable Major Lawrence Smith and Captain William Bird to seate certain Lands " be "forthwith suspended; and no proceedings had thereon till His Majesty shall signify his further pleasure." As no further action was taken in the matter, the law stood virtually repealed.[2] An act for the "Encouragement of Trade and Manufacture" condemned as impractical by the commissioners of customs, was sent back to the colony for reconsideration, with an order that the clause fixing the time of its enforcement as to the landing of goods and shipment of tobacco "be immediately suspended." [3] The Privy Council took like action upon two laws, (1) for " Ports and Towns," and (2) " Reviving a former Act regarding Manufactures," passed ten years later, except that in the latter case it wholly suspended the operation of the laws in question.[4] The important subject-matter of these acts, together with the fact that they were to go into operation at

---

[1] *CO*/5-1357, p. 219. *C. S. P.*, 1689-92, p. 78. *B. T. J.*, vol. vi, p. 254. In 1716 Secretary Cook of Virginia in writing to the Board mentions an act of 1676 regarding tobacco payments, and says: " In spite of repeal by Proclamation, lawyers think the clause regarding who shall not bear office is still in force." *B. T. J.*, vol. xxvi, p. 40.

[2] *A. P. C.*, vol. i, p. 861 ; 6 August 1679.

[3] *CO*/5-1356, pp. 3, 4. *C. S. P.*, 1681-5, pp. 157, 158; 21 December 1681. Hening, *Statutes*, vol. ii, p. 508.

[4] The Assembly refused to take further action. *CO*/5-1358, p. 272; 10 October 1693.

a future date, goes far to explain why this action was taken. The more legitimate course, and the one which ultimately prevailed, was that taken in 1685 in regard to a Virginia law for " Holding Courts." This was neither confirmed nor disallowed, but simply permitted to remain in force, the governor being instructed to propose to the assembly the passing of an amendment to safeguard the rights of the crown.[1] In like manner six Pennsylvania acts were returned to the colony for reconsideration, with the express understanding that they continue in force until repealed or amended there.[2] The object of the government in these cases was to avoid the ill feeling and inconveniences resulting from the disallowance of laws beneficial in intent, by inducing the assemblies themselves to eliminate certain objectionable features.

Attempts to impose laws unaltered upon the assemblies, or to repeal acts except in their entirety and by order in council, were a natural outworking of the policy of Charles II. Both ceased, for the most part, with his reign; while after the " Glorious Revolution " there was a complete tolerance of the assemblies and a fairly scrupulous respect for their autonomy.

[1] *C. S. P.*, 1681-5, p. 747. *B. T. J.*, vol. v, 54. Instructions, *CO/5-1357*, p. 20; 13 August 1685.

[2] *CO/5-1114*, p. 134; 9 August 1694.

CHAPTER II

THE PROCEDURE OF THE ENGLISH GOVERNMENT IN LEGISLATIVE REVIEW—THE BOARD OF TRADE AND COMMITTEE OF THE COUNCIL

IN May, 1696, the old committee of the Privy Council was dissolved and the center of English colonial administration was shifted to the newly-formed " Lords of Trade and Plantations," more commonly known as the " Board of Trade." [1] Although subject to vicissitudes in influence and efficiency, this body continued, until its final dissolution eighty-six years later, to be the chief adviser of the Privy Council in matters relating to trade and plantations. In addition to numerous other activities, it examined all acts received from the colonies. It heard complaints regarding them from persons who felt that their interests were adversely affected. It obtained from the law officers of the crown an opinion as to their legality and, if necessary, referred them to other departments of the government for a special report as to their probable effect and expediency. In the light of information thus obtained, the Board of Trade formally advised the Privy Council regarding the confirmation or disallowance of the acts considered. And in the great majority of cases its recommendations were

[1] Books and papers in the plantation office relating to the committee on trade and plantations were ordered to be delivered to Popple, Secretory of the new board, " and all matters depending before the former Committee to be referred to the said Council of Trade." The appellate jurisdiction of the Privy Council, however, was retained in a standing committee of the Council. *A. P. C.*, vol. ii, p. 299; 7 July 1696.

accepted and made effective by orders in council. A study
of the administrative machinery and the procedure by which
the English government scrutinized colonial legislation,
therefore, begins naturally with some account of the history, functions and working habits of the Board of Trade.

The formation of the Board of Trade was due to a
movement in Parliament inspired by the English merchants
for the appointment of a special board of experts for colonial and commercial affairs.[1] The crown opposed this
project as an encroachment upon its prerogative; but as a
concession to the sentiment of Parliament, it commissioned
the new Council of Trade and Plantations, with a salaried
membership controlled not by Parliament, but by itself.
The first Board was composed of the eight officers of state;
the lord chancellor, the lord president, the lord treasurer,
the lord high admiral, the principal secretaries of state and
the chancellor of the exchequer; together with eight members of Parliament, two lords and six commoners, who
were more or less versed in colonial affairs. Among the
members of the first Board were William Blathwayt, who
had been secretary of the old committee for trade and plantations, John Pollexfen, brother of the chief justice and a
merchant of the city, John Locke, the philosopher, who was
interested in Carolina, and Abraham Hill, whose collections
on trade and colonies were later deposited in the British
Museum.[2] Any three members constituted a quorum, while
the great officers attended only when summoned to a "full
Board" for the consideration of important matters.[3] The

---

[1] Andrews, a study of " British Committees, Commissions and Councils
of Trade and Plantations," in the *J. H. U. Studies*, vol. xxvi, pp. 9-151.

[2] *N. Y. Col. Docs.*, vol. iii, Introd., p. xv. Chalmers, George, *Opinions
of Eminent Lawyers on points of English Jurisprudence*, (Burlington,
N. J., 1858), p. 7, note.

[3] In 1702 the Bishop of London was added to those "not obliged to
constant attendance." They were expected to attend "only so often

greater part of the work was done by the more active among the commoners—usually a group of from three to five. A secretary, appointed by the crown, and several clerks, appointed by the Board itself, performed a great amount of routine business and carried on the ordinary work of the office when their lordships were not in session.[1] At different times, Matthew Prior the poet and playwright, Addison the essayist, and Gibbon the historian were members. Although the average duration of membership was considerably less, several influential commissioners spent over fifteen years in the service. Such were Paul Docminique, Thomas Pelham and Saome Jenyns. Martin Bladen and Thomas Ashe sat twenty-nine and twenty-six years, respectively.

During the first sixteen years of its existence the Board of Trade showed great activity and enjoyed much influence. Meetings were frequent and well attended, and the scrutiny accorded colonial laws was comparatively prompt and exacting. Amid the uncertainty and party struggle of the last two years of Queen Anne, however, this vigilance relaxed and its activity was confined largely to matters of trade.[2]

as when the presence of them or any of them shall be necessary and requisite and as their other public service will permit." *N. Y. Col. Docs.*, vol. iv, p. 148.

[1] For a full account of the Board's organization see an article entitled "The Board of Trade at Work" by Mary P. Clarke, in the *Am. Hist. Review*, vol. xvii, p. 17, October 1911.

[2] An anonymous pamphlet of 1755 styled *A Miscellaneous Essay*, which is in the British Museum, says: "The Opposition given to those employed in the administration of public affairs, in the latter end of Queen Anne's reign, and the struggles for power, which then subsisted, did, in a great measure, take off the attention of the Ministry from the concerns of America. From which cause the reports of the Board of Trade were often silenced, and lay in the Secretary's Office, without any notice taken of them. * Such persons as had any concerns depending, in relation to America began to apply to the Council Board, or to the Treasury or Admiralty, as the nature of the business might require."

The accession of George I and the triumph of the Whigs in 1714 resulted in a complete change of membership,[1] and throughout the era of Walpole the efficiency of the Board steadily declined, to continue at a low ebb for several years under the government of Newcastle.[2] This state of affairs was the result partly of the laxity of the secretary of state and the Whig administration, and partly of a renewed and increasing activity and influence upon the part of the committee of the Privy Council. In 1752 the colonial governors were directed to address their general correspondence directly to the Board of Trade, instead of in duplicate, as had been the custom previously, to the Board and to one of the principal secretaries of state.[3] As a result of this order the Board transacted more business and enjoyed for several years a revival of its former prestige. At the beginning of the next decade, however, its action had again become indecisive and dilatory, and it was further weakened by the loss of its power to nominate colonial officers.[4] By an order in council of August 8, 1766, the commissioners were directed to consider in the future only such matters as were referred to them by the Privy Council or one of the principal secretaries of state. At the same time the governors were instructed to correspond with the secretary

[1] *N. Y. Col. Docs.*, vol. iii, Introd., p. xvi. In place of Meadows, Monckton and Moore, who had been long active, Chetwynd, Cooke, Docminique and Bladen became the leading spirits at the Board. Martin Bladen was appointed July 13, 1717.

[2] " The Board of Trade during Sir Robert Walpole's administration had very faultily been suffered to lapse almost into a sinecure, and during all that period the Duke of Newcastle had been Secretary of State. It would not be credited what reams of papers, representations, memorials, petitions from that quarter of the world lay mouldering and unopened in his office." *Memoirs of George II*, vol. i, p. 396.

[3] *B. T. J.*, vol. lix; 11 March, 1752. *A. P. C.*, vol. iv, p. 156.

[4] *B. T. J.*, vol. lxviii, p. 265; 15 May 1761.

of state, sending duplicates only to the Board. These orders, which originated in the desire of Pitt to reduce the evils of a divided responsibility in colonial administration, deprived the Board of initiative and reduced it to a mere advisory and consulting body.[1] Lord Hillsborough was now commissioned as " Secretary of State for the Colonies," and thereafter he and his successors sat as presidents of the Board, directing its activities with no uncertain hand. Many journal entries of this period begin with the statement: "The Earl of Hillsborough laid before the Board," while the drafting of letters to the governors regarding legislation was left almost entirely to his discretion. The weakness of the Board is occasionally shown, also, by a tendency to state the points for and against a law, without itself making any definite recommendation for confirmation or disallowance.[2] Until finally abolished in 1782, its initiative and vitality remained at a very low ebb.

The commission of the Board of Trade empowered it to assume a general oversight over colonial legislation. Among other duties, it was " to examine into and weigh such Acts of the Assemblies . . . as shall from time to time be transmitted; and to . . . represent . . . the Usefulness or mischief thereof to our Crown, and to our Kingdom of England, or to the Plantations themselves, in case the same shall be established for Lawes there; and also to consider what matters may be recommended as fitt to be passed in the Assemblys there." [3]   In other words, the Board might

---

[1] *B. T. J.*, vol. lxxiii, pp. 299, 337. Fitzmaurice, *Life of William, Earl of Shelburne*, (London, 1876), vol. ii, pp. 1-3. Andrews, " British Committees, Commissions and Councils of Trade and Plantations," *J. H. U. Studies*, vol. xxvi, pp. 113, 114.

[2] *CO/5-1296*, p. 363. *A. P. C.*, vol. v, p. 163.

[3] *N. Y. Col. Docs.*, vol. iv, p. 147; 6 July 1697. *B. T. J.*, vol. xii, p. 74. The Board's first commission issued May 15, 1696 was renewed from time to time.

examine, consider and make reports to the Privy Council, but of real executive power it had very little. In important matters its wishes were binding upon no one unless embodied in an order of the Privy Council.

The Board, probably because of other duties, did not undertake the examination of colonial laws until some months after its formation. Among the books and papers bequeathed to it by the former committee of trade and plantations were certain acts of Massachusetts, together with an opinion of the attorney general and the draft of a committee report upon them. These the Board examined at several meetings in October, 1696. A report urging the repeal of the two laws was signed on November 5, and on the following day it was announced, apparently not without satisfaction, that his majesty, at a council held the previous evening, had " entirely approved " their " representation " regarding the Massachusetts laws. Several days later an engrossed copy of the order in council repealing these acts was brought to the Board from the clerks of the Privy Council. After having the order read, the Board directed its secretary to deliver it to the agent for Massachusetts and to obtain a receipt for it.[1]

The Board of Trade received laws sometimes by reference from the Privy Council, but usually by letter directly from the governor.[2] Upon days allotted to the considera-

---

[1] *B. T. J.*, vol. ix, pp. 191, 192, 206, 211, 242.

[2] After 1735 the former course was followed in the case of laws of Pennsylvania and Massachusetts, both of which colonies were compelled by charter to submit their enactments to the Privy Council. All acts passed during one session of a provincial assembly were, as a rule, transmitted together, each separate law bearing an imprint of the provincial seal in wax. After 1766 acts as well as other communications were sent by the colonies to the secretary of state, and by him were brought or sent to the Board of Trade. *B. T. J.*, vol. lxxiv, pp. 43, 111.

tion of colonial legislation,[1] the secretary presented to their lordships acts lately received, noting the colony whence they came and the date of their passage. At first the Board was accustomed to read the laws at this time, laying aside such as were found to be temporary or expired. But this practice was soon discontinued, and upon their presentation the secretary was at once authorized to send them to the law officer.[2]

After being returned with a report " in point of law," acts were considered by the Board of Trade. Each in turn appears to have been read aloud, probably by the secretary, and to have been made the subject of discussion.[3] Laws fell naturally into three classes, those which were (1) temporary or expired, those (2) unobjectionable, and (3) those clearly objectionable or of doubtful expediency. If difficult or important questions were raised by the latter, their consideration might be postponed and some future time set for a hearing, to which the agent of the colony and persons in a position to be well informed regarding the law, or interested in its operation, would be summoned.

It sometimes happened that the attention of the Board was first called to particular laws by petitions from persons whose interests were effected thereby. The merchants trad-

---

[1] The Board's programme varied from time to time. In 1717 it fixed upon the following routine: " Monday's for reading letters and papers from the Colonies, Tuesday and Wednesday for Plantation business, Thursday for Trade, and Friday for Colonial legislation." *B. T. J.,* vol. xxvi, p. 438.

[2] By this term was meant the attorney or solicitor general, or, after 1718, the king's counsel. Subsequent to 1755 presentation by the Secretary became so much a matter of formality that he often referred acts to the law officer at once, notifying the Board of his action at their next meeting. *B. T. J.,* vol. lxix, p. 218.

[3] There is no authoritative statement of the exact course pursued by the Board in considering laws. The above inferences are drawn from the wording of the journal entries.

ing to the colonies and the Quakers were particularly active in this respect. Such petitions were addressed not to the Board but to his majesty in council, and were referred to the former by an order in council. In 1717 the Board refused to receive a petition presented by the memorialist and addressed to itself. But memorials frequently were brought to the Board and presented in person when the matter at issue was already in due course under consideration there.[1]

If the petitioners were adverse to the confirmation of the law, the agent usually presented a memorial in reply. At first the contestants seem to have relied mainly upon written briefs for the presentation of their cases, attending the Board to furnish additional information when desired. But hearings gradually became more formal and elaborate, each side being represented not only by an agent, but also by a solicitor. Thus, to cite one example among many, when in 1725 the Board considered several acts of New York regarding the Indian trade, the hearings extended over several days and the agent for the province and a solicitor for the merchants each addressed their lordships at considerable length. The Board also examined under oath[2] two fur-cutters of London and a late inhabitant of the province, and consulted an ex-governor.[3] When the proprietors of Pennsylvania complained of several acts passed by the

---

[1] *B. T. J.*, vol. xxvi, pp. 196, 284. Petitions were sometimes made while the law in question was yet with the law officer, or even before it had been received from the colony. In such cases petitioners were assured that they would be notified in ample time for the presentation of their case when the act came before the Board in the usual course. A more speedy consideration of the matter usually resulted, although the Board was reluctant to take up acts out of their usual order without good reason. *B. T. J.*, vol. x, p. 352.

[2] The solicitor general rendered an opinion in 1720 that the commission of the Board of Trade impowered it to administer an oath upon examination. *B. T. J.*, vol. xxix, p. 82.

[3] *B. T. J.*, vol. xxxiv, pp. 110-114, 122-155.

assembly, in 1760, they were represented by the attorney
and solicitor general; while for the colony appeared two
agents, one of whom was Benjamin Franklin, and two
solicitors.[1] The procedure observed at the Board upon
these occasions seems to have been informal. Usually the
petitioners against a law opened the discussion and its defenders replied. Sometimes the speakers were heard in
rebuttal. Each side was afforded ample opportunity to
present its case. Indeed, postponements for the convenience
of one or more of the parties interested were so common
as to constitute the rule rather than the exception.

At the conclusion of a formal hearing, the non-members
withdrew and the Board arrived at a decision on the questions at issue. From minutes taken down during the discussion the secretary composed the draft of a report or
" representation," which he submitted to the Board at a
subsequent meeting.[2] After having been considered and,

---

[1] *B. T J.*, vol. lxvii, pp. 136-138. At a hearing upon a North Carolina
act in 1751 the defenders of the law included both a solicitor and a
counsel. The latter refused to plead when it appeared that his op-
ponents were represented by a solicitor only; and they agreed to procure counsel. *B. T. J.*, vol. lviii, pp. 43, 44.

That Board " hearings" were regarded somewhat in the nature of a
trial at law is shown by an order in council of November 30, 1738. This
directed that no appeal to the Council against reports of the Board
upon hearings of parties upon plantation affairs should be admitted
without security to pay cost. *B. T. J.*, vol. xlvii, pt. ii, p. 59. *A. P. C.*,
vol. iv, p. 440.

[2] "At first there seems to have been a distinction between a report
and a representation. The latter was the more formal paper addressed
to the King in Council, while a report was less formal and was addressed to the committee of the Council. As time went on and the
Committee came to act in place of the Council, the words were used
more or less interchangeably. Thus on June 29, 1731, the Board signed
what in the text is called a representation, but in the margin, a report.
B. T. J., vol. xli, 169. Communications to the Secretary of State were
usually called letters." Clarke, " The Board of Trade at Work," *Am.
Hist. Rv.*, vol. xvii, p. 36, note 130.

perhaps with minor alterations, " agreed to," this was re-
copied or "transcribed fair" by one of the clerks and signed
by the members who chanced to be present on the following
day,[1] although if there were need of haste, representations
were sometimes written, agreed to and signed at a single
meeting. The great majority of Board reports covered acts
passed at a single session of a colonial assembly. But they
were made, as well, upon single acts, upon collections of
laws, and in a few instances upon those of several different
colonies. After mentioning such laws as were temporary,
expired, or without objection, the representation called
attention to those which were objectionable, usually quoting
at length from the opinion of the law officer, and conclud-
ing with a definite recommendation that they be disallowed,
or perhaps that they be permitted to remain in operation
notwithstanding their defects.

In course of time two important changes occurred in the
customary procedure of review: (1) In 1718 a special officer known as the " King's Counsel " was designated to
pass upon the legality of colonial legislation, and thenceforth, in the usual course, acts were referred to him instead
of the attorney or solicitor general. (2) Early in the century the Privy Council gradually relinquished its discretion
in confirming the recommendations of the Board of Trade,
to a committee of its own members, and the Board, in consequence, addressed the majority of its reports to that body.[2]
After 1720, therefore, laws received by the Board of Trade[3]

[1] See, for example, the progress of a New York act at the Board in
1719; B. T. J., vol. xxviii, pp. 244, 247, 249, 253. Or of a North Carolina
act in 1761; B. T. J., vol. lxviii, pp. 378, 379, 381, 395, 412.

[2] As a matter of formality, however, practically all reports of the
Board, whether addressed to the Council or the committee, appear to
have been delivered to the Council and by it referred to the committee.

[3] Laws received, as was often the case, by the Privy Council in the
first instance, were referred by order in council to the committee and
by the committee to the Board.

were referred at once to the king's counsel. The Board, after considering the acts, together with the law report upon them, reported to the committee, and the latter, in turn, to the Privy Council, which confirmed the recommendations of the committee by an order in council.

Having signed the representation upon a law, the Board had no further part in its review [1] until a copy of the order in council for its confirmation or disallowance was received from the Privy Council office.[2] It then informed the governor, or the colonial agent, of the action taken, and the reasons for it. A copy of the order in council, and usually of the representation or of the law report as well, were enclosed.

Not more than one-fourth of the laws considered at the Board of Trade were recommended for confirmation or disallowance. A few had been repealed by the assemblies, and many had expired of their own limitation before action upon them could be taken by the government. But the majority were either neglected or suffered to " lye by pro-

---

[1] Two exceptions may be made to this statement. (1) If, after the Board had made its report, a new petitioner, whose case had not been heard, appeared before the committee of the Council, or if some question arose upon which additional information was desired, the whole matter might be re-referred to the Board for reconsideration. This occurred, for example, in the case of several Massachusetts acts for erecting townships. *A. P. C.*, vol. v, p. 33. And (2) the committee sometimes summoned the Board to its own office for a joint meeting. *Cf. infra*, p. 84, note 2.

[2] Soon after the formation of the Board one of the clerks was instructed to call at the Council from time to time for their determination upon colonial laws. *C. S. P.*, 1696-7, p. 215. But this plan seems to have proved unsatisfactory, for in 1697 the secretary of the Board made arrangements with the clerks of the Council for the transmission to the Board of such orders as concerned trade and plantations. *B. T. J.*, vol. x, p. 125. In 1724 the Board requested the president of the Council to give directions that orders for the confirmation or repeal of acts be sent to their office. *B. T. J.*, vol. xxxiii, p. 135.

bationary." The latter course was sometimes taken as a means of eliminating certain objectionable features from an otherwise beneficial law, the act being allowed to stand provisionally while the governor either was instructed to procure an amendment remedying its defects, or to obtain the repeal of the old law and the enactment of a new. This was especially true of acts involving the collection or payment of money, the provisions of which had been at least partially fulfilled before action upon them could be taken by the Board of Trade. A Massachusetts act of 1764, for example, the Board found objectionable " in no other respect . . . than as it directs a double Impost . . . for all goods . . . imported by inhabitants of other Colonies." They accordingly proposed "an instruction to the Governor for procuring the amendment of this particular clause." [1] In some cases it was stated that, if the request for an amendment were not complied with, the act would be immediately disallowed; [2] and that a Pennsylvania law might remain unrepealed, the agents signed a written agreement that a desired alteration would be made. [3]

In other cases the period of probation was temporary pending the receipt of further information from the colony. After considering a petition of the merchants against an Indian trade act of New York, for example, the Board " being doubtful of the facts alleged and considering how far the British trade may be affected, . . . and how much the security and interest of Your Majesty's Colonies . . . May be concerned," advised that no direction be given on the subject until the governor had been acquainted with

[1] Goodell, *Acts and Resolves*, vol. iv, p. 698. *A. P. C.*, vol. iii, p. 553; South Carolina, 1737. *A. P. C.*, vol. iv, p. 416; North Carolina, 1759.

[2] *CO/5-401*, p. 146. *N. Y. Col. Docs.*, vol. vi, p. 33. Board Representation to the House of Lords, 1734, in the British Museum. 8223. 1. 5.

[3] *A. P. C.*, vol. iv, p. 442; 2 September 1759.

the objections of the merchants, and had made answer.[1] Again, probation amounted merely to a brief delay in confirmation to insure ample time for the presentation of petitions against legislation. For this purpose it became the settled policy of the Board to hold probationary for several months all " private acts " or laws conferring special rights or privileges upon individuals or small groups of persons. Public acts affecting in an unusual manner or special fashion the rights or property of private individuals might also be laid by. Thus, in reporting upon a New Jersey law for running a boundary between East and West Jersey, the committee said: "This is an act wherein private Property is concerned. The Lords Commissioners have lett the same lye by for some time, that in case any Person should have been aggrieved thereby, they might have Sufficient oppertunity to lay their objections before them. . . . As it is now about ten years since the act was passed, and it will be of advantage to the inhabitants," it may be confirmed.[2]

In the great majority of cases, however, acts were laid by indefinitely as a precaution to safeguard the rights of private individuals or the interests of the crown. Inasmuch as the government conceded that laws once confirmed could never thereafter be disallowed,[3] the advantage of the practice is obvious. Acts which presumably embodied local sentiment could remain in force, while the crown, never-

---

[1] *N. Y. Col. Docs.*, vol. v, p. 709; 14 July 1724.

[2] *A. P. C.*, vol. iii, p. 222.

[3] In 1703 Attorney General Northey delivered an opinion to the effect that a law "having been approved absolutely and not for any time or with any reservation to the Crown to repeal it, will be in force till the same be repealed by another act of the General Assembly of the Colony. * the passing of an act there with the absolute confirmation of Her Majesty having the force of an act of Parliament made in England." *CO/5-323*, F, 14. Board of Trade to Hunter, *CO/5-995*, p. 327; 22 March 1716. *A. P. C.*, vol. iv, p. 144.

theless, remained uncommitted and free to repeal them at
any time if unexpected objections arose. As to such laws
as are not directly repugnant to the laws or interests of
Great Britain, against which no complaint is made, and
where the Board are doubtful of the effect they may have,
says a report of that body, " it has always been usual to
let them lye by probationary, being still under the power
of the Crown to be repealed, in case any inconvenience
may arise from them." [1]   Either from neglect or design,
fully one-half of the laws passed between 1690 and 1699
were allowed to remain in force without formal confirmation or disallowance. Of those enacted between 1700 and
1710, about three-fourths, and of those passed during the
decade following, about ninety per cent were unaffected by
orders in council.[2]   Despite the growing tendency to dispense with a definite decision, however, the phrase " to lye
by probationary" did not come into use until about 1718.[3]

[1] Representation to the House of Lords, in the British Museum, 23
January 1734.

[2] The approximate percentages of acts submitted which were confirmed
or disallowed by orders in council are as follows: of laws enacted between 1690 and 1699, 48%, thereafter by decades, 26%, 10%, 5½%, 18%,
20%, 19%, 9%. Between 1770 and 1775, 6%. The increased percentages between 1730 and 1760 are due to the confirmation of a large
number of Massachusetts laws, and have, therefore, no great significance. By colonies the percentages of acts confirmed or disallowed
are: South Carolina 6%, New Jersey 7%, New York 8½%, North
Carolina 9½%, Georgia 11%, New Hampshire 11%, Virginia 18%,
Massachusetts 25%, and Pennsylvania 29%. The laws of Massachusetts and Pennsylvania were subject to rather closer scrutiny than those
of other colonies because of the charter provisions by virtue of which
they were confirmed by lapse of time unless disallowed within a stated
period. Moreover their early attempts to base legislation upon the
word of God resulted in the annulment of many laws during the first
two decades of review. Thereafter the proportion of their acts disallowed was not appreciably larger than that of other colonies.

[3] In 1708 the Board made inquiries of Lovelace regarding a New
Jersey act of 1704 for "Regulating Elections," ordering that "in the

It first appeared, and continued to be most often employed, in connection with the laws of Massachusetts, probably because their probation meant no more than the postponing of confirmation until three years after presentation, when acts not disallowed were placed beyond the reach of the crown by the terms of the provincial charter. The practice continued in frequent use at the Board of Trade, and became very common after 1760, when many laws which appeared unobjectionable were ordered collectively " to lye by till their further effect may be known."

As an advisory council upon colonial affairs, the Board of Trade served not only the Privy Council and the secretary of state, but also Parliament. Upon receiving an order from either house for laws or documents relating to the colonies, the Board, by one of its members, would dispatch copies.[1] For several years it rendered annual reports to the house of Commons regarding " the Laws, Manufactures, and Trade of the Plantations." These made brief mention of such laws only as concerned trade, shipping or manufactures. Apparently they were put to no very important use, and after a time the custom was allowed to lapse.[2] In 1740 the Board reported to both houses regard-

meantime the act remain in force, without being confirmed." *N. Y. Col. Docs.*, vol. v, p. 46. In May 1710 it agreed to let a Massachusetts act of 1705 " remain as Probationary for some time longer." *B. T. J.*, vol. xxi, p. 454. With a few exceptions all the Massachusetts laws passed between 1706 and 1714 were confirmed by lapse of time. *Acts and Resolves*, vol. i, p. 616, note. In 1716 a New York law was " left probationary " until the governor should be heard from; while in 1718 two acts of Barbadoes, two of New Hampshire, and nine of Massachusetts were ordered to " lye by." *CO/5-1123*, p. 431. *Acts and Resolves*, vol. ii, p. 31. *B. T. J.*, vol. xxvii, pp. 166, 310. The phrase appears commonly thereafter.

[1] *B. T. J.*, vol. xl, pp. 84, 91. *B. T. J.*, vol. xli, pp. 54, 56, 92. *B. T. J.*, vol. lxxxi, p. 44.

[2] *B. T. J.*, vol. xli, pp. 36, 37, 38, 40.

ing the state of the paper money in the various plantations, and upon request it drafted an act of Parliament for "Raising a Revenue" in New York.[1] Official communications from the Board to Parliament, however, had as their object either the transmission of desired documents, or the communication of information regarding the colonies in general. Unlike representations to the committee or the Council, they did not contain definite recommendations that any particular course of action be pursued.

Turning from the Board of Trade itself, we shall consider briefly the various sources of counsel and information available to it in forming opinions and recommendations upon colonial laws. Legislation upon matters under the jurisdiction of the treasury or the admiralty was referred to one or the other of these departments; while laws affecting the interests of the Anglican Church were sent to the Bishop of London. And careful attention was accorded alike to the complaints and representations of the merchants, to the arguments of colonial agents, and to the recommendations of the governors. But none of these exercised upon the deliberations and policy of the Board so constant and persuasive an influence as did the opinions delivered by the legal advisers for the crown, the attorney and solicitor generals, and later by the king's counsel.

The commission of the Board of Trade empowered it to "desire the advice of the Attorney and Solicitor General or other Counsel at Law,"[2] and of the privilege the Board, like its predecessor the committee, continually availed itself. References were commonly made for one of two purposes: either to obtain an expert opinion as to the general fitness of legislation " in point of law," or to secure advice upon

[1] *B. T. J.*, vol. xlviii, pp. 3, 23. *B. T. J.*, vol. xxii, pp. 255, 257, 264.

[2] *B. T. J.*, vol. xii, p. 74; 19 June 1699.

definite legal problems arising out of the consideration of acts.

For the former purpose the services of the attorney and solicitor proved, upon the whole, unsatisfactory. From the first the procrastination and delay with which they rendered their reports were a cause of annoyance and of serious inconvenience to the Board of Trade. In spite of repeated solicitations, several acts of Massachusetts, referred in September, 1696, were not returned until June, 1698.[1] In June, 1699, the Board was still without a desired opinion upon Pennsylvania laws which had been with the attorney and solicitor general eighteen months; and notwithstanding a request for a " speedy report," acts of Virginia referred in May, 1703, remained in the law office four years.[2] Occasionally the attorney and solicitor acted with commendable promptness.[3] But in the majority of cases they did not do so, and much needless uncertainty and delay re-

[1] These acts were among "all laws of the Plantations now before this Board" which were ordered to the attorney and solicitor on September 5, 1696. *B. T. J.*, vol. ix, p. 92. On December 11th the Board ordered its secretary to desire of the attorney his report upon "Laws already in his hands, as soon as he can." *B. T. J.*, vol. ix, p. 277. And again on April 8, 1697 the Board requested a "dispatch of the acts of the Assemblies (but most especially those of Massachusetts Bay) which lye in your hands. It being for His Majesty's service that they be dispatched." *CO/5-1287*, p. 64. Later they asked the agent of Massachusetts to look into the matter, "as it is not right these acts should be kept so long in suspense." *CO/5-907*, p. 372; 3 May 1698. He did so, and reported that they had been mislaid, but were now "found by Mr. Attorney." *B. T. J.*, vol. xi, pp. 43, 54, 68. *CO/5-908*, p. 4. Other acts referred at the same time were reported on in January 1698, after having been with the law officers a year and a half.

[2] *C. S. P.*, 1699, p. 140. *B. T. J.*, vol. xi, p. 438. *B. T. J.*, vol. xvii, pp. 36, 37.

[3] Some forty acts of New Hampshire, for example, sent to the attorney general on July 22, 1703 were considered together with his report on August 13.

sulted. Judging from their spasmodic manner of examining the colonial laws, they regarded the task as an unlucrative addition to more important duties. In excusing the failure of the attorney to dispatch plantation laws, the agent for Virginia mentions " some difficulties in relation to his fees," while the attorney himself urges the fact that not one of the agents have attended him.[1] While the agents, no doubt, gave necessary information regarding the purpose of legislation, their influence in securing law reports was due in part to a judicious distribution of fees — the lack of which caused much of the delay at the law offices.

Moreover, the fact that the examination of laws was entrusted to two officials of equal authority resulted in divided responsibility and consequent confusion. The first acts referred by the Board of Trade were sent " to the Attorney and Solicitor General for their advice thereon."[2] Several months having passed without a report, the Board, in order to expedite matters, requested the attorney to give his opinion upon the acts already in his hands, at the same time directing that such laws as had been lately received be sent to the solicitor.[3] In July, 1697, the Board ordered its secretary to urge the dispatch of laws already referred, as a matter of great importance to his majesty's service. "And that hereafter in sending any such acts to them, he direct them to the said Attorney and Solicitor General, or either of them; And send the Packets, as they shall happen to consist of many or few, with that Direction, alternately first to the one and then to the other."[4] This arrangement failing to secure the desired promptness and regularity, the

---

[1] *B. T. J.*, vol. xvii, p. 37. *CO/5-1360*, p. 470; 11 May 1704. *CO/5-323*, F, 18; 19 October 1703.

[2] *B. T. J.*, vol. ix, p. 92; 5 September 1696.

[3] *B. T. J.*, vol. ix, pp. 277, 278; 11 December 1696.

[4] *B. T. J.*, vol. x, p. 156; 8 July 1697.

Board suggested that the secretary propose to them, " if they saw fit, to agree between themselves about the acts of what particular Plantation they will each of them henceforwards take care." [1]   But this plan, if adopted at all, did not remain long in operation, for acts of each colony were sent now to the solicitor and now to the attorney.   No general rule was followed, apparently, although in the long run the number of references to each was about equal.

For a time the Board sent practically all the acts received to the attorney or the solicitor; but after 1700 the proportion referred begins to show a marked decline, the tendency being to dispatch only those of more questionable expediency or of unusual importance, until gradually the Board gave up attempting to exact from the attorney and solicitor a general examination of colonial legislation, contenting itself with an occasional reference of isolated acts.   Such a course was in harmony with the growing practice of allowing unobjectionable acts " to lye by," and was, no doubt, partly the result of the general laxity of administration then setting in.   On the other hand, the regularity of the references made to the king's counsel a few years later, and the importance attached to his reports, would indicate that the fault at this time lay not so much in the failure of the Board to refer, as in that of the attorney and solicitor to report.[2]   Despite the increasing volume of legis-

[1] *B. T. J.*, vol. xi, p. 278; 8 November 1698.

[2] All Massachusetts laws enacted between 1696 and 1706 were referred; while those passed between 1706 and 1716 were allowed to lye by.   Only about one-half of the New York laws passed between 1696 and 1714 went to the attorney and solicitor, though all enacted previous to 1700 were referred.   The laws of New Hampshire enacted prior to 1704 were sent to the attorney or solicitor, but none thereafter. The last acts of each colony to be referred collectively were passed by New York in 1701, New Hampshire in 1703, Massachusetts in 1706, Virginia in 1710, and Pennsylvania in 1712.   No laws of New Jersey were so referred.   After 1718 acts were allowed to lye by, as a rule, only after having been approved by the king's counsel.

lation, the process of review was almost at a halt, when in April, 1718, a special attorney known as the " King's Counsel " was designated to act as legal adviser to the Board; and upon him were conferred the burden and routine of reporting as to the fitness of colonial acts " in point of law." The attorney and solicitor, however, continued to advise the Board, upon request, regarding acts of unusual importance and legal questions of unusual difficulty.[1]

In many instances prior to the appointment of a king's counsel, and in a great majority of instances thereafter, the Board, in referring acts to the attorney and solicitor, requested not merely an opinion " in point of law," but a reply to one or more definite questions. The point most frequently raised in this manner was the legality, or what might now be termed the constitutionality of legislation. Had the colonial legislature exceeded its power and authority in passing the law? Were its provisions unwarranted under the terms of the provincial charter, or in conflict with an act of Parliament? The Board inquired, for example, whether two acts of North Carolina were " proper consistently with the just rights of the inhabitants and the Constitution of said Province." [2] And three private acts granting decrees of divorce, they referred to the attorney and solicitor upon " a matter of doubt whether the legis-

---

[1] In 1770 Jackson, the King's Counsel, recommended that a Pennsylvania act be sent to the attorney and solicitor " inasmuch as the exercise of this power [the granting of divorce] may frequently effect other parts of His Majesty's Dominions out of the limits of the Province, and very important consequences may therefore be drawn from the allowance of such an act." *CO*/5-1278, Z, 1.

It is perhaps worthy of note that whereas, prior to 1718, references had been made, as a rule, either to the attorney or the solicitor a great majority of those thereafter were made neither to the one nor the other, but to both; while the majority of their reports which formerly had been signed separately were after this time rendered jointly.

[2] *CO*/5-323, p. 353; 30 April 1750.

lature of the Province of Massachusetts Bay or any other Colony has a power of passing Laws of this nature, and consequently whether these acts are not of themselves null and void." [1]   And, to give one example among many, a naturalization law of New Jersey was sent to the solicitor with an inquiry as to how far it was "consistent with the act of Parliament of 12 Charles II, . . . or other acts of Parliament." [2]   Many queries had to do with the interpretation of some puzzling or obscure provision of a colonial law. [3]   The Board also passed on to them several questions propounded by the governor of Rhode Island regarding his powers under the provincial charter; and they inquired whether certain acts of Parliament extended to the plantations, and whether the charter of Pennsylvania entitled both Penn and his lieutenant governor to exercise a veto upon laws passed there. [4]   Other questions were of a more general nature.   The attorney and solicitor were requested, for example, to report upon the granting of letters of denizenship by the governors, and by what authority it was done. [5]   Also, whether the crown might not settle rates of coin in the plantations by proclamation; whether foreigners naturalized by the assemblies gained thereby all the privi-

[1] CO/5-918, p. 490; 6 June 1758. CO/5-920, p. 209; 13 March 1767. B. T. J., vol. xix, pp. 84, 85; 27 February 1701.

[2] CO/5-995, p. 450; 10 December 1718.

[3] Question as to the effect of an act suspending the operation of a former law. CO/5-726, pp. 345, 348; Maryland, 5 December 1705. Inquiry regarding a Massachusetts tax act: "Whether the Commissioners and other Officers of the Customs are liable to be taxed * for their salaries paid out of money not granted to the Crown by the General Court." CO/5-920, p. 276; 9 February 1770.

[4] CO/5-1294, p. 57; 5 September 1732. B. T. J., vol. lxxix, p. 176; 5 June 1767. B. T. J., vol. xviii, p. 52; 9 October 1705.

[5] CO/5-714, p. 348; 3 November 1698. This request came from the Privy Council.

leges of persons naturalized by the act of Parliament in
Great Britain; and by what authority the colonies claimed
the power to make temporary laws.[1]

In addition to their examination of laws, the attorney
and solicitor considered the tentative drafts of acts, or
" bills," which governors sometimes presented to the Board
with a request for permission to give their assent.   When
requested to do so by the Board they drafted amendments
to such bills; and in a few cases they " prepared the heads "
of a law which the Board wished to have passed by an
assembly.[2]   After 1718 they rarely attended at the Board,
and when they did so it was usually to act as counsel for
one of the parties to a hearing.   In March, 1738, the Board
" had discourse " with both regarding quit-rents in North
Carolina.[3]   The solicitor attended and spoke at length as
counsel for the petitioner against a New York act " Making void a fraudulent Conveyance to William Davenport ";
and in 1760 both acted for the proprietors of Pennsylvania
at a hearing upon several laws.[4]

In April, 1718, Richard West was designated as " King's
Counsel " with a yearly salary of three hundred pounds.
He was commissioned to attend to such " Law Business
regarding Trade and Plantations as the Board should not
conceive of that importance to require the opinion of the

---

[1] *B. T. J.*, vol. xvi, p. 142; 1 June 1703. *B. T. J.*, vol. xlv, p. 29;
2 March 1736.   Chalmers, *Opinions*, pp. 338, 339; 22 July 1714.

[2] *C. S. P.*, 1693-6, p. 647. *CO/5-1360*, p. 469. *B. T. J.*, vol. xxvii,
p. 118. *B. T. J.*, vol. xli, p. 191. *B. T. J.*, vol. lxv, (unpaged) ; Jamaica,
5 July 1758.

[3] *B. T. J.*, vol. xlvii, p. 29.

[4] *B. T. J.*, vol. xlvii, p. 52; 3 April 1734. *B. T. J.*, vol. xlvii, p. 148.
CO/5-1295, p. 297 ; 24 June 1760.   One of the two appeared for Carolina
against an act of Georgia for regulating the Indian trade. *CO/5-366*,
F, 59.

Attorney and Solicitor General."[1]   West held the office
until he was appointed chancellor for Ireland in June, 1725.
His successor was Francis Fane, who retired in 1746 and
subsequently became a member of the Board of Trade.
He was succeeded by Sir Matthew Lamb, an exceedingly
able man, who held the position for over twenty years.
After a short intermission, during which the post was
vacant, Richard Jackson was appointed.   He served until
after 1776.

In obedience to a summons from the Board, West attended for the first time on May 7, 1718.   After considering several acts of Antigua, they desired him to put his
observations upon them, or any other acts of the plantations, in writing, and he agreed to do so from time to time
accordingly.[2]   For a time West attended all meetings of the
Board at which acts were considered.   He appears to have
rendered oral advice while they were under consideration
and to have submitted a written report at a subsequent meeting upon those which involved questions of special difficulty
or importance.[3]   Gradually, however, West's attendance became less frequent, and in the course of a year or two the
Board had returned to the procedure formerly observed in
referring laws to the attorney and solicitor general.   In
other words, they sent all acts to the counsel and deferred
the consideration of them until returned with a written re-

[1] Chalmers, *Opinions*, pp. 9, 10. *B. T. J.*, vol. xxvii, pp. 206, 213.

[2] *B. T. J.*, vol. xxvii, p. 231; 7 May 1718. He was given "Liberty at
any time to peruse such papers in this Office as relate to any of these
acts of Plantations, * * or which concern the Trade of this Kingdom."
B. T. J., vol. xxvii, p. 222; 2 May 1718.

[3] A New York act, after being considered with the king's counsel
attending was "referred to Mr. West for his opinion in writing
thereon." *B. T. J.*, vol. xxviii, p. 129, 140; February 1719. Others
were sent to him, "for his particular consideration and report."
B. T. J., vol. xxviii, p. 218.

port. The king's counsel continued, nevertheless, to attend meetings of the Board whenever he was requested to do so.[1]

Law reports, whether submitted by the attorney and solicitor general or by the king's counsel, often consisted of the simple statement that certain acts, having been examined, appeared unobjectionable " in point of law." Or the law officer began by stating that certain acts were temporary and had expired, and that others were liable to no objection. The remainder he listed separately, with comments following the title of each. After a short discussion of an act there followed, as a rule, a definite recommendation that it be confirmed, or, in spite of objectionable features, allowed to lie by, or that it be disallowed. Criticisms were based primarily upon grounds of legality, although general considerations of policy and expediency were discussed as well. In the latter case, however, the law officer was more restrained in making definite recommendations as to the course which, in his judgment, should be pursued.

From the first, it was usual for the agents or for representatives of persons interested in particular laws to solicit from the law officers the consideration of and report upon legislation. They appear to have explained the purpose of laws by stating the special circumstances which led to their enactment, to have advanced arguments for or against their confirmation, and to have expedited matters by the payment

---

[1] The Board sometimes propounded queries to the counsel as well as to the attorney and solicitor. They were, however, comparatively few in number, and generally had to do with matters of lesser scope and significance. The Board asked, for example, whether the Pennsylvania charter permitted the re-enactment of laws disallowed in England; whether a clause of a law repealed by a temporary law revived upon the expiration of the repealing act; and whether under an act of Parliament colonial privateers were entitled to bounties. *B. T. J.*, vol. xxviii, p. 167. *CO/5-873*, p. 507. *B. T. J.*, vol. li, p. 129.

of fees.[1] In rare instances they employed counsel and a preliminary hearing was held. There is no record of the proceedings. But apparently the arguments were concerned both with matters of law and of policy, and were, therefore, scarcely more technical or less broad in scope than those advanced at hearings before the Board of Trade.[2]

The content of the law report usually determined the trend of discussion upon an act at the Board of Trade, and not uncommonly, apart from any other consideration, determined its fate. In no instance was a recommendation of the attorney or solicitor general as to the confirmation or disallowance of an act rejected; although laws were sometimes re-referred for additional information or further elaboration of points previously made.[3] Advice given by the king's counsel was sometimes, though not often, disregarded.[4] Even after the appointment of a king's counsel,

[1] A representative of the commissioners of the customs appeared before the solicitor against a Massachusetts act " Prohibiting the Exportation of Money." *C. S. P.*, 1700, p. 475; 9 August 1700. The report of the solicitor upon a New York law "Vacating Several extravagant Grants of Lands" contains a statement of the arguments advanced to him both for and against the law by parties interested. *CO/5-1044*, p. 132; 27 June 1700. Also regarding an act of Jamaica see *B. T. J.*, vol. xvi, p. 205; 9 September 1703.

[2] The report upon two laws of North Carolina stated that the officer had "taken the same into consideration and heard Counsel for and against the said acts." *CO/5-296*, C, 1; 1 December 1750. In 1737 the Georgia trustees entered a caveat with the attorney general that no report be made upon some queries of the Board regarding an Indian trade act until they had been given an opportunity to be heard by their counsel before him. *CO/5-366*, F, 59; 29 June 1737. Fane was attended by a solicitor for the merchants, who argued against the confirmation of a New Jersey impost act that great detriment would arise to the trade of the kingdom from a clause laying a duty on copper ore exported. *CO/5-973*, F, 9.

[3] *CO/5-1361*, p. 1; 15 August 1740.

[4] *CO/5-1296*, p. 363; Pennsylvania, 20 July 1770. *A. P. C.*, vol. v, p. 282; New Hampshire, 9 December 1770.

the Board did not invariably secure a law report upon acts which it considered. An important bankruptcy law of Massachusetts was disallowed without a reference to Lamb, because he was absent from the city, and a quick disposal of it was deemed advisable.[1] An act of New York, " Declaring certain Persons incapable of being Members of the Assembly," appears to have escaped legal examination because the law was so flagrantly bad as to render it superfluous.[2] After 1718, however, such cases constituted the rare exception and not the rule. Upon the other hand, in adopting a recommendation of the law officer, the Board nearly always incorporated parts of his opinion in its representation. And copies of his report were often sent to the governors as a guide in enacting future legislation.[3]

The influence of the Board's legal advisers upon its policy in legislative review can scarcely be over-emphasized. The king's counsels, holding office as they did for comparatively long periods, and reviewing practically the entire volume of colonial legislation, were veritable watch-dogs of legality. Their practised eyes were quick alike to note undue encroachments upon the domain of individual liberty, unwarranted violations of the security of private property and unseemly infringements upon the prerogatives of the crown. They strove, not always successfully, but certainly not without effect, to keep the enactments of the assemblies within a fair degree of conformity to the acts of Parliament and the common law.

For advice regarding the confirmation or disallowance of legislation which in any way affected the revenues of the crown, the Board of Trade turned to the lords of the treas-

[1] *B. T. J.*, vol. lxv, unpaged; 21 June 1758.

[2] *B. T. J.*, vol. lxxvii, pp. 83, 92; 4 April 1770.

[3] *B. T. J.*, vol. xxvii, p. 92; 28 January 1718.

ury and the commissioners of the customs. From the latter body they requested an opinion upon many laws imposing restrictions upon trade or navigation. Among these were acts levying customs duties and prescribing the manner of their collection by establishing ports of entry or fixing collectors' fees. Laws regulating the production or the exportation of commodities, such as hides and tobacco, or levying imposts upon goods imported from Great Britain, or tending in any way to diminish the volume of trade between the mother country and the colonies, and consequently to impair the crown revenue, were also referred to them from time to time.[1]

Until 1715 the Board, as a matter of formality, sent these acts to the secretary of the lords of the treasury with a request that they " move the Lord High Treasurer that the Board may have the opinion of the Commissioners of the Customs." And in due time the report of the commissioners was returned through the same channel. Subsequently, however, the Board addressed letters to the secretary of the commissioners of the customs, and communications, as a rule, passed directly between the two bodies.[2]

---

[1] Among the acts referred were laws of Massachusetts, " To Restrain the Exportation of Raw Hides," " Establishing Sea Ports," " Establishing a Naval Office," "Ascertaining Fees," and " Rates and Duties of Tonnage," *Acts and Resolves*, vol. i, pp. 153, 336, 364. *B. T. J.*, vol. xvi, p. 45. *CO/5-260*, p. 261. They examined laws of Virginia for " Preventing Frauds in the Customs," " Establishing Ports," and several acts for " Improving the Staple of Tobacco." *B. T. J.*, vol. xiii, p. 14. *B. T. J.*, vol. xix, p. 157. *CO/5-1322*, R, 135. *CO/5-1366*, p. 532. Various acts from Maryland, Carolina and the Island colonies were referred as well. *CO/5-1273*, V, 110. *CO/5-403*, p. 9. *B. T. J.*, vol. lxvi, p. 22.

[2] There were two variations from this procedure. In 1752 two acts of Virginia "Amending the Staple of Tobacco" and " Preventing Frauds in the Customs " were sent, together with an act for " Settling the Titles and Bounds of Lands " to the lords of the treasury. *CO/5-1366*, p. 531. Action in this case may have been determined by the fact

An interesting episode occurred in 1730, when the Board referred an act of Virginia, "Amending the Staple of Tobacco and Preventing Frauds in His Majesty's Customs," to the commissioners of the customs. They returned it and asked to be excused from giving their opinion upon acts of the assemblies "unless commanded by the King in Council or the Lords of the Treasury." The Board replied by sending a list of acts upon which such an opinion had been rendered in the past. The commissioners then expressed a willingness to consider any measure that might effect the revenue under their management, and asked that the act be returned, at the same time insisting that they be excused from considering matters of trade unless commanded by his majesty or the lords of the treasury. The Board returned the act with a request for an opinion " so far as the act may relate to the revenue under their management," which was doubtless all that they had expected in the first instance. After submitting a report, the secretary for the commissioners wrote to the Board saying that they were informed that the agent for Virginia had complained in a memorial of not receiving an opportunity to be heard while the matter was under consideration before them. The Board sent them a copy of the memorial, to which the commissioners replied at length, defending themselves from the allegation of unfairness and answering the agent's arguments in favor of the act.[1]

To the lords of the treasury the Board applied also for advice upon legislation affecting quit rents or the revenues

that the latter act was one with which the commissioners of the customs had no concern. In 1753 a law of Pennsylvania for " Regulating Fees " was referred to the commissioners and a report returned through the lords of the treasury. *CO*/5-1273, V, 110.

[1] *B. T. J.*, vol. xxxix, pp. 301, 313, 326. *B. T. J.*, vol. xl, pp. 15, 17, 32, 41, 100. *CO*/5-1322, R, 133, R, 135, R, 137, R, 141. *CO*/5-1366, pp. 55, 58.

derived from the crown lands. In 1732 their lordships reported upon an act of this kind passed in South Carolina; but in subsequent cases they delegated the task to the auditor general of the plantations. Communications between the Board and the auditor continued, as a rule, to pass through the hands of the lords of the treasury; though here again there was a tendency upon the part of the Board of Trade to resort to a simpler procedure.[1] The lords of the treasury also examined and gave their approval to three private acts of New York relating to a contract for farming the excise there.[2]

Although it was the general policy of the Board to consult the treasury regarding laws which pertained to the royal revenue, the matter was wholly within their discretion and many acts apparently germane to the subject were never referred. Upon the other hand, the treasury, unlike the law officers, was actively engaged in the administration of the colonies and had subordinate officials there who frequently furnished information regarding questionable legislation. Upon the strength of their complaints the treasury sometimes took the initiative and brought the laws in question to the attention of the Board of Trade. As such commu-

---

[1] The treasury condemned a law of South Carolina " For the Remission of the Arrears of Quit Rents," and to their solicitor was entrusted the task of drafting a new one. *CO*/5-362, D, 33; 6 October 1732. *B. T. J.*, vol. xlii, p. 137. An act of Virginia " Settling the Titles and Bounds of Lands" was referred to the auditor in April 1751. But he failed to report and in December 1757 the Board wrote directly to the auditor and asked for an opinion. *CO*/5-1367, p. 321. *CO*/5-1329, X, 28. His report was addressed to the Board of Trade. An act of New York for the " More Easy Recovery of Quit Rents" was referred in December 1758 with the request that it be laid before the auditor general. *B. T. J.*, vol. lxv; 13 December 1758. *CO*/5-1129, p. 142. The auditor reported upon another quit rent act of New York in December 1770. *CO*/5-1075, p. 131.

[2] *CO*/5-1053, Cc, 124; 9 April 1724.

nications carried, either by statement or implication, the endorsement of the treasury, no further reference to it was usual.[1]

Although relatively few laws from the colonies came within the cognizance of the lords of the treasury, or their subordinates, their opinion upon such as concerned the crown revenue appears to have carried great weight. An act of Virginia for regulating the growth and shipment of tobacco, upon which they had reported unfavorably, was suffered to lie by because of the earnest solicitations of the governor. But this is the only instance in which their condemnation of an act did not result in its disallowance.[2]

From the Bishop of London the Board obtained advice upon laws concerning morality, religion and the Anglican Church. Unlike its other counselors, the bishops were members of the Board, and as such entitled to participate in discussions there and to sign its representations. They seldom attended, however, and when they did do so they generally came in response to a special request from the Board.[3] In all, the bishops submitted written reports upon

[1] The treasury referred to the Board a complaint from one John Taylor regarding a duty levied upon his ships by the government of New England; a complaint regarding the decrease in the revenue of the post office caused by the issuing of bills of credit in Massachusetts; and a complaint from the surveyor general of customs in Carolina, against an act laying a 10% impost upon British manufactures. *CO*/5-911, p. 404; 4 January 1705. *CO*/5-913, pp. 383, 399; June 1713. *CO*/5-1293, p. 141; 20 March 1717. Walpole, Surveyor General of the revenue, presented a representation regarding a New York quit rent act; and the secretary of the treasury forwarded a memorial of John Stewart, a contractor for transporting felons, against acts of Virginia and Maryland which imposed restrictions upon the importation of convicts. *B. T. J.*, vol. lii, pp. 1, 17; 1 February 1745. *A. P. C.*, vol. v, p. 115; 7 October 1767. An act of Florida was disallowed upon the complaint of the collector at Pensacola. *A. P. C.*, vol. v, p. 346; 19 June 1772.

[2] *CO*/5-1366, p. 72; 27 May 1731.

[3] The Bishop of London appears to have been in attendance not over

more than twenty acts of the assemblies. The majority of these were referred by the Board with a request for an opinion. But in several cases the bishops took the initiative by requesting that no action be taken upon a law until they had presented their views upon it. The majority of the acts upon which they reported provided for the establishment of the Anglican Church, the organization of parishes or the settlement and maintenance of ministers. They submitted opinions, also, regarding three acts for regulating marriage, two allowing affirmations in place of oaths, and one act for the suppression of vice and immorality. A good example of the activity and influence of the Bishop of London is afforded by the fate of a New York act " Declaring the Town of East Chester a distinct Parish from West Chester." After repeatedly calling the attention of the Board to this law, the bishop finally secured its consideration in January, 1703. He reported that it was " prejudicial to the Church, in that (without establishing any fixed maintenance for a minister in East Chester) it does impeach a former act which did make a convenient settlement for Ministers of that and several other Churches named." The law was accordingly disallowed in February, 1703.[1] In but few cases, however, were laws repealed upon the sole urgence of the Bishop of London. Those regulating matters of a more general nature, such as marriages or affirmations, were, as a rule, open to objections from other sources. In 1727 the bishop secured the promulgation of instructions to the governors in America, directing that they

half a dozen times between 1696 and 1776. Twice, in regard to the Maryland act " For the Worship of God" he was accompanied by the Archbishop of Canterbury. *B. T. J.*, vol. xiii, p. 343. Once he sent a personal representative. *B. T. J.*, vol. xv, p. 16; 12 May 1702.

[1] *CO*/5-1047, R, 33. *B. T. J.*, vol. vii, p. 86. *CO*/5-1119, p. 362. *CO*/5-1048, V, 27.

cause all laws against blasphemy, profaneness and immorality to be vigorously executed.[1]

In a few instances the Board of Trade referred laws to the post-master general. Upon his recommendation an act of North Carolina was disallowed in 1772, and the governor instructed to secure a new law free from the objections which he had raised against the former.[2] Upon two acts, one from Carolina, " Regulating the Court of Admiralty," and another from Massachusetts, " Regulating Fees," the Board obtained an opinion from the admiralty.[3]

Aside from the law officers, no opinion carried more weight with the Board than did that of the English merchants engaged in colonial trade. The upbuilding of commerce between the plantations and the mother country was one of the chief ends of the British colonial policy; and no one had a better practical knowledge of the subject than they. Moreover, the fact that their financial interests fre-

[1] *B. T. J.*, vol. xxxvi, pp. 111, 127, 128, 130, 139; 6 June 1727.

[2] *CO*/5-302, p. 187. *CO*/5-305, p. 147. *A. P. C.*, vol. v, p. 34; 6 May 1772. The chief objection was against allowing post riders in certain cases a fee of one shilling a mile. This was deemed exorbitant. In 1703 the Board referred to the post master general three laws of New York for " Encouraging a Post Office." He replied with observations at considerable length, but the Board appears to have taken no further action in the matter. *B. T. J.*, vol. viii, p. 67. *CO*/5-1119, p. 412. *CO*/5-1048, W, 6. He also reported upon the draft of an act for a post office in Pennsylvania. *CO*/5-1263, N, 57; 20 November 1705.

[3] In transmitting the Carolina act the Board inquired as to its consistency with his majesty's commission to the judge, with the rights of the crown, and the methods of proceeding which ought to be observed there. The reply was unfavorable and some correspondence with the proprietors followed; but apparently no action was taken by the crown. *B. T. J.*, vol. xiv, p. 312. *CO*/5-1261, p. 44; 3 February 1702. The lords of the admiralty offered no objection to the Massachusetts law regarding fees. *B. T. J.*, vol. xxviii, p. 236. *CO*/5-867, W, 56; 8 May 1719.

quently were affected adversely by colonial legislation upon
matters of finance and trade, caused them to keep close
watch for the enactment of such laws, and quickly to regis-
ter objections against those of which they did not approve.
Indeed, in some cases, their complaints reached the Board
before copies of the acts themselves had arrived from the
colony. Occasionally, on the other hand, the Board took
the initiative, and, despite the fact that the merchants possessed no official status, requested from them advice or information. Because of their proximity, the merchants of
London were most often in evidence. But certain acts concerning the slave and tobacco trades called forth remon-
strances, as well from those of the " out ports," Bristol,
Liverpool and Glasgow.[1] Usually several of the merchants
appeared at the Board whenever one of their memorials
came up for consideration, and one or two of the more
prominent spoke in support of their petition, or to refute
arguments advanced by the agent. At the more important
" hearings," when the proceedings assumed the formality
of a trial at law, the merchants intrusted the management
of their case to a solicitor, and did not address the Board
unless requested to give an opinion or to impart additional
information.

Precisely how much influence the merchants exerted in
determining the fate of any particular enactment, it is difficult to say. Their petitions were, for the most part, in
accord with established commercial policy, and doubtless
many acts disallowed at their request would have met the
same fate eventually without such interposition. But
others which were free from legal objection would certainly

[1] Such petitions had, upon an average, about ten signers. In some
cases their wording is so similar as to suggest that the merchants of
different ports, acting in concert, entrusted the writing of them to the
same person.

have passed unnoticed. Moreover, the fact that laws regarding trade and finance were being brought continually to the attention of the Board contributed, in turn, to the development of a more effective and consistent policy upon those subjects. The protests of the merchants were most numerous and at the same time most effective against laws imposing obstacles to the collection of their debts. These include bankruptcy legislation, stay laws, and acts regulating bills of exchange and executions upon judgments. Next in point of number were petitions for the disallowance of acts authorizing the emission of bills of credit. These, however, seldom accomplish their whole purpose, because the Board came to realize that some form of currency was an economic necessity in the colonies, and because they hesitated to annul laws under which bills had already been issued. The merchants complained also against many acts levying duties upon the importation of liquors, slaves or goods of British manufacture. Here they generally accomplished their object by securing the disallowance of the offensive law, or at least an instruction for the passage of an amendment repealing the particular duty in question. Other memorials had to do with acts of Virginia and Maryland for regulating the growth and export of tobacco, laws governing the conduct of the fisheries or the Indian trade, or providing for the erection of ports and towns. The activity and influence of the merchants at the Board of Trade did not escape notice in the colonies, and letters from the governors sometimes betray the presence of considerable ill feeling against them occasioned by the disallowance of a popular law.[1]

For information regarding the aim and purpose of colo-

[1] Gooch of Va. to the Board, *CO*/5-1322, R, 160; 22 December 1731. Fauquier of Va. to the Board, *CO*/5-1330, Y, 85; 29 June 1763.

nial legislation and the special circumstances leading to its enactment, the Board of Trade was dependent upon two principal sources: the representations of the agents in England, and letters received from the governors.[1] Soon after its formation the Board, wishing to discuss the raising of levies with representatives of the various colonies, noted a want of authorized agents with whom to consult. Accordingly it was ordered that the next letters to Virginia, Maryland and New York should intimate that various other places had agents, and that the want of them was an inconvenience, " and may happen in some occasion to prove prejudicial to them, by delays in their public affairs, and loss of opportunities for their public advantages." And in like manner the Board on other occasions urged upon Massachusetts, Maryland and New Jersey the expediency of maintaining accredited agents in England.[2] Eventually all the colonies complied with this advice. From time to time the Board required agents to appear and present their credentials, apparently in order that there might be available a correct list of persons serving in that capacity.[3]

[1] The official journals of the council and assembly were also to a certain extent useful for this purpose.

[2] *B. T. J.*, vol. x, pp. 310, 311; 15 October 1697. *C. S. P.*, 1700, p. 629; 30 October 1700. The Board wrote to Gov. Blackiston of Maryland: " It will be for the service of the Province that an Agent be constituted, with authority * to solicit the dispatch of acts * * and all other public business. * The charge need not be great. It is a thing done by most of the Plantations, and proves very useful to them * " *C. S. P.*, 1700, p. 709; 3 December 1700. Also *CO/5-726*, p. 99. *CO/5-1123*, p. 441.

[3] *B. T. J.*, vol. xxvii, p. 34; December 1718. *B. T. J.*, vol. lxi, unpaged; 19 December 1754. In 1740 the Board summoned all the agents to attend for a discussion " at large of the Problem of Paper Currency in the Colonies." They, however, proved non-committal, saying that they had received no instructions in the matter. *B. T. J.*, vol. xlviii, p. 94.

In regard to local disputes caused by agents being appointed by the lower house without the concurrence of the governor and council, the

The most important duty of the agent was that of over-
seeing and furthering the review and confirmation of legislation. As a rule, public acts progressed with reasonable
promptness from the Board to the law officer without the
necessity of urgency upon the agent's part. Having informed himself regarding legislation by letters from the
colony or any other means at his disposal, it behooved the
agent to wait upon the law officer and solicit a report. After
obtaining this he sometimes attended the Board to ask for
an early consideration of acts there. When they were taken
up he was on hand once more to furnish whatever information was required and to explain away objections. If
opposition to the confirmation of an act led to a formal
hearing before the Board, the agent either defended the interests of the colony in the matter or, in the more important
cases, employed a solicitor to do so. The work of the agents
in preventing delays, and in explaining legislation to the
Board in the most favorable light, was of the greatest importance.[1] Unfortunately, however, the position was often
held by Englishmen with little first-hand knowledge of colonial conditions, or by Americans who having been long
resident in England, were out of touch with colonial affairs,
and consequently dependent upon information and instructions from the colony. Having failed, either from mishap
or neglect, to receive these, they were obliged either to ask
the Board for a long delay, or to defend the act in question

Board took no decisive stand, although it insisted in a general way
that agents representing a colony should be appointed by the governor,
council and assembly. In 1771 Governor Hutschinson was instructed
to that effect. *CO*/5-920, p. 309.

[1] On May 28, 1754 the Board made a representation for the repeal of
nine acts of South Carolina. On June 26 Mr. Crockatt, the agent, was
called in. After he was gone the Board agreed to allow the acts to
lye by. Dickerson, *Am. Col. Govt.*, p. 267, note 628.

without an adequate knowledge of the subject.[1] Moreover, the agent spoke with the professional bias of a solicitor bound to further the interests of clients rather than to give an unprejudiced opinion based upon the best information at his disposal.

Of far greater value to the Board of Trade were the comments which, in accordance with their instructions, the governors transmitted upon all legislation. Their fullness and accuracy varied considerably according to the ability and political insight and prejudice of the different governors, and they were subject necessarily to a strong official bias. Nevertheless, such comments came first-hand from one in close touch with the colony, and therefore informed in regard to local need and sentiment. Regarding acts of unusual importance or of doubtful propriety, governors were apt to write at considerable length. Others they often grouped, attaching brief comments, such as " beneficial," " customary," or " fit to be allowed." Consequently, it was not unusual for the Board to allow an act to lie by, while they wrote to the governor for a more detailed account of his reasons for passing it. In some instances governors betrayed a naïve and amazing unconsciousness of defects in laws which they recommended for confirmation. Again, they frankly acknowledged the existence of grave faults, stating, in effect, that having resisted popular clamor for legislation even more objectionable, it seemed best to assent and so place the burden of refusal upon the government in England. Or again the governor protected himself by securing the inclusion of a suspending clause, and then

---

[1] On July 24, 1735, Guerin, Agent for New York told the Board that he was not ready to offer reasons for passing an act regarding bills of credit. *B. T. J.*, vol. xliv, p. 151. Furie, agent of South Carolina, failed to speak in defence of a fee act, because he had no instructions regarding the law, and did not know the reasons for it. *B. T. J.*, vol. xlvi, p. 40; 10 March 1737.

damning the act by faint praise. A governor who stood well with the Board, and could justify his recommendations in an able fashion, was in a position to exert no inconsiderable influence upon the fate of legislation. A conspicuous example of this fact is afforded by the manner in which Governor Gooch of Virginia secured legislation regulating the growth and exportation of tobacco, although his law was opposed by a considerable body of local sentiment and, in no uncertain terms, by the commissioners of customs.[1] Notwithstanding strong objections from the king's counsel, a New Hampshire law for " Restraining the Taking of Excessive Usury " was confirmed because the governor had written that it was of the greatest importance to the province.[2] An opportune letter from Governor Shirley secured the confirmation of a Massachusetts excise act, despite strong opposition from the province; while in 1761 Governor Ellis, of Georgia, appeared before the Board and saved a law concerning the recovery of debts, for the disallowance of which a representation had already been drawn.[3]

In conclusion, a study of the Board of Trade reveals a small group of expert colonial advisers, in close touch with the high officials of state, with the legal advisers of the crown and with the several administrative departments of the government; a body sensitive to conflicting interests, fair, painstaking and laborious, but possessing withal no very great powers.

---

[1] *A. P. C.,* vol. iii, p. 326. *Cf. infra,* p. 118.

[2] *CO*/5-930, p. 77. *CO*/5-943, p. 16. *A. P. C.,* vol. v, p. 282; 9 December 1770.

[3] *CO*/5-918, p. 325; 6 August 1755. *B. T. J.,* vol. lxviii, pp. 281, 282; 6 June 1761. These examples, however, should not be accorded undue weight. A much greater number might easily be given in which laws recommended by the governor in the strongest terms, were found objectionable and forthwith disallowed.

Unless neglected or laid by probationary at the Board of Trade, laws progressed, together with the report or representation upon them, to the Privy Council, by an order of which they were confirmed or disallowed, or in some cases left conditionally in force.[1] For several years subsequent to 1696 the Council scrutinized the findings and recommendations of the Board rather closely. In one instance it sent a representation to the attorney and solicitor general with the request that they report upon it;[2] but in no case during this period was its final action upon a law contrary to that recommended by the Board. After 1710, however, the Council gradually acquired a habit of delegating the examination of legislation, and the recommendations from the Board pertaining to it, to a committee of its own members, whose findings it invariably indorsed without question. The proceedings of the Council in this connection were thenceforth purely formal. The part taken by the committee in legislative review becomes, therefore, of sufficient importance to warrant a somewhat detailed consideration.

During the early part of the eighteenth century the Privy Council for the most part relinquished the exercise of its discretion to a small group of its own members, retaining to itself little authority save in matters of formal and customary procedure. The process by which this change came about is obscure, and lies without the limits

[1] The precise wording of the order in council varies considerably from time to time. In some cases the act was inserted in full. But the usual course was to give only the title and date of passage. The action is represented as being taken by " His Majesty in Council," or by " His Majesty with the advice of the Privy Council," or by the " Lords Justices with the advice of the Privy Council." It is usually stated, also, that the Council has acted upon the advice of the Board of Trade, or of the Board and a committee of the Council.

[2] *C. S. P.*, 1697-8, p. 523; 3 November 1698.

of this study.[1]   Suffice it to say that after 1710 acts were referred by the Council with increasing frequency to "the Committee on Appeals," "the Committee of the Whole Council," "a Committee for the Plantations," or simply to "the Committee"—terms which were sometimes used interchangeably.[2]   The body thus designated seems to have had no fixed membership, but rather to have consisted of members of the whole Council working now upon one kind of business and now upon another, for the time being. In 1702 a representation of the Board upon several Barbadoes laws was referred to the "Lords of a Committee of the whole Council," and upon their recommendation one of the acts was disallowed.[3]   And on the same day a committee of the whole, having obtained an opinion from the attorney general, recommended that Governor Lord Cornbury of New York be instructed to induce the assembly to repeal an objectionable clause of their enactment.[4]   The next reference involving colonial legislation occurred in 1714, when the "Committee for hearing Appeals" returned a representation upon several Pennsylvania laws to the Board, with the request that they investigate and report back "by what grants or authorities several of His Majesty's Plantations do claim a power of making temporary laws."[5]   After the accession of the Whigs to power in 1714, references to the committee become some-

---

[1] For a full discussion of the matter see an article by E. R. Turner, entitled "The Development of the Cabinet, 1699-1760," in the *American Historical Review*, vol. xviii, pp. 756-768, and vol. xix, pp. 27-43. Pages 758 and 759 of the former volume are in particular germane to the subject. See also, Andrews and Davenport, *Guide to the MS. Material in the British Museum*, pp. 172, 173.

[2] *A. P. C.*, Introd., vol. ii, pp. vi, xi, and vol. iii, pp. viii, ix.

[3] *A. P. C.*, vol. ii, p. 415; 6 July 1702.

[4] *A. P. C.*, vol. ii, p. 413; 9 July 1702.

[5] *B. T. J.*, vol. xxiv, pp. 228, 229. *CO*/5-1292, p. 418; 2 September 1714.

what more frequent. There occurred one in October, 1714, one in 1715, one in 1719, and two in 1720. During the decade following the increase is gradual though constant, until by 1731 the reference of acts by the Council to the Board through the committee had become the rule, and reference directly to the Board the rare exception.[1] The Board, in turn, came gradually to address its reports to the " Lords of the Committee " rather than to " His Majesty in Council." In the great majority of cases the committee, after examining acts, simply endorsed the recommendations in regard to them already made by the Board of Trade. Indeed, their reports which appear in the *Acts of the Privy Council* consist almost exclusively of Board representations adopted with little or no alteration.

Various deviations from the customary procedure, however, emphasize the fact that the increasing initiative and activity of the committee necessarily resulted in a corresponding decrease in the prestige and authority of the Board of Trade. The former sometimes sent acts and representations back to the Board for further consideration.[2] Or again it referred them to the treasury, or the attorney and

[1] After about 1758 the Council sometimes referred business directly to the Board, with directions to report to the committee. *A. P. C.*, vol. iv, Introd., vol. vi. *A. P. C.*, vol. iv, p. 367.

[2] *A. P. C.*, vol. iii, p. 225; 22 May 1729. The committee sometimes attained much the same result by summoning the Board to meet with itself in joint session. The journal for 1731, for example, contains the following entry: " The Board at the desire of the Lords of the Committee having attended them this morning, the Committee took into consideration the following reports of this Board. [Three reports upon acts of New Jersey, Jamaica and South Carolina.] The Lords of the Committee then desired the Board would please to attend again tomorrow Senight to hear what the Agent for New England had to offer regarding two articles in the Governor's instructions." *B. T. J.*, vol. xl, pp. 287, 288. See also *CO/5-870*, Z, 71; 15 October 1729. *B. T. J.*, vol. xl, pp. 196, 202; 28 July 1731. *B. T. J.*, vol. xliv, p. 102; 17 June 1735.

solicitor general, with instructions to report, not to the
Board, but to itself.[1] The committee sometimes overruled
the Board's suggestions for instructions to governors, or
took the initiative in suggesting new ones.[2] In some cases
it even reversed the recommendations of the Board in regard to the confirmation or disallowance of acts. A conspicuous example of this is afforded by the course of a New
York act levying a two per cent tax upon the importation
of European goods. The Board, while objecting to the tax
imposed, recommended its confirmation because of the
" present necessity of the government." But the committee,
influenced probably by the merchants, insisted upon its disallowance.[3] In like manner, an act of Antigua, constituting
a court of attachments, was disallowed upon the recommendation of the attorney and solicitor generals, although the
Board had urged its confirmation.[4]

Parties dissatisfied with the outcome of a hearing at the
Board could continue the contest before the committee.
There the procedure was more formal, each side filing a
written brief and being heard by counsel only. If new and
important facts were brought out, the committee might refer
the whole matter to the Board for further consideration.[5]
As the work done in committee became of more importance,
the attendance there seems to have increased, until often
after the middle of the century a committee was merely the
Council sitting as such, a transition from one to the other

[1] *A. P. C.*, vol. iii, pp. 55, 350. *CO*/5-1366, p. 344. *CO*/5-879, Cc, 4.

[2] *A. P. C.*, vol. iii, Introd., pp. xix, 605, 606, 695. *A. P. C.*, vol. iv, pp.
153, 712. *B. T. J.*, vol. lix; 15 February 1752.

[3] The act contained a suspending clause and two years elapsed between the Board's representation and the report of the committee.
CO/5-1124, p. 283. *CO*/5-1053, Cc, 125.

[4] *A. P. C.*, vol. iii, pp. 180; 23 November 1728. *A. P. C.*, vol. iii, p. 63;
Barbadoes, 21 February 1724.

[5] *A. P. C.*, vol. v, p. 351; Jamaica, 19 December 1772.

being indicated in the *Acts of the Council* by the words,
" afterwards their Lordships sat as a Committee." [1] The
committee report upon a Massachusetts act of " Indemnity "
in 1767, was signed by twenty-six persons, including the
lord chancellor, the lord president and the chancellor of the
exchequer, while the order in council carried thirty-one
names. Thirteen signatures appear upon both documents.[2]
This law, however, had aroused much interest. The usual
attendance in committee was probably not so large, even
during this later period.

[1] *A. P. C.*, vol. iv, Introd., p. ix, p. 207.
[2] *CO*/5-892, p. 447.

CHAPTER III

THE PROCEDURE OF THE GOVERNMENT IN LEGISLATIVE REVIEW (CONTINUED)

By means of instructions limiting the discretion of governors in giving assent to proposed legislation, the the government exercised a considerable restraint upon the law-making power of the legislatures in the royal colonies. At the close of the seventeenth century it had already imposed general rules regarding the form of enactments and the manner of their transmission. It was insisted that enacting clauses should read "by the Governor, Council and Assembly," and that each separate act should deal with but one subject, and contain no clause foreign to its title.[1] Unless passed for a temporary end, acts must be of indefinite duration; while laws for levying money were not to continue for less than one year.[2] Governors were not to re-enact any law except upon very urgent occasions, and in no case more than once without his majesty's express consent. Acts altering, confirming or suspending other acts must indicate by title and date of passage the precise laws effected.[3]

Governors were instructed to transmit laws within three months from the time of their enactment and to send duplicates by the next conveyance, upon pain of

[1] *CO/5-1362*, p. 141; Virginia, 22 April 1717.

[2] *CO/5-726*, p. 177. *CO/5-914*, p. 378.

[3] *C. S. P.*, 1669-1674, p. 625; Jamaica, 1674. *CO/5-914*, p. 378; instruction to Shirley, 18 July 1716.

forfeiting one year's salary.[1]   Each act was to bear in wax a separate imprint of the provincial seal.   It was to be carefully abstracted in the margins, and to bear the dates of its passage by the governor, council and assembly.   The governor was to be " as particular as may be " in his observations upon every act ; " whether . . introductive of a new Law, declaratory of a former Law, or whether [it] does repeal a Law then before in being ; . . and to send . . the reasons for the passing of such law, unless the same do fully appear in the preamble." Copies of the official journals of the council and assembly were to accompany acts.[2]

Other instructions of a more detailed and specific nature forbade the governor's assent to laws for the accomplishment of certain ends, such as laying a duty upon European goods imported in English vessels,[3] or placing inhabitants of the colonies upon a more advantageous footing than those of Great Britain, or affecting the trade or navigation of Great Britain, or levying duties upon British shipping or the product of British manufactures.[4]

---

[1] *C. S. P.*, 1677-80, p. 608; 30 September 1680. *N. Y. Col. Docs.*, vol. iii, p. 378.   The governor of Jamaica was instructed in 1670 to transmit laws " at the first opportunity."   *C. S. P.*, 1669-74, p. 625.   This phrase was used also in the case of New Hampshire, possibly because communication with England was uncertain.   But the form quoted above was the usual one after 1680.

[2] *CO*/5-1293, p. 339; Pennsylvania, 1724. *N. Y. Col. Docs.*, vol. v, p. 127; 27 December 1709. *CO*/5-907, p. 103; Massachusetts, 30 January 1697.   The Board suggested to Bellomont that acts be in a form convenient for binding. *CO*/5-1118, p. 120.   After the first quarter of the eighteenth century most of the laws were transmitted in print.

[3] *N. Y. Col. Docs.*, vol. v, p. 706. *CO*/5-1053, Cc, 125; 30 April 1724.

[4] *A. P. C.*, vol. iii, p. 348; 27 January 1732. *N. H. St. Papers*, vol. xviii, p. 45; 5 May 1732.   There were prohibitions against acts making duties upon negroes payable by the importer, or imposing duties upon

In other cases the prohibition was conditional, usually upon the insertion of a clause suspending the operation of the act until his majesty's pleasure concerning it could be known. Thus, for many years governors were forbidden to pass laws emitting bills of credit without a suspending clause; and it was a standing rule that there should be no laws " of an unusual or extraordinary nature, wherein his majesty's prerogative or the property of his subjects might be predjudiced" without consent previously obtained or the insertion of a suspending clause.[1] While the greater part of these instructions were of a general nature, and binding upon all the governors, others had to do with local concerns and were issued only to governors of particular colonies. In 1770, for example, Virginia was forbidden to pass any law increasing the duty already established upon the importation of slaves ;[2] while Massachusetts was forbidden to appoint an agent otherwise than by an act of the whole legislature, or to levy a tax upon the salaries of government officials, except such as were paid by the assembly.[3]

This method of controlling the assemblies was more effective than the disallowance of laws already passed because its operation was more uniform in all the colo-

---

the importation of felons. *CO*/5-1128, p. 139; 5 July 1753. In 1767 acts by which the number of members in the Assemblies were enlarged or diminished were forbidden; (*B. T. J.*, vol. lxxix, p. 250. *N. Y. Col. Docs.*, vol. viii, p. 175) in 1771 laws by which the property of non-residents was made liable for the payment of debts; (*CO*/5-999, p. 246) and in 1773 laws for naturalization or divorce, or the confirmation of land titles. *CO*/5-930, p. 563. *B. T. J.*, vol. lxxx, p. 142. *A. P. C.*, vol. v, p. 552. This list is not exhaustive.

[1] Instruction to Shirley *CO*/5-914, p. 378; 18 July 1716.

[2] *CO*/5-1334, Cc, 8; 9 December 1770. *A. P. C.*, vol. iv, p. 746; 11 July 1766.

[3] *CO*/5-920, p. 309; 16 March 1771.

nies, and because it was preventative and served to check abuses at their source. A legislative indiscretion upon the part of one or two of the assemblies was apt to be met by a general instruction, which more or less effectively locked the stable door so far as the other colonies were concerned. Instructions once issued were continued in succeeding documents unless it became evident that because of changed conditions or circumstances they were no longer required. In 1738 the Board "digested under several heads, such as Council, Assembly, Militia" all general instructions. In this manner a recognized form became established, and the Board in making its representation upon the draft of a new governor's instructions noted only such articles as were added to or differed from those issued to his predecessor.[1]

Other instructions were mandatory rather than prohibitive, bidding the governors to urge upon the assemblies the passage of certain salutary laws. In this fashion the Board recommended the enactment of laws to secure the humane treatment of negro slaves and Indians, and to obtain permanent acts for regulating the militia.[2] The governor of Maryland was instructed to "do all that in you lyes" to secure the enactment of a law prohibiting the export of bulk tobacco, while the governor of South Carolina was directed to urge upon the assembly the necessity of pro-

---

[1] *B. T. J.*, vol. xlvii, p. 24. Instructions were suggested either at the Board, or in the Council or its committee. In any case a draft of the instruction proposed was prepared by the Board, approved by the committee (or prior to about 1720 by the Council) and issued by an order in council.

[2] *B. T. J.*, vol. iv, p. 213; 6 October 1683. *CO/5-403*, p. 76. *CO/5-1073*, p. 17.

viding a jail and of keeping the same in repair.[1] Instead of allowing an objectionable act to lie by and instructing the governor to obtain its repeal or amendment, the Board sometimes secured the same result in a more emphatic and effective fashion by disallowing the law and stating specifically in an instruction the modifications which would serve to make it acceptable to the government. Thus it was stated that if in the act disallowed for " Securing the Administration of Pennsylvania " a clause be inserted that on the death of the Lieut. Governor, the Proprietors do name another and obtain her Majesty's approbation within six months, then the act will be confirmed." [2] In the case of a Jamaica act which had been disallowed because, contrary to the governor's instructions, it enlarged the number of the assembly and contained no suspending clause, permission was given to pass " a new law corresponding in all respects to that repealed." [3]

In several instances the Board, disapproving an act submitted, drafted a measure more to their liking and sent it to the colony for enactment. But it was not insisted that these drafts be accepted unaltered. Rather were they sent to show what the Board conceived " his Majesty might not be unwilling to approve of in case the General Assembly think fit to enact it accordingly." [4] In the most conspicuous instance of this kind a Maryland act " For the Service of God and the Establishment of a Religion " was replaced by a new bill, containing " proper alterations "

---

[1] *CO/5-724*, p. 47; 12 October 1691. *B. T. J.*, vol. xlv, p. 90.

[2] *A. P. C.*, vol. ii, p. 615; 24 October 1709. Similar action was taken regarding an act of North Carolina, *A. P. C.*, vol. v, p. 341. *CO/5-305*, p. 155; 12 May 1772.

[3] *A. P. C.*, vol. v, p. 351; 5 March 1773.

[4] *B. T. J.*, vol. ix, p. 351.

agreeable to the toleration allowed in England, together with a clause for repealing the act then in force.[1]

When the enactment of a law was forbidden unless it contained a suspending clause, or unless his Majesty's assent had been previously obtained, the governor or the assembly sometimes chose the latter alternative and submitted the tentative draft of a desired law to the Privy Council. In this manner, for example, Governor Bernard secured permission to approve an act which established a lottery for the benefit of Harvard College.[2] Though such bills were approved, amendments were sometimes suggested by the Board. In 1704 they considered the draft for a revision of the laws of Virginia prepared by the governor and a committee of the council, and suggested many changes to be made before its final enactment.[3] And permission was accorded New Jersey to issue certain bills of credit providing a clause regarding the disposal of interest,

---

[1] *A. P. C.*, vol. ii, p. 362; 13 February 1701. *CO/5-726*, p. 170. Some English Quakers objected, esteeming themselves "under hard usage that a Law contrary to their fundamental settlement and the ancient Law of that Province should be prepared here and sent over there." They complained that it was not customary for the King to prepare money Bills and give directions to have them passed into acts. *C. S. P.*, 1701, p. 211. The Massachusetts council refused assent to the draft of a law regarding "Pirates and Privateers" because it enlarged the jurisdiction of the admiralty. *Acts and Resolves*, vol. i, p. 263; 3 June 1699. In 1735 an act was drafted by the attorney and solicitor to replace a South Carolina quit-rent law. But the agent and the governor so strongly defended the act in force that the matter appears to have been dropped. *B. T. J.*, vol. xliii, pp. 149, 162, 163; vol. xliv, pp. 229, 232, 233, 240. *CO/5-364*, E, 44.

[2] *CO/5-920*, p. 148; 24 December 1762. *B. T. J.*, vol. lxix, p. 317.

[3] *B. T. J.*, vol. ix, pp. 12, 13, 14; April 1704. *CO/5-1361*, p. 4. The Board informed the attorney and solicitor that these bills might "be altered in any part thereof as Bills transmitted from Ireland." *CO/5-1360*, p. 469.

to be prepared in England, should be inserted *verbatim* in the act for emission.[1]

From time to time the colonies were urged to gather and to transmit a complete collection of their laws in force, for convenience in reviewing new acts and in judging colonial appeals. With this request all the colonies, royal, charter and proprietary, at rather long intervals complied.[2] The order, long a standing instruction to the governors that they coöperate with the councils in revising the laws and in sending home a complete body with an opinion upon each, met with less response. It was expected that the revisions would be examined and approved by the Privy Council, and then returned to the colonies for re-enactment—a procedure of which the lower houses, from whence must come the necessary appropriations, strongly disapproved.

Complaints from the Board regarding the confused state of the Maryland laws, led to a general revision by the assembly, in 1699, and the passing of a blanket act "Ascertaining the Laws." But this was disallowed, because the Board had contemplated a revision by the governor and council only, and because the inclusion of so many acts under one title constituted a violation of the governor's instructions.[3]

Because of opposition or indifference upon the part of the burgesses, and of procrastination upon the part of the

[1] *A. P. C.*, vol. iv, p. 228; 1755. The Board insisted that the submission of drafts in this manner be approved by the governor, although it did not require that he approve of the subject matter. *B. T. J.*, vol. xxxvi, p. 230; 1727.

[2] *A. P. C.*, vol. iv, p. 153. Collections of the acts of New York were made in 1699, 1711, 1740, of Massachusetts in 1713, of New Hampshire in 1702, 1741, 1761 and 1768, and of Virginia in 1700, 1741 and 1761. New York, New Hampshire, South Carolina and Virginia complied in 1740-1; South Carolina, New Hampshire, Virginia and Pennsylvania in 1761.

[3] Board to Blackiston, *CO/5-725*, p. 468; 4 January 1700.

members of a joint committee of the council and the house, chosen by the governor to perform the task, a revision of the Virginia laws commenced in 1698 consumed several years.[1] In January, 1704, Secretary Jennings of Virginia attended the Board of Trade with two books, the large one containing " a complete collection of all laws in force." The lesser contained copies of bills prepared by the committee of revision, and comprehended all that was material in the other book. When once the latter were " enacted and confirmed," then the other was to "determine and become voyd." After the Board had proposed sundry alterations, the bills were returned to the colony, where fifty-eight laws were enacted in October, 1705.[2] In 1713 Governor Spotswood wrote the Board that, notwithstanding the great length of time spent in securing the late revision, and its cost of upwards fifteen hundred pounds, the work was still imperfect and unsatisfactory.[3] He accordingly intrusted the task of making a further revision to the secretary, attorney general, judge of the admiralty and clerk of

---

[1] The "Account of the present State and Government of Virginia" signed by Hartwell, Blair and Chilton, sets forth the need of a revision there. " There being great scarcity of able Lawyers and wise Politicians in that country—very few of the Laws have been as well drawn and framed in the Beginning, but that Experience has discovered many errors and Imperfections, which they have endeavored to patch up and mend with subsequent laws, and sometimes by repealing the old law and making a new one. [So] the body of their Laws is become not only long, and confused: But it is a very hard matter to know what laws are in force, and what not. * * " *CO*/5-1359, p. 130; 20 October 1697.

[2] *B. T. J.*, vol. viii, pp. 356, 357; 11 January 1704. Five of these acts were afterwards disallowed in England because of " many disagreeable clauses foisted in both by the Committee and the Assembly that passed the late revised laws." Spotswood to the Board, *CO*/5-1363, p. 500; 11 February 1713.

[3] *CO*/5-1363, pp. 500-502; 11 February 1713.

the council, who as remuneration sought, apparently without success, a royal grant of the sole privilege of printing it.[1]

In 1746-8 the laws of Virginia were revised once more by a joint committee of the two houses,[2] and a " body " of eighty-nine acts were approved by the assembly and dispatched to England. In October, 1751, the Privy Council confirmed fifty-seven of these acts, and disallowed ten. The Council also approved a committee report representing the action of Virginia, " as a method worthy of imitation and which we could wish to see followed in all Your Majesty's Colonies in America, since nothing can more effectually tend to promote Order and good Government, secure the Properties and Possessions of your Majesty's subjects, and prevent litigious Controversies and Disputes than a clear and well digested body of Laws." Accordingly the governors were instructed, " jointly with the Council and Assembly, . . . to consider and revise all laws, . . . excepting only such as relate to private property, . . . and in lieu thereof to frame and pass a complete and well digested body of new laws, . . . taking care that no law be passed without a clause suspending its execution.[3]

The instruction, however, proved ineffectual, for the assemblies had no mind to risk the disallowance of laws

[1] Spotswood to the Board, *CO*/5-1364, p. 403; 31 July 1716. This revision differed from the former in that the laws therein were fully enacted by the assembly before being dispatched to England. *CO*/5-1318, P, 144; 25 October 1717.

[2] A " joint committee of some of the principal members best acquainted with the business and living nearest the capital, to perform the work in vacation times, all bills from them are to be reported to the Assembly where they are to be formally ratified and passed. Nor is any law to be abrogated or altered but by act of the Assembly." *CO*/5-1326, V, 90; Gooch to the Board, 4 July 1746.

[3] *A. P. C.*, vol. iv, p. 132; 31 October 1751. *B. T. J.*, vol. lix, unpaged; 14 February 1752. *N. Y. Col. Docs.*, vol. vi, p. 755.

already confirmed and established, and were loath to resort
to such an extensive use of the suspending clause.   The
laws of Massachusetts, by reason of the many temporary
acts annually renewed and others many times amended,
were particularly in need of revision.   The assembly there
having rejected such a proposal, Governor Shirley was instructed to lay the matter " in the strongest manner " before them.[1] With difficulty he succeeded in securing the
appointment of a joint committee empowered merely to
suggest amendments " necessary in any particular Laws." [2]
Nothing further was done, and shortly after the instruction
was omitted from those issued to all the governors.   Later
developments had revealed considerable inconvenience resulting from the Virginia revision, at first so cordially approved.   The house of burgesses issued formal protests
both against the confirmation and the disallowance of so
many acts; against the former because it deprived them of
the power to make necessary amendments, and against the
latter because of the importance and popularity of the laws
annulled.   The Board, upon the other hand, in recommending that the instruction be discontinued, complained that
the legislature in framing the new laws had " availed itself
of the opportunity, either totally to set aside or to alter in
part several of the former laws, which had been confirmed
by the Crown."   Moreover, an act regarding " Executions
for the Relief of Debtors," against which the merchants
bitterly complained, was found to have been confirmed,

[1] *A. P. C.*, vol. iv, p. 207; 19 April 1753.   *B. T. J.*, vol. lx, unpaged;
1 May 1753.

[2] *CO*/5-887, Hh, 19; 20 April 1754.   Shirley admitted that if the new
laws were acted on two or three years and then disallowed inconveniences would arise.   But this, he said, was guarded against by
the provision that each act contain a suspending clause!   He referred
to the instruction as a " Remarkable instance of His Majesty's paternal
care over his subjects."   *CO*/5-887, Hh, 12.

among others, and so placed beyond the possibility of disallowance.[1]

None of the proprietary colonies save Pennsylvania regularly submitted its legislation to the Privy Council for review. Upon several occasions, however, the Council disallowed, either directly or through the proprietors, acts of
Carolina against which complaints had been received. It
also dictated to the proprietors the purport of instructions
forbidding the governors to enforce objectionable laws or
to permit the enactment of similar ones in the future. This
was done upon the ground that the acts annulled or forbidden were repugnant to the laws of England, and therefore constituted a violation of the proprietary charter.
Thus, in 1706, the Council declared two acts for the " Establishment of Religious Worship " " not consonant to
reason and repugnant to the laws of England, and therefore not warranted by the Charters," and accordingly issued
an order directing the proprietors to declare them null and
void.[2] In 1709 the proprietors were ordered to forbid the
enforcement of an act levying a duty upon skins taken
across Carolina by Indian traders of Virginia.[3] In 1718
the Council went a step further and itself declared a law,
which had not yet been transmitted to the proprietors, to
be " null and void," and directed that the governor be
ordered not to pass any such act in the future.[4] Laws

[1] Representation upon draft of instructions to Bernard, *CO*/5-920,
pp. 46-52; 24 April 1761. *B. T. J.*, vol. lviii, unpaged; 26 November 1751.

[2] These acts came before the Board of Trade in connection with an
address from the House of Lords upon complaints made by the settlers
of Carolina against the proprietors. *A. P. C.*, vol. ii, p. 506; 10 June
1706.

[3] *A. P. C.*, vol. ii, p. 610; 26 September 1709. *CO*/5-1316, O, 40.

[4] An act additional to an " Impost upon liquors, goods etc." passed
in 1717 and disallowed May 14, 1718. *CO*/5-1265, Q, 154. The agita-
tion which resulted in the overthrow of the proprietary government
had already begun.

passed by the proprietary governments of New Jersey and Maryland appear to have met with no objections from the English government. The same was true of the North Carolina laws during the proprietary régime. After the Carolinas had become royal provinces, however, many of the proprietary acts remaining in force were disallowed.[1] When, as was the case in Maryland, Carolina and New Jersey, the proprietors after relinquishing their rights of government retained property interests in the colony, they often continued to exert considerable influence upon the fate of legislation at the Board of Trade. The proprietors of South Carolina were consulted in regard to an act for the sale of the governor's mansion, and several acts of Maryland were disallowed at the instigation of Lord Baltimore, because they were prejudicial to his revenue or property.[2]

The Georgia charter of 1732 granted to a corporation for twenty-one years a power to make laws not repugnant to those of England. Acts were to be submitted to the Privy Council and to be in force only after receiving its approval.[3] Accordingly the trustees from time to time submitted proposed enactments, together with petitions or statements setting forth their reasons for desiring confirmation. The trustees not infrequently were represented at the Board by their secretary, or by some of their members, and upon several occasions by counsel and solicitor. In

[1] Among the acts of North Carolina annulled by the Privy Council were: "For Biennial Assemblies," "Attornies from Foreign Parts," "Disposal of Goods on Execution," "Disputes regarding Lands," "Regulating Abuses regarding Lands," "Escheats and Escheators," and "The Public Treasurer to Give Account," all of which were passed in 1715. An act to "Encourage the Settlement of South Carolina," passed in December 1696, was disallowed April 3, 1734.

[2] *B. T. J.*, vol. xxxiii, p. 68; March 1724. *A. P. C.*, vol. ii, p. 235. *B. T. J.*, vol. xv, p. 402; 1 February 1703. *B. T. J.*, vol. xx, pp. 302, 313, 314; November 1708.

[3] Macdonald, *Select Charters*, pp. 241-243; June 1732.

1750 they conceded to the freemen of the colony an assembly "with power to consider and propose . . . what laws they might think beneficial to the welfare of the Province." At its first meeting this body requested the privilege of making " Bye Laws, to be in force till the Trustees should disapprove thereof " — a power which " had been found necessary elsewhere." [1] But the trustees thought it too early to grant the favor, and the first acts of a Georgia assembly did not reach the Board until 1755, after the colony had became a royal province.

For a time Penn, like the other proprietors, exercised a veto upon acts approved by his governor.[2] But in 1705 Attorney General Northey, in answer to queries from the Board, gave an opinion that under the terms of the Pennsylvania charter Penn or his deputy could accept or reject laws where the assembly sat, and not elsewhere; and that Penn's instructions to the governor, saving to himself and heirs a final assent, were void and of no avail.[3] Thenceforth the proprietors possessed no check upon legislation save by instructions to the governors or by appeals to the crown. Because of the constant encroachments and increasing prestige of the assembly, the former tended to become less effective, while recourse to the latter became more frequent.[4] In 1760, after the house had offered to indem-

---

[1] CO/5-671, pp. 221-224; 19 June 1752.

[2] In December 1699 Penn vetoed an act for " Preventing Frauds and Regulating Abuses in Trade," "in consequence of one disagreeable clause." C. S. P., 1697-8, p. 578. The Privy Council, nevertheless, proceeded to disallow the act because "his simple disallowance" was not "sufficient for the discountancing of such like attempts for the future." CO/5-1288, p. 20.

[3] Report, CO/5-1263, N, 48; 19 October 1705.

[4] Petition in behalf of the widow of Penn, for the disallowance of an act whereby fines and forfeitures were taken from the proprietors. A. P. C., vol. ii, p. 771; 8 January 1720. A memorial desiring the repeal of three acts. B. T. J., vol. xxxv, p. 134; 26 April 1726.

nify the governor in case the proprietors sued to recover security upon his bond, the proprietors petitioned for the disallowance of eleven acts which they considered highly injurious to their political and landed interests. As a result, the Board recommended the annulment of several laws, and administered a severe rebuke to the proprietors for waiting until their property was endangered before protesting against encroachments upon the prerogative of the crown.[1]

Until disabled by ill health in 1712, Penn took charge of the Pennsylvania acts in England, seeing to it that they were duly presented to the Council and the Board, and reported upon by the law officers, and that they were considered in as favorable a light as possible. In short, he performed all the duties of an agent, and because of his disinterestedness, prestige and wide acquaintance among officials he was far more influential than an agent designated by the colony could have been. Penn's successors sometimes addressed the Board in writing regarding the confirmation or disallowance of acts. But their interests were in the hands of solicitors, and they seem to have exercised little personal influence there.

The charters of Massachusetts and Pennsylvania contained provisions regarding the submission and confirmation of laws which caused some variation in the procedure of their review, and proved a considerable limitation upon the veto power of the crown. Massachusetts was not obliged to submit laws to the Privy Council until one year, and Pennsylvania until five years after their enactment. Acts of the former, if not disallowed, were confirmed by lapse of time three years after presentation, and those of the latter six months after presentation. Thus the government

---

[1] Representation, *CO/5-1295*, pp. 295-385; 21 March 1760. Root, *Relations of Penn with the British Government.*

was forced to a decision upon their laws within a comparatively short time, and was prevented from allowing them to lie by until the full effect of their operation could be observed. In 1735 the Board resolved that all Massachusetts acts should remain " two years (from the time of their being presented to the Crown) Probationary (unless objected to in the meantime) and then to report upon them." [1] This was the longest possible period in view of delays incident to their proper consideration, and the three-year limitation.

In reply to queries from the Board, the law officers ruled that the limitation upon the time allowed for review did not begin until laws were presented to the Privy Council.[2] Consequently acts delivered by the colony to the Board of Trade could be considered there without regard to the time-limit. In order to avoid the consequences of this decision, the agents of Massachusetts and Pennsylvania delivered laws, as a rule, to the clerk of the Privy Council, and the Council, in turn, referred them to the Board of Trade. In 1746 the Board proposed that two objectionable acts of Pennsylvania passed in 1722 and 1729 respectively should be disallowed, upon the ground that they had been delivered

---

[1] *B. T. J.*, vol. xliv, p. 151; 10 July, 1735. *Acts and Resolves*, vol. ii, p. 790, note.

[2] Opinion of the king's counsel regarding the laws of Pennsylvania in 1719: ". . . the six months during which Pennsylvania laws are repealable are to be counted from the time of their being delivered to the Privy Council, unless agents of the Province deliver duplicates to the Privy Council at the same time they are delivered to your Lordships. The time during which they remain with your Lordships Can make no part of the six months, but from the time delivered to the Privy Council subsequent to your Lordship's report." *B. T. J.*, vol. xxviii, pp. 167, 185; *CO/5-1265*, O, 171; 24 March 1719. Chalmers, *Opinions*, pp. 336, 337. In 1722 the attorney and solicitor rendered an opinion to the same effect in regard to the laws of Massachusetts. *B. T. J.*, vol. xxxi, pp. 113, 116. *CO/5-915*, pp. 341, 342. Chalmers, *Opinions*, pp. 337, 338.

to the Board of Trade in the first instance, and had never been laid before the Council. But the proprietors protested against the establishment of such a precedent, and upon their promise that the acts would be repealed by the assembly, no further action was taken.[1]

The needlessly long period allowed Pennsylvania for the submission of her acts, together with the short time allotted for their consideration, placed the government at a serious disadvantage, and afforded the assembly and proprietors considerable opportunity for neglect and evasion. Inertia, and probably in some cases deliberate intent, caused the proprietors to delay transmission, and then to submit the accumulated enactments of four or five years. But if the Privy Council and its subordinate officials moved at their usual leisurely rate of procedure, six months was hardly an adequate time for the consideration of so many laws. In 1739 the Board made a strong protest to the proprietors against this and other abuses, and the submission of Pennsylvania laws was accomplished with greater promptness and regularity thereafter.[2]

The charters of Connecticut and Rhode Island, like that

---

[1] *A. P. C.*, vol. iv, p. 21. *Pa. Sts.*, vol. iii, p. 511. Root, *Relations of Pa. with the British Government*, p. 135.

[2] Representation, $CO/5$-1294, pp. 116-118; 2 February 1739. In strict conformity with the original charter Pennsylvania laws should have been disallowed under the Privy Seal. But as the result of an error in copying the charter they were annulled, as were those of other colonies, by orders in council. When the fact was brought to light in connection with a judicial hearing upon the appeal of Hamilton *v.* Richardson in 1733 the assembly, fearing action by Parliament, passed a law which was intended to correct any informality or illegality in the previous repeal of acts by orders in council. In spite of a report from the king's counsel in connection with this act that " by the express terms of the Charter [Pennsylvania acts] must be declared void under Privy Seal "—the use of orders in council continued as before. $CO/5$-1268, S, 46; 13 January 1734. Root, *Relations of Pa. with the British Government*, pp. 134, 135.

of Maryland, did not require the submission of laws to the crown. But to the recurrent insistence of the government that they send home complete copies of their acts, both colonies yielded a somewhat reluctant and dilatory compliance.[1] Apparently the Board of Trade never made any very careful examination of these laws. Upon several occasions collections of Connecticut acts were sent to the king's counsel with the request for an opinion, " whether some of them are not repugnant to the laws of this Kingdom." But his reports, made at considerable length, were not read at the Board.[2] They show that many acts were " repugnant " if measured by the standard of conformity applied to those of the royal colonies. Yet in only three instances were acts of Connecticut or Rhode Island disallowed by virtue of the charter requirement that legislation be " not contrary, but as near as may be agreeable to the laws of England." A Rhode Island law which established a court of admiralty was annulled upon the opinion of the attorney general that the charter conferred power to erect courts only for trying matters arising within the colony.[3] Upon complaint of the Quakers, a Connecticut law against " Heriticks " was adjudged " contrary to the Liberty of Conscience indulged to Dissenters by the law of

[1] Collections of Connecticut laws were transmitted in 1699, 1706, 1710, 1732, 1740 and 1752; of Rhode Island in 1699, 1700, 1710. Other collections were perhaps sent, of whose receipt the journal makes no mention.

[2] *B. T. J.*, vol. xli, p. 104. *CO/5-1271*, V, 16; Fane on 133 acts of Connecticut, 10 August 1733.

[3] The Board was in search of a pretext for annulling the Rhode Island charter, and inquired whether putting the act in force would not be a good cause for forfeiting it. The attorney replied that the law was void, but that such action would not be warranted because the act was only provisional until his majesty's pleasure could be further known. *CO/5-1262*, M, 3. *CO/5-1290*, pp. 403, 413. *A. P. C.*, vol. ii, p. 852; 28 January 1704.

England, as likewise to the Charter " of that Colony.[1]
And, finally, a Connecticut act of 1699 for the settlement
of intestate estates was declared void in connection with an
appellate decision in the famous case of Winthrop *vs.* Lechmere.   That the government was alive to the desirability
of subjecting the legislation of these colonies to review by
the Privy Council is evident from the various attempts
made to annul the charters, and from resolutions offered in
the house of Lords, that the acts of all colonies should be
sent home within a year after passage, and that no law
should be in force till approved by the crown.[2]

In a few instances the exercise of appellate jurisdiction
in cases from colonial courts involved a decision by the
Privy Council upon the validity of legislation.   As a rule,
the act involved, together with petitions praying relief from
its operation, were referred by the committee for appeals
to the Board of Trade, and in accordance with their recommendation the law was upheld or condemned.   Thus an
appeal of Col. Bayard from a conviction of treason under
a New York act for "Quieting and Settling Disorders,"
was referred to the Board, together with papers from the
governor and council, copies of the act and the warrant for
commitment.   After considering the Board's report, the
committee recommended that the governor be instructed to
secure the repeal of the clause under which the appellant
had been convicted and that sentence be reversed.[3]   The
most notable instance of an appeal to the king in Council

[1] *CO*/5-1291, p. 210.   *CO*/5-1263, N, 54.   *A. P. C.*, vol. ii, p. 832;
11 October 1705.

[2] *CO*/5-1291, p. 238; 23 January 1706.   *B. T. J.*, vol. xxiv, p. 411; April
1734.   Root, *op. cit.*, p. 145.

[3] *A. P. C.*, vol. ii, p. 413; 2 July 1702.   *B. T. J.*, vol. xiv, pp. 413, 428,
429, 430, 435, 453.   *C. S. P.*, 1702, p. 255, 267.   " * the meaning of which
clause having been Misinterpreted to the Oppression of His Majesty's
subjects."

involving the validity of a colonial law was the Connecticut case of Winthrop *vs.* Lechmere. The respondent relied upon a law of 1699 under the terms of which the real estate of an intestate was to be divided equally among the children, except that a double portion was to be allotted the eldest son. The appellant contended that this act was invalid because repugnant to the English common law, which made the eldest son sole heir. By an order in council of February 15, 1728, the Connecticut law was declared invalid and the appellant given the whole estate.[1] This is probably the only case in which a colonial law was declared invalid without a reference to the Board of Trade.[2] Had Lechmere's counsel or the agent for Connecticut petitioned to be heard in defense of the act, the matter, no doubt, would have been referred to the Board and there considered upon other than strictly legal grounds. That no action was taken by the agent was perhaps due to the consistent reluctance of Connecticut to acquiesce in the review of her laws by the home government. After the act had been declared void the agents petitioned to have previous proceedings under it made valid. The matter was gone into at length before the Board, and a report rendered upon which no action was taken.[3] In 1738 the case of Phillips

---

[1] Dickerson, *Am. Col. Govt.*, pp. 275-277. Hazeltine, "Appeals from Col. Courts," *Am. Hist. Rv.*, 1894, pp. 319, 320. For an able discussion of the matter from another point of view see, Schlesinger, "Colonial Appeals to the Privy Council," *Pol. Sci. Quart.*, vol. xxviii, pp. 440-446. Andrews, "The Influence of Colonial Conditions as Illustrated by the Connecticut Intestacy Law," in *Select Essays in Anglo American Legal History*, vol. i, pp. 431-463.

[2] "It was declared void at once, without any Reference to the Board of Trade, a thing that was never done in any other case, before or since, to my knowledge," Paris to Allen, 26 July 1738, *Conn. Hist. Coll.*, vol. v, p. 81 ; Citd. by Dickerson, *Col. Govt.*, p. 276.

[3] *B. T. J.*, vol. xxxix, pp. 95, 96, 104, 111, 209, 295, 299, 316, 323, 339. Memorial of Winthrop contending for the invalidity of the act, *CO/5-1267 R, 109*; 28 April 1730.

vs. Savage called in question the validity of a similar act of Massachusetts. But here the law, together with several acts additional thereto, had been confirmed by lapse of time under the terms of the provincial charter. Its validity was consequently upheld and the appeal dismissed, a result diametrically opposite from that attained in Winthrop *vs.* Lechmere.[1] Several years later, when Samuel Clark, of Connecticut, appealed to vindicate a claim at common law to lands settled upon one Tousley according to the laws of the colony, the appeal was dismissed, and the validity of the act of 1699 finally established.

The great number of " private " acts, affecting the legal rights or the property of some particular person or group of persons therein named, which were passed by the colonial assemblies, led to the imposition of various restrictions upon their enactment, transmission and review. It was insisted that every such law should contain a " saving clause " protecting the rights of the crown and of all persons other than those mentioned in the act.[2] In 1719 the Board proposed that no private act passed in America should be in force " till confirmed here by His Majesty." This prohibition had been incorporated in the instructions to the governors of the Island colonies when, in 1723, at the suggestion of the committee, it was made general and sent to all colonies.[3] Moreover, governors were forbidden to approve private acts affecting real property until proof had been made before them in council that public notification of in-

---

[1] Hazeltine, "Appeals from Col. Courts," *Am. Hist. Rv.,* 1894, pp. 319, 320. Schlesinger, " Col. Appeals," *Pol. Sci. Quart.,* vol. xxviii, p. 442. *Acts and Resolves,* vol. i, note, p. 667.

[2] *CO/5-*1271, V, 13. *N. Y. Col. Docs.,* vol. v, p. 126; 27 December 1709. In 1718 the Board resolved that " such private acts as shall in the future be transmitted without said clauses, will be laid before His Majesty for disapprobation." *B. T. J.,* vol. xxviii, p. 35.

[3] *B. T. J.,* vol. xx, pp. 260, 267. *A. P. C.,* vol. iii, p. 42; 27 June 1723.

troduction into the assembly had been given for three successive Sundays in the several parish churches where the premises in question were situated.[1]

Governors transmitted private laws " under Separate Seals, Separate and distinct " from those that were public; and in England further safeguards restricted their progress. Although the Board referred public acts to the law officers as a matter of course, it did not, as a rule, so refer those of a private nature until some one appeared to stand sponsor for them. Time and again the Board urged upon governors the absolute necessity of having some one—not necessarily the colonial agent — appointed to give information upon every private bill and to pay the required fees in the various offices.[2] After having secured a law report, it was necessary for the person in charge of a private law to wait upon the secretary of the Board and urge him to move for a favorable report upon it. In 1727 it became the settled policy to leave all private acts against which there seemed to be no objection probationary for six months after their

---

[1] Instruction to all governors. *B. T. J.*, vol. xlii, pp. 95, 96; 29 June 1733. The form of notification used in Virginia follows: " Notice is hereby given that the subscriber does intend to petition the next Assembly that an act may pass empowering me to dispose of my Estates in the same manner as if I had never been married, that any person who hath anything to object may appear." *CO/5-1325*, V, 31. Governors were required to transmit with private acts certificates showing that these precautions had been duly observed.

[2] " If there be nobody here to follow such [private] acts they [the attorney and solicitor] will not report upon them, and frequently upon the Removal of Attornies or Solicitors said acts are liable to be lost." Board to Hunter, *CO/5-995*, p. 327; 22 March 1716. " Some persons should be appointed here to solicit the dispatch of this and all other private acts, and to pay the fees in the several offices, * " *CO/5-915*, p. 20; 4 June 1719. *CO/5-915*, p. 276. *CO/5-726*, p. 99. *CO/5-1360*, p. 24. A general instruction was issued to the same effect, 8 July 1720. *B. T. J.*, vol. xxix, p. 246.

consideration at the Board.[1] If during the period of probation no objection was raised against them, a representation was signed, stating that they had passed through all the forms prescribed by instructions, that they contained a suspending clause, had met with no objection from the law officer or from parties concerned in their operation, and were fit to be confirmed.[2]

The requirement that private acts contain a suspending clause was never acquiesced in by Pennsylvania or Massachusetts because of the charter provisions that laws, unless disallowed, should be in force from the time of enactment. Massachusetts, which had passed forty-seven private laws prior to 1724, when the governors were instructed to insist upon the inclusion of a suspending clause, enacted none during the twenty years following. After 1743 she submitted seventeen private acts, most of which were disallowed for want of the required clause. New Hampshire was also negligent in this respect. Virginia and other southern colonies, however, made extensive use of private laws to dock entails upon lands, and generally complied with all the required forms.

[1] A New York act was ordered to lie by for six months, and "if during that time no objections shall be made thereto, their Lordships would represent the same to His Majesty as proper to be confirmed, and that the same method shall be observed in respect to all private acts for the future." *B. T. J.*, vol. xxxv, p. 8; 12 January 1727. In view of the charter limitation it was scarcely practical to subject Pennsylvania laws to this delay. *CO*/5-1294, p. 84. But that colony passed comparatively few private acts.

[2] Favorable representations upon such acts approached a formula. Representation upon thirteen acts of Virginia, *CO*/5-1366, pp. 103, 107; 29 June 1733.

CHAPTER IV

The Policy of the British Government in Legislative Review: Trade, Shipping and Finance

The British government, by means of colonial charters, and commissions and instructions to the governors, imposed various restrictions upon the law-making power of the assemblies. But upon no occasion did it formulate a positive or comprehensive statement of its policy in regard to colonial legislation. Summarized in a general way, the documents mentioned above yield a series of negations. Laws were to be not repugnant to those of England, not inimical to the acts of Parliament regarding colonial trade or to the commercial policy of the British Empire, and not detrimental to the royal prerogative. The varied interests by which the government consciously or unconsciously was influenced, and the general principles by which it was guided, are revealed more plainly in the many " opinions in point of law," Board representations, committee reports and orders in council. These show that under normal conditions each individual law was scrutinized not only for violations of the instructions, but also with a view to its probable expediency for the colony and the Empire, possible injury to other colonies, and unseemly infringements upon rights to private property or individual liberty.

There was no conscious cleavage between the political and economic aspects of the government's policy toward legislation. In their larger sense the terms " conformity " and " repugnant " included breaches of the acts of trade, as well as cases of divergence from the common law. Revenue acts were regarded with a double concern—their probable effect upon British trade and shipping, and the establishment of adequate salaries for royal appointees. Unless properly susbservient to the crown, the contribution of the colonies to the economic well-being of the Empire was uncertain and of little value. It is difficult to say, therefore, whether the government gave to the one or the other the greater emphasis in its treatment of colonial legislation. Issues raised by questions of taxation and revenue, which affected the interests of the merchants, were brought to the attention of the Board in a particularly speedy and insistent fashion. Moreover, they were more clear-cut and susceptible to settlement by anticipatory instructions than were those growing out of encroachments upon the prerogative. The fact that the colonists learned, in a large measure, to acquiesce in a consistent policy regarding matters of trade, while the assemblies, responsive to popular sentiment and strong in their control over appropriations, continued to encroach upon the "twilight zone" which lay beyond their proper field of legislation, explains, at least in part, why the economic aspect appears to have been the more prominent prior to 1750 or 1760, and why the emphasis was perhaps political thereafter.

In so far as the government's economic policy toward the colonies rested upon theory, its cardinal point was the idea of a self-sustaining empire, in which the colonies should be useful primarily to furnish raw commodities, and to consume the products of British manufactures. Commercial restrictions, it was claimed, were intended not to benefit the mother country at the expense of the colonies or *vice versa*, but to work for the economic stability and integrity of the Empire as a whole. Commercial relations between the two were to be reciprocally beneficial. The attitude of the Board of Trade toward colonial enactments regarding matters of trade, shipping and finance was determined, in a large measure, by this conception of an economically self-sufficient empire.

At first the colonies were allowed to levy imposts upon English goods, provided that such acts contained a suspending clause and were calculated to furnish necessary revenue without adversely affecting the trade and shipping of Great Britain.[1] In 1718, however, the proprietors of North Carolina were ordered to veto an act laying a duty of ten per cent upon all goods of British manufacture imported, and to direct the governor not to assent to its like in the future.[2] Following the enactment of a three per cent impost without the required suspension by the Leeward Islands, and a New York act levying two per cent, the government, at the instigation of the merchants, issued general instructions forbidding the governors' assent to any law laying a duty upon European goods imported in English vessels.[3]

This prohibition was strictly enforced, even when the colonists attempted to attain their result in an indirect manner. The Council, for example, disallowed a Massachusetts excise which was payable by the retailer, upon the ground that it would lessen the value of goods imported and so affect the trade of Great Britain.[4] Objection was raised to a North Carolina act subjecting pedlars to an impost of ten per cent upon the sworn value of their goods, because "the tax seemed calculated to discourage, if not Prohibit, the free Circulation of petty Trade and Traffic" and to be

[1] Board to Hunter, *N. Y. Col. Docs.*, vol. v, p. 501. Board to Shute, *Acts and Resolves,* vol. ii, p. 69; 4 June, 1719.

[2] *A. P. C.,* vol. ii, p. 740.

[3] *A. P. C.,* vol. iii, p. 40; 6 October, 1722. *CO*/5-1124, p. 238.

[4] *Acts and Resolves,* vol. iii, pp. 495, 508.

No content available

" restrictive upon Trade [and] the dispersion of British manufactures throughout the Continent." [1]   The Council instructed Massachusetts to amend an act which laid a double impost upon goods imported by inhabitants of other colonies, so that British goods would not be subject to duties as upon foreign commodities.   Because of a Georgia law which was intended to lay an equal assessment upon property of every kind, the governor was directed to see that similar acts in the future should clearly express the tax " to be *ad valorem* upon stock in trade and not upon goods and merchandise imported." [2]

In regard to export duties the government was more liberal.   The colonies appear to have used them quite extensively for purposes of revenue.   But they were not countenanced if unreasonable, if adverse to the interests of British manufacturers in that their operation served to raise the price of raw materials, or if so levied as to nullify bounties paid by the English government upon colonial products.   Thus, the Council disallowed a Georgia law which imposed an export duty upon raw hides, because by its operation " an article of general use and importance to the manufacturers of this Kingdom would be enhanced in price."   The act " could not but be prejudicial to the interests of the Mother Country and tends to give a preference to the manufactures of the Colony against [those] of Great Britain." [3]

In like manner the government made no objection to the imposition of duties upon the importation of slaves and convicts, provided the charges fixed were calculated to raise a necessary revenue without placing a prohibitory burden

[1] *A. P. C.*, vol. v, p. 127.

[2] *CO*/5-651, p. 381; 16 June, 1772. A similar case arose in 1774. *A. P. C.*, vol. v, p. 403.

[3] *A. P. C.* vol. v, p. 316; June, 1771.

upon the traffic. The amount of duty permitted upon
negroes seems to have depended largely upon the forbearance of the Royal African Company and the English merchants. Several acts of Virginia levying twenty shillings
sterling passed without notice; but a law of 1723 carrying
a duty of forty shillings, to which they objected, was
disallowed. Against this act the merchants urged that
lessening the number of negroes would increase the price
of labor and decrease the production of commodities, with
consequent injury to the customs and trade of Great Britain. The representation of the Board emphasized the prob-
ability that the act would discourage the production of naval
stores, especially in the two new counties where his majesty
had remitted the payment of quit rents for seven years in
order to encourage settlement. In recommending the disallowance of a similar act passed in 1728, the king's counsel
carried the argument a step further by stating that a decrease of the tobacco crop caused by a scarcity of slaves
would lessen the purchasing power of the colony and
" amount to a duty upon the importation of British manufactures." [1] After considering several negro acts of Barbadoes, South Carolina, New York and Maryland in 1729,
the Board instructed the governors to procure laws substi-
tuting other duties in lieu of those upon slaves, inasmuch
as they "do in some measure enhance the price of Labour,
and consequently [that] of several commodities produced
in the Plantations wherein our neighbors rival us in foreign markets." [2] The number of acts imposing negro duties
which were subsequently disallowed shows, however, that
this manner of raising money was popular with the assem-

---

[1] *CO*/5-1319, O, 49; 5 December, 1723. *CO*/5-1365, p. 269. *CO*/5-
1366, p. 28. *CO*/5-1321, p. 28.

[2] *B. T. J.*, vol. xxxviii, pp. 246, 262; October, 1729.

blies, and that there existed, as well, considerable sentiment in favor of restricting the importation of blacks. Indeed, Virginia went so far as to declare that this impost was the only one which without oppression could be laid upon the imports or exports of the colony.[1]

For the protection of slave dealers, the government insisted that no duty be laid upon negroes brought into a colony and re-exported within one year,[2] and that all duties be payable by the purchaser rather than by the importer. When levied upon the latter, he was often obliged to hold the negroes at great expense on shipboard pending their sale. The expedient of placing the duty upon the purchaser, which was adopted at the suggestion of the merchants, lessened the outlay and consequent risk to be borne by the dealer, and was at first thought to be of less burden upon the trade. In 1770, however, the king's counsel pointed out that the distinction between dues paid by the importer and the purchaser was largely fallacious, since " all such duties must in the end be paid by the purchaser, raise the price and thereby lessen the demand." [3]

Alleging that transported convicts committed numerous crimes and caused the local governments great expense, several colonies sought to lessen the number sent over from England. Toward laws aimed to accomplish this object by the imposition of duties, the attitude of the English gov-

---

[1] An early act of South Carolina which imposed a duty of ten pounds was ordered " to be repealed ". *B. T. J.*, vol. xxxix, p. 72. *CO/5-361*, C, 79. Acts of Virginia which levied as high a duty as 25 per cent were disallowed in 1768 and 1770. *A. P. C.*, vol. v, pp. 164, 286. A law of Pennsylvania was disallowed in 1773. *A. P. C.*, vol. v, p. 398. Other acts were ordered to be amended, or allowed to lie by. *B. T. J.*, vol. xl, p. 217. *A. P. C.*, vol. iii, pp. 422, 393. *A. P. C.*, vol. v, p. 362.

[2] *CO/5-1128*, p. 139; 5 July, 1753.

[3] *B. T. J.*, vol. xxxix, p. 72. *B. T. J.*, vol. xl, p. 217; 1723. *CO/5-1332*, Aa, 79.

ernment was similar to that regarding duties upon slaves. To a reasonable tax for revenue it offered no objection; but several acts it disallowed because their provisions would have placed a prohibitive burden upon the traffic. The policy of the government, however, was in this case more firm and consistent because such laws came into conflict with acts of Parliament providing for the transportation of convicted felons. Complaining that the difficulties imposed upon importers amounted " almost to a prohibition," the Council disallowed an act of Virginia which provided that no convict should be sold or disposed of for a less term than that for which he had been transported. For the convict's good behavior, the law required one hundred pounds security from the dealer and ten pounds from the purchaser.[1] For the same reason the Council insisted upon the amendment of several Pennsylvania acts which levied a duty of five pounds upon each convict and required of the importer fifty pounds security for good behavior.[2]

In the interests of British shipping, the government strongly objected to the practice of allowing exemptions on imposts or tonnage dues to vessels owned by inhabitants of the colonies. A Virginia law of 1684 was annulled in part because it contained an exemption in favor of local shipping.[3] The Board complained that a Massachusetts

---

[1] " Amending the act regarding Servants and Slaves, and the better Government of Convicts," *A. P. C.*, vol. iii, p. 54; Disallowed 6 August, 1723. This law was brought to the Board's attention by a contractor for transporting convicts. *CO*/5-1319, Q, 36. *CO*/5-1365, p. 252. *CO*/5-1319, Q, 37.

[2] The original act to which the others were supplementary was passed in 1738 and confirmed by lapse of time. *Pa. Stats.*, vol. iii, p. 501; vol. iv, p. 467. A similar law passed in 1742 was disallowed in 1746. *A. P. C.*, vol. iv, p. 20. An act of New Jersey was annulled in 1732. *CO*/5-972, E, 70. *A. P. C.*, vol. iv, p. 140. *CO*/5-1278, Z, 8.

[3] Hening, vol. iii, pp. 23, 38. Beer, *Old Col. System*, vol. i, p. 208.

act which exempted sloops and other vessels under twelve tons made "the duty lie singly upon ships belonging to England."[1]   A Virginia law of 1730 granted vessels belonging solely to Virginians a reduction of fifty per cent in an impost upon liquors.   This was disallowed upon a complaint from the merchants that it was "a very partial stipulation to the inhabitants of that Colony" and "manifestly designed to encourage their trade and navigation in opposition to that of Great Britain."[2]   Shortly after the governors were forbidden to pass any law whereby colonial inhabitants were put on a more advantageous footing than those of Great Britain; and as a result of the enactment of a South Carolina law which contained exemptions partial to local shipping, they were commanded more explicitly in 1755 to allow "no greater duties upon ships and goods of non-residents than upon natives of the Province."[3]

The British government conceded to each colony a right of supervision over the Indian trade within its own borders. But it insisted that such control be so exercised as to further the economic interests of the Empire as a whole, by enforcing order and preventing frauds and abuses, without injuring the trade of neighboring colonies or imposing undue restraint upon the distribution and consumption of British manufactured articles.   Otherwise, the government feared, prices would increase and the Indians would turn for trade to the French and Spanish.[4]   It was insisted, also, that such regulation should not constitute a monopoly, either by granting exclusive rights to a company of traders, or to inhabitants of the colony, or by vesting arbitrary

[1] *CO/5-909*, p. 281.

[2] *CO/5-1366*, p. 75.

[3] *A. P. C.*, vol. iii, p. 348; 27 January, 1732. *N. H. St. Pap.*, vol. xviii, p. 45.   *CO/5-403*, p. 41.

[4] *A. P. C.*, vol. ii, p. 610; 26 September, 1709.

powers in a local commission. All British subjects, the Board declared, were free under English law and the acts of Parliament to avail themselves of a share in the plantation trade with his majesty's allies.[1] A Virginia act was disallowed in 1767, for example, because the powers granted to trustees did " in effect institute a monopoly." Such restrictions, said the Board, " we consider destructive of that general freedom of Trade and Traffic which both by the Law of this country and the policy of all commercial nations is and ought to be accessible to every individual." [2]

In like manner the government permitted colonies to regulate the cultivation and shipment of tobacco, provided that in doing so they caused no undue inconvenience to English shipping or marked decrease in the revenue of Great Britain. For the convenience of shippers, the Board prevailed upon Maryland to reduce the size of the tobacco hogshead prescribed by law, to conform with that adopted by Virginia, and to decrease the penalty for defacing or breaking open the casks.[3] At the instigation of the merchants a Virginia law to " Prevent Frauds in the Tobacco Trade " was disallowed because the taxes and restrictions imposed were "a burden and a clogg to the trade." [4] Later, however, both the merchants and the Board conceded the

---

[1] Report of the solicitor upon an act of Virginia which granted exclusive privileges to a local company. CO/5-1364, p. 463; 21 June, 1717. A. P. C., vol. ii, p. 721.

[2] A. P. C., vol. v, p. 36. The king's counsel expressed a similar opinion in connection with an act of South Carolina. CO/5-371, H. 55; October, 1722. Arbitrary powers vested in commissioners were responsible in part for the disallowances of ten acts of New York in December, 1729. A. P. C., vol. iii, p. 209.

[3] CO/5-727, p. 245; 8 May, 1711.

[4] CO/5-1364, pp. 463, 474. A. P. C., vol. ii, p. 721; June, 1717.

necessity of strict supervision over the marketing and shipment of tobacco, and a law passed in 1730 for "Amending the Staple of Tobacco," which provided that the weight of each hogshead should be stamped thereon by an inspector, and that unmerchantable tobacco should be destroyed, remained in force.[1]

Since the continental colonies were supposed to benefit the mother country and to contribute to the well-being of the Empire chiefly by their consumption of British manufactured articles, it was inevitable that the government should discourage all colonial enterprise which might compete with home industries. Otherwise, it was feared, the colonies would become more and more self-sustaining, with consequent loss to British shipping, decrease of imperial revenue and injury to English manufactures. To keep the American market open to British enterprise, acts of Parliament forbade intercolonial trade in woolen goods and hats, and the manufacture of iron ware. By its commission, the Board was directed to consider means whereby the colonies could be prevented from furnishing themselves or other colonies with what could be supplied from the mother country; and the governors had strict instructions against assenting to any laws encouraging the establishment of manufactures which might compete with those of England.[2] Largely as a result of the government's determined attitude in the matter, comparatively few laws for this purpose were enacted in the Plantations. In passing upon

[1] The commissioners of the customs urged that the act would decrease the king's revenue and should be disallowed. The merchants petitioned against its confirmation, but did not press their case, and it was allowed to lie by at the earnest solicitation of Governor Gooch. *CO*/5-1322, R, 126, R, 152, R, 135, R, 141, R, 142. *CO*/5-1366, p. 61. *A. P. C.*, vol. iii, p. 326; 1 July, 1731.

[2] *CO*/5-918, p. 295. *A. P. C.*, vol. iv, p. 482.

an act of South Carolina to " encourage the making of flax, linnen and thread," the Board commended a bounty upon the production of flax. But, continued the report, " there is also thirty pounds for every hundred weight of linnen made in the Colony, which being a manufacture of this Kingdom . . . the Establishment of it in the Colonies ought . . . to be discouraged." [1] An act of Virginia allowing a drawback of export duties upon dressed hides was disallowed as " an express and avowed Act for the promotion and management of a Manufacture as an article of Exportation and Commerce. Every such attempt ought in policy and Reason to be discouraged and suppressed." [2]

Indeed, the argument that a particular line of action would work to the advancement of colonial manufactures never failed to command attention at the Board of Trade, and it was used frequently both by colonists and the merchants with telling effect. By a clever stroke the supporters of the long-contested Connecticut intestate law urged that if the English rule which gave all real estate to the eldest son was forced upon the colony, the younger sons would be driven from agriculture, and from sheer necessity would turn to trade and manufacturing.[3] The Council forbade Virginia to close her ports to the trade of North Carolina lest the inhabitants of the latter community be forced to adopt a similar course.[4] With this motive the Board also discouraged the establishment of ports and towns in Maryland and Virginia. At the instigation of the merchants, and with the concurrence of the commissioners of

[1] *A. P. C.,* vol. v, p. 320; 15 January, 1772.

[2] *A. P. C.,* vol. v, p. 37; 26 June, 1767.

[3] *Select Essays in Anglo American Legal History,* vol. i, pp. 431-463. An essay by Andrews upon the " Influence of Colonial Conditions as Illustrated by the Conn. Intestacy Law."

[4] *A. P. C.,* vol. iii, p. 346; 25 November, 1731.

the customs, the governors of these colonies were urged to secure the designation of certain ports exclusive of others for the lading and unlading of ships. But the assemblies, with a largeness of vision characteristic of frontier communities, went further than either the Board or the customs desired, by setting up incorporated towns as well as ports, and granting extensive privileges to their inhabitants. It was feared that the growth of towns would cause the inhabitants to take up manufacturing and neglect tobacco raising to the consequent detriment of British shipping, revenue and industry, and the laws passed by both colonies were disallowed.[1]

No other question within the realm of trade and finance caused the English authorities greater perplexity or affected the economic interests of the colonists in a more vital fashion than did the issue of paper currency. The traditions of the British government furnished no sanction for fiat money, while the merchants and other creditors clamored to be relieved from losses caused by unnecessary depreciation. Upon the other hand, the colonies were permitted neither to establish mints for making their own coins, nor to regulate shipping and commerce in such a manner as to obtain for themselves a favorable balance of trade, and so prevent the further exportation of such coin as they possessed to England. Letters from the governors dwelt continually upon the lack of currency in the colonies, and the necessity for securing some constant and recognized medium of exchange for commercial transactions and the payment of taxes. Consequently the government conceded with reluctance that a reasonable amount of paper currency with ample provision for its refunding might prove a benefit rather than a detriment to trade, and spent its efforts

[1] *CO*/5-1362, p. 432; 18 November 1709.

chiefly in attempting to secure a proper regulation of the bills issued. To safeguard the interests of creditors and protect the colonies from the evil effects of depreciation, the Board came gradually to insist: (1) that the amount of bills issued be limited to the minimum which would serve the legitimate needs of the colony for a circulating medium, (2) that ample provision be made for refunding and that such provision be strictly observed, (3) that the bills be of definite and limited duration and that they be not re-issued, and (4) that they should not be made legal tender for the payment of debts or taxes.

The fact that bills once issued and placed in the hands of private individuals could not be recalled or annulled without creating confusion in the provincial finances and bringing great hardship upon innocent holders, saved many laws for the issue of paper currency from disallowance, and caused the Board to insist that acts for this purpose contain a suspending clause.[1] This check proved only fairly effective, and during the third and fourth intercolonial wars the Board admitted that unforeseen circumstances might arise which would necessitate an immediate supply, and make it inadvisable for the governor to insist upon a suspending clause. Of this concession the colonies were not slow to take advantage.[2]

[1] CO/5-996, p. 175; September, 1727. This instruction was based upon that already issued to the governor of Jamaica. To facilitate the collection of necessary revenue, Massachusetts and New Hampshire were allowed to issue each year an amount sufficient to pay the running expenses of the government. CO/5-916, p. 269. N. H. St. Pap., vol. xviii, p. 25.

[2] The Board to Shirley, CO/5-918, p. 135; 28 August, 1744. A. P. C., vol. iii, p. 706; 30 June, 1743. In 1758 permission was given the governor of New Jersey to issue bills without the suspending clause "in case of emergency for military purposes." A. P. C., vol. iv, p. 372. CO/5-998, p. 257.

The forcing of provincial bills as legal tender upon English merchants, even at a rate of exchange which allowed for their depreciation, was, in the eyes of the Board, " an intolerable hardship." [1]   Although it had discountenanced legal tender provisions from the first, the government took no decisive stand in the matter until in 1751 some inhabitants of Rhode Island petitioned the crown to restrain the further emission of paper currency in that colony. Because Rhode Island acts, unless contrary to the charter or repugnant to the laws of England, were not subject to disallowance by the Privy Council, Parliament intervened and passed an act " To regulate and restrain Paper Bills of Credit in Rhode Island, Connecticut, Massachusetts and New Hampshire, and to prevent the same being legal tender in payment of money." This act forbade the enactment of any law postponing the time set for calling in bills already subsisting, or whereby any of them should be depreciated in value, or re-issued or obtain further currency. [2]

For a time the Board endeavored to compel all the colonies to comply with this act. But under the strong necessity of war, this resolution also broke down. Against a law of Virginia passed in July, 1755, which provided for the re-issue of twenty thousand pounds of paper currency which was to " be legal tender for a limited time," no objection was made. [3]   And it was so hard to obtain grants of supplies from Pennsylvania that the government permitted the confirmation of acts which violated all instructions to the governors regarding the emission of bills.

---

[1] *CO*/5-1121, p. 460; 29 November, 1709.

[2] *B. T. J.,* vol. lviii, pp. 13, 32, 37, 38, 39; 25 June, 1751. Board to Wentworth, *CO*/5-941, p. 297. Pickering, *Stats. at Large*, 1751, chapter 53.

[3] *CO*/5-1329, X, 24.

Thus, in 1757, an act which made thirty thousand pounds legal tender for ten years, and contained no suspending clause, was confirmed because "of the great exigencies of the present conjuncture, when supplies are so absolutely necessary for Your Majesty's service." [1] And in the year following, two acts for the emission of sixty and fifty-five thousand pounds to be legal tender were allowed because, the bills having been issued and circulated, the repeal of the laws would cause the greatest confusion. [2] In like manner an act of Georgia was confirmed despite the fact that the bills were to be legal tender for all debts between people within the Province, and to be current for seven years. [3]

In 1764 the Board conferred with the various colonial agents regarding the state of the paper currency in America, and it was agreed " on all hands, that putting a stop by act of Parliament to all further emission as legal tender, declaring all bills now existing not legal tender after periods fixed for Redemption, and fixing a period for legality of tender for those having no fixed period, would be highly expedient and proper." [4] The agents asked in vain that the matter be delayed until they could consult their constituents. On March 9, 1764, the Board submitted to Parliament an elaborate report upon paper money in the colonies. While disclaiming any intention of conveying censure upon particular colonies, the Board stated in conclusion that "complaints lately made by Merchants of the principal trading cities of Great Britain of the prejudice they have sustained . . . do call for that redress from Parliament, which . . . the Crown has in vain endeavored to obtain for them

---

[1] *A. P. C.*, vol. iv, p. 347; 8 July, 1757.

[2] *A. P. C.*, vol. iv, p. 341; 16 June, 1758. *CO/5*-1295, p. 248.

[3] *CO/5*-674, p. 198; 23 June, 1761.

[4] *B. T. J.*, vol. lxxi, pp. 57, 58, 60; 2 February, 1764.

by its own authority." [1]   In accordance with this recommendation, Parliament passed an act which declared all laws making bills legal tender, or prolonging the legal tender of bills already issued, to be void after September 1, 1764.[2]   This act was strictly enforced against all the colonies, and effectively deprived the paper currency there of its worst feature.

In dealing with the problem of paper money the Board found itself placed squarely between two opposing sets of interests, those of the debtor class predominant in the colony and its assembly, and those of the British merchants.   The latter sought redress many times from adverse financial legislation, in the great majority of cases with success.   In spite of the losses they sustained because of paper money, however, the merchants conceded the necessity of its use and made no stand for its abolition.   Their complaints were directed in almost every case against legal-tender provisions, or else against inadequate measures for refunding and the consequent depreciation of the bills.   In several cases the merchants even exerted their influence upon the Board in favor of an issue under proper restrictions.   In 1730 they requested that the governor of South Carolina be allowed to re-issue one hundred thousand pounds for seven years, applying the proceeds to the encouragement of new settlers.[3]   They approved an issue of sixty thousand pounds under stringent regulations in Massachusetts; and urged the confirmation of three acts from New Hampshire because the whole sum to be emitted would not be more than was " absolutely necessary to carry on the trade and business of the Colony," and because such an emission

[1] *A. P. C.*, vol. iv, Preface xix.

[2] *Statutes at Large*, 1764, chapter 34.

[3] *CO*/5-361, C, 63, C. 64; 4 February, 1730.

would be the best means to prevent the use of the base currency of neighboring colonies as a medium of trade there.[1] Like the merchants, the Board regarded paper currency with dislike and apprehension, as a necessary evil of which the best must be made. They felt the colonists to be mistaken in their expectation that bills of credit would prove an economic panacea, and believed that in permitting their issue only under stringent restrictions and careful regulations, they were advancing the true interests not only of British traders, but of the colonies as well.

Conflict between the interests of English merchant creditors and of colonial debtors resulted also from the enactment of laws which regulated and sometimes impeded the collection of debts. In this case the Board of Trade, always solicitous for the security of private property and mindful that a sound credit was requisite as a basis for the plantation trade, regarded the creditor's right of recovery as axiomatic, and conceded very little to colonial sentiment. Massachusetts in 1757, and Virginia in 1762, passed elaborate bankruptcy acts which allowed debtors, voluntarily confessing themselves insolvent and surrendering their assets, exemption from imprisonment and a certain percentage of the proceeds from the disposal of their property. The Board acknowledged the beneficial intent and inherent justice of these laws, but insisted, nevertheless, upon their disallowance because of fear that their operation by colonials would surely work injustice to absent English creditors. " Upon the whole," says the Board's representation upon the Massachusetts act, " a bankrupt law, even though just and equitable in abstract principle, has always been found in its execution to afford opportunities for fraudu-

---

[1] CO/5-917, p. 259; 11 April, 1739. CO/5-925, A, 11; 26 November, 1742. The merchants took a similar position regarding two acts of Pennsylvania. B. T. J., vol. xlviii, p. 26; 18 March, 1740.

lent practice. And even in this country where in most cases all creditors are resident on the spot, it may well be doubted whether the fair trader does not receive more detriment than benefit from such a law. But in a Colony where not above one tenth of the Creditors are resident, and where that small proportion of the whole, both in money and in value, might (as under this act), upon a commission being issued, get possession of the bankrupt's effects and proceed to make a dividend before English merchants could ever be informed of bankruptcy, such a law is beneficial to a small part of the Creditors resident only." [1]

Toward acts designed to relieve debtors who were already charged in execution and suffering imprisonment, and who chose to surrender their property for the benefit of creditors, the Board was more tolerant; and all of the colonies passed such laws from time to time. It was insisted, however, that settlements be not concluded without the consent of creditors holding at least the major part in value of the claims presented, and that insolvents should not be granted exemption from debts which they might contract in the future.[2] Several acts providing for the release of individual debtors were disallowed because, in the opinion of the Board, the process of liquidation was not surrounded with adequate safeguards for protecting the interests of creditors against fraud and concealment. In framing an

---

[1] Regarding "Bankrupts and their Creditors." *CO/5-430*, p. 1. *A. P. C.*, vol. iv, p. 388; Disallowed 28 July, 1758. *Acts and Resolves*, vol. iv, p. 29. The Virginia law " For the Relief of Insolvent Debtors " was disallowed July 20, 1763. *A. P. C.*, vol. iv, p. 563. *CO/5-1369*, p. 234. *CO/5-1330*, Y, 84, Y, 87. Hening, vol. vii, p. 549. The law of Virginia was more objectionable than that of Massachusetts in that it did not permit debtors to be petitioned into involuntary bankruptcy.

[2] *CO/5-379*, p.37. *CO/5-979*, p. 45. *CO/5-1295*, p. 249. *CO/5-1277*, Y, 3. *A. P. C.*, vol. v, p. 311.

act of New Jersey, for example, the assembly neglected to make the notification of all creditors obligatory upon the trustees, and provided merely that the insolvent should lose the benefit of the law if he secreted any part of his estate— a penalty which the Board deemed " much too light and trivial for an offence commonly enacted a felony." [1] In like manner an act of St. Vincent was annulled because it allowed two prisoners for debt full benefit of the English bankruptcy laws, without subjecting them to the penalties contained in those laws, in case they should not in good faith comply with them.[2]

Most of the objections made to debtor legislation had to do with provisions which, under the guise of uniformity, did in fact impose particular obstacles to a just recovery by English creditors. Many acts discriminated against the British merchants by so fixing the time for the final settlement of insolvent estates that they were not allowed a sufficient period for presenting and proving their claims. The Virginia bankruptcy law of 1762 provided that the effects of insolvents should be sold at auction within three months after the assignment, and a final dividend declared within eighteen months.[3] An act passed by North Carolina in 1773 was disallowed because it allowed only sixty days between the appointment of commissioners and the examination of creditors, and permitted no further delay for absent persons: and a law of Antigua, which was annulled "for the sake of precedent," though it had probably taken effect, provided that the entire estates of two insolvents should be applied in payment of executions already in the

[1] An act of New Jersey " For the Relief of Francis Goelet." *CO/5-999*, p. 125; Disallowed 2 January, 1762.

[2] " Relief of John Earls and Robert Hunter," *A. P. C.*, vol. v, p. 364; 7 April, 1773.

[3] *CO/5-1369*, p. 234.

hands of the provost marshal.[1]   Some months notice of
distribution and eighteen months to make the distribution
in, the Board stated, would be fair to British creditors.[2]
But it is doubtful, to say the least, whether a delay of two
years, or more, between the insolvency of a debtor and the
declaration of a dividend would have been satisfactory in
all cases to colonial creditors.

In addition to bankruptcy legislation, the assemblies presumed to regulate the collection of debts in ways detrimental to the interests of the English merchants. Especially objectionable were provisions compelling the accept-
ance in payment for debts of commodities of uncertain
value, or of depreciated currency at an unduly low rate of
exchange. An act of Virginia for the " Encouragement
of Manufactures " was held objectionable because it provided that for all debts, contracted in money or tobacco,
the debtor could, upon taking oath as to his substance (in
money or tobacco), tender the same in payment and the
residue in certain commodities.[3]   Notwithstanding the fact
that the depreciation of paper currency had advanced the
rate of exchange to forty per cent, it required more than ten
years of urgence from the Board of Trade to secure the
amendment of a Virginia law, inadvertently confirmed, by
which the tender of paper at twenty-five per cent was made
a legal discharge for sterling debts.[4]   Declaring it "unjust

[1] *A. P. C.*, vol. v, p. 396; 1 June, 1774.   *A. P. C.*, vol. v, p. 313; 15
January, 1772.

[2] *A. P. C.*, vol. v, p. 311.

[3] *CO/5-1358*, p. 162.   A report of the commissioners of the customs,
15 March, 1692.

[4] *A. P. C.*, vol. iv, p. 389.   The order in council stated that "though
the Courts find means by way of damages to decree the whole amount
of the debt according to the actual value of it in sterling, yet in cases
of executorship where minors are concerned the Courts are under the
necessity of adhering to the letter of the law."

to enact that Debts already contracted shall be hereafter discharged according to an accidental rate of exchange," the Council disallowed a Jamaica act which fixed an arbitrary rate of forty per cent.[1]

Equally objectionable and even more discriminatory against English creditors were the offers of exemption from arrest for previous debts, made by some of the frontier colonies for the purpose of hastening settlement. An early act of Virginia was disallowed because it barred British creditors from recovery unless the debtor had carried over to the colony effects to the value of his debts;[2] and, as well, a South Carolina law, which by granting a five-year exemption from arrest to all newcomers, enabled certain "evil persons" from other colonies to "live in great splendor and influence on the property of their Creditors."[3] A subsequent law of Georgia which granted a similar exemption of seven years, excepted amounts owing in Great Britain, but it was disallowed, nevertheless, on the ground that the establishment of an asylum for the protection of debtors against lawful creditors appeared "inconsistent with the principles of justice, as well as of good policy."[4]

The government objected also to laws insuring a priority in the payment of local debts. An act of North Carolina which provided that no foreign debts, not even excepting those due the crown, should have executions until

---

[1] *A. P. C.,* vol. iv, p. 455.

[2] This act for regulating the collection of foreign debts, was passed in 1663 and disallowed in February, 1718. *CO/5-1318,* p. 106. *CO/5-1365,* pp. 36-38, 46-47. *B. T. J.,* vol. xxvii, p. 121.

[3] *CO/5-362,* D, 64. *B. T. J.,* vol. xliii, p. 2. *A. P. C.,* vol. iii, p. 395; 3 April, 1734.

[4] *CO/5-646,* C, 8. *CO/5-676,* C, 63. *A. P. C.,* vol. iv, p. 408; 3 March, 1759. In 1707 the Board reported to the same effect upon a similar act of South Carolina. *CO/5-1292,* p. 17.

amounts owed in the colony at the time of the suit had been paid, was characterized by the merchants of London as " unjust, illegal, and a bare-faced fraud," and was annulled as " contrary to reason, inconsistent with the laws, and greatly prejudicial to the interests of this Kingdom." [1] Two Pennsylvania laws of similar intent were condemned with a declaration that all "Creditors should stand on the same foot as to recovery." [2] The Board objected, however, to any imposition of equality among creditors after legal proceedings for the collection of a debt had begun. A private act of Jamaica providing for the sale of an infant's estates to pay the father's debts, was annulled because it stipulated that the money thus obtained should be applied " in equal shares and Proportions," whereas it should have directed that all debts be paid " according to the several Degrees and Priority and to the usual and due Course of Law," thus preserving the legal priority of judgment and bond creditors.[3] A like objection proved fatal to an act of New Hampshire which provided for an equal distribution among creditors of insolvent intestate's estates " without regard to the nature of the debts." [4]

In several instances acts providing for a speedy recovery of debts were objected to because they endowed with a final and exclusive jurisdiction, courts which the Board feared would prove partial or incompetent. When Antigua attempted to establish a court like that of London for holding pleas of foreign attachments, the act was disallowed

[1] This act " Regarding Attornies from Foreign Parts and giving Priority to Country Debts," was passed in 1715 by the proprietary government and disallowed in August, 1747. *CO*/5-296, B, 71, B, 73. *CO*/ 5-323, p. 303. *A. P. C.,* vol. iv, p. 43.

[2] *Pa. Stats.,* vol. ii, ch. 52, p. 63. *CO*/5-1263, N, 40. *Stats.,* vol. ii, ch. 176, p. 364. *CO*/5-1264, Q, 37.

[3] *A. P. C.,* vol. v, p. 165 ; 12 August, 1768.

[4] *CO*/5-912, pp. 156, 186, 210.

upon the ground that it would "occasion many inconveniences in commerce," and might "discourage British merchants from giving credit to persons residing" there.[1] An act of South Carolina which gave two justices and three freeholders final jurisdiction over all actions of debt whatsoever not exceeding twelve pounds sterling, was disallowed because the sum named was "too large to be determined in so summary a way."[2] At the earnest solicitation of the governor, a Georgia law "For the Easy and speedy Recovery of Small Debts" which established a court for the trial of actions not exceeding eight pounds sterling, was allowed to lie by "until the Colony is in a situation to admit of more constitutional and less exceptionable Regulations for the attainment of so desirable an end."[3]

The Board regarded with disfavor laws which prejudiced creditors by setting a time-limit to the validity of certain debts. Such was an act of Antigua which extended the statute of limitations to judgments, a provision which could only "operate in favor of the careless or ignorant Debtor" and might defeat the just creditor.[4] Similar objection was taken to a Massachusetts law which barred action for debts on account after the expiration of two years from the contracting thereof; and to an act of North Carolina which decreed that no real estate should be liable for the payment of debts unless suit was brought within five years after the passage of the act, or the death of the alleged debtor.[5]

---

[1] *A. P. C.*, vol. iii, p. 180; 23 November, 1728.

[2] *A. P. C.*, vol. iv, p. 59; 4 May, 1748. The law was liable to other objections as well.

[3] *CO*/5-648, E, 25. *B. T. J.*, vol. lxviii, p. 281.

[4] *A. P. C.*, vol. iv, p. 412; 29 March, 1759.

[5] *B. T. J.*, vol. xxviii, p. 256. *CO*/5-915, p. 285. *A. P. C.*, vol. v, p. 39; 26 June, 1767.

In a few cases laws were condemned because they appeared grossly unfair or excessively burdensome either to the debtor or the creditor. A Maryland act of 1704 provided that the deposition of a witness before a notary, made in any foreign part without notice to the debtor, should be evidence to prove any debt against an inhabitant within the province. A deposition, the attorney general objected, should not be allowed as evidence when the opposing party could not cross-examine, and was without previous notice of the claim.[1] Upon the other hand, the Board rejected, as an undue hardship upon the creditor, a Maryland act which required him, when summoned, to appear and show cause why his debtor, having taken oath to the possession of no estate exceeding five pounds sterling, should not be discharged, and to furnish security for the debtor's further maintenance in prison. For failure to respond, the creditor was liable to a fine of ten pounds sterling, and if he failed to establish a case the debtor was to be released at the expiration of sixty days.[2] In behalf of creditors' heirs, the Board urged the modification of a Massachusetts law which compelled the creditor to accept a life interest in land as a full discharge of an execution for debt.[3]

The government permitted acts making lands and tenements liable for the payment of debts, provided they were in essential particulars conformable to the law of England upon the subject.[4] From time to time, however, many colonies passed laws making the property of absentee deb-

---

[1] CO/5-716, H, 48; 12 November, 1707.

[2] CO/5-727, p. 132. B. T. J., vol. xxi, p. 244. This law " For the relief of Poor Debtors" was passed in December, 1708, and disallowed October 18, 1709.

[3] CO/5-915, pp. 168-170, 276. B. T. J., vol. xxvii, p. 348; 4 June, 1719.

[4] CO/5-300, F, 4. A. P. C., vol. v, p. 38; 26 June, 1767.

tors liable for the payment of colonial debts. To these the Board objected, except in so far as they were aimed against debtors who, having dwelt in the colonies, had absconded to avoid payment. Such laws, administered by colonials, it was complained, deprived the English debtor of the opportunity for a fair defense and left him exposed to fictitious claims—a proceeding " contrary to the principles of English law and highly dangerous to commerce." [1] Their prevalence led, in 1771, to a general instruction forbidding the governors to assent to any law by which the property, real or personal, of any persons who had never resided within the colony should be made liable for the recovery of debts.[2] Upon the other hand, instructions to the governors urged, apparently without much success, the passage of laws whereby creditors of English bankrupts having estates in the colonies, could be satisfied for the debts owing to them.[3]

In August, 1731, several merchants of London petitioned the crown for relief from colonial acts which impeded the collection of their debts or placed them at a disadvantage in the payment of duties. They complained that as the laws stood in some of the plantations, his majesty's subjects residing in England were unable to recover just debts, or had " such remedy only as was very partial and precarious." [4] After a protracted hearing, the Board reported in the following January, that while several laws upon the subject were unreasonable, they were of long standing, had never been complained of before, and might properly lie

---

[1] *A. P. C.*, vol. v, pp. 312, 314, 390. *CO*/5-1078, p. 206.

[2] *CO*/5-999, p. 243. *B. T. J.*, vol. lxxix, p. 12. *A. P. C.*, vol. v, p. 320.

[3] Commission to Dudley, *CO*/5-910, p. 33; 11 December, 1701. *CO*/5-726, p. 177. Board to Gooch, *CO*/5-1366, p. 3; 16 February, 1728.

[4] *B. T. J.*, vol. xl, p. 221.

by for the present.[1]   Apparently both the merchants and
the Board had in view the possibility of interposition by
Parliament, for on November 24th the merchants had
stated that " all they desired was an act to be passed here
to enable them to recover their debts in the Plantations."
Shortly after each house of Parliament requested copies
of the merchants' petition and the Board's report thereon.
There followed the enactment by Parliament of a law
tending " to revive the Credit . . . formerly given by the
trading subjects of Great Britain to the Natives . . . of
the Plantations, and to the advancing of the trade of this
Kingdom thither."   It provided that thenceforth, in any
action or suit in the Plantations regarding a debt, wherein
a resident of Great Britain should be a party, he as plain-
tiff, defendant or witness might make an affidavit in writing, upon oath or affirmation, before a magistrate.   This,
when transmitted to the colony under the seal of a city,
borough or township, was to have the same force as though
made in open court.   The act also declared lands, tenements
and negroes owned by Plantation debtors, liable for the
payment of debts, in like manner as these properties were
liable in England, and made them subject to the same reme-
dies and proceedings in colonial courts as though they were
personal estates.[2]

The provision that slaves should be regarded as chattels
when used as security for debts, was a departure from the
traditional British policy which annexed them to the soil
in colonies dependent upon their labor.[3]   But the fact that
as real property they were often entailed, or settled for life
with a remainder over, injured their usefulness as a secur-

[1] *B. T. J.,* vol. xli, p. 27.

[2] Pickering, *Statutes,* vol. xvi, p. 272, ch. 7; 1732.

[3] *CO/5-1368,* p. 226.

ity, and caused Virginia in 1728 to anticipate the act of
Parliament in making them personal for the payment of
debts.[1] In 1740 South Carolina passed an act declaring
slaves personal property in all respects, and as such, presumably subject to division among the children upon the
settlement of an estate.   The king's counsel called the
Board's attention to the fact that this was inconsistent with
the laws of other colonies and with the act of Parliament,
and recommended that the law be disallowed.[2] But nothing was done and it remained in operation.   Meanwhile
Virginia found her compromise, by virtue of which slaves
were personal as security for debts but real as to inheri-
tance, unsatisfactory.   The fact that a sale for the debts of
a tenant in tail served to bar the entail, resulted in many
suits.   When the land became overstocked, slaves held in
tail were a manifest prejudice to the tenant; while their
intermarriage with those held in fee simple caused great
confusion as to title.[3]   Consequently the assembly made
two attempts, both defeated by the Privy Council, to follow
the example of South Carolina in making slaves personal.[4]
In 1767 a similar act of Georgia was disallowed, upon the
ground that slaves were a necessary part of the plantations,
which might become valueless to the heir, and suffer
neglect if they were separated from the land.[5] But Governor Wright refused to accept this reasoning as conclu-
sive.   He wrote to Hillsborough, citing the act of Parliament to show that it was the obvious intention to make

[1] *CO*/5-1326, V, 60; 10 January, 1729.

[2] Report of Lamb, *CO*/5-372, I, 43; 2 November, 1748.

[3] A memorial of the Council and Burgesses, *CO*/5-1327, W, 90; 21
December, 1752.

[4] *A. P. C.,* vol. iv, p. 138; 1751.   *CO*/5-1368, p. 226; 6 May, 1763.

[5] *A. P. C.,* vol. v, p. 40; 26 June, 1767.

both lands and negroes personal for the payment of debts, and mentioning the fact that South Carolina had long enjoyed a law similar to that desired by Georgia.[1] As a result, the Board yielded, and Georgia was permitted to pass a law making slaves personal, " especially as it would be conformable to the act [of Parliament] for the more easy recovery of debts in the Plantations." [2] We may conclude, therefore, that because slaves were used extensively in some colonies as a basis for credit, the government agreed with the English merchants that they should be subject to attachments and executions for the payment of debts; but that it consented only with manifest reluctance to any change in their status which might decrease the value of lands and prove detrimental to the pursuit of agriculture.

The regulation of exchange rates upon foreign coins was another phase of colonial finance which provoked the interposition of Parliament. Because the colonies had no mints, and because their imports from England exceeded their exports, they were continually being drained of coin and were unable to keep a supply sufficient for the ordinary needs of trade. To meet the difficulty, the assemblies ascribed to the various English and foreign coins values somewhat greater than their intrinsic worth would warrant, in order that bullion and coin might be drawn from the other colonies or the West Indies and kept from exportation. But this expedient conflicted, not only with a well-founded belief in England that the best interests of British commerce demanded a uniform value upon coins throughout the colonies, but also with the common mercantilist idea that the commercial welfare of the mother country depended upon the importation of specie, resulting

[1] *CO*/5-650, p. 155; 5 October, 1768.
[2] *A. P. C.*, vol. v, p. 176; 6 March, 1769.

from a favorable balance of trade.[1] Accordingly in 1703
the crown issued a proclamation fixing the values of coins
in the plantations, and soon after Parliament passed an act
for the same purpose.[2] This manner of regulation proved
an effective check upon the colonies, because laws whose
provisions were deemed in conflict with an act of Parliament could be disallowed forthwith. That it failed to
afford a satisfactory solution of the difficulty from the
point of view of the colonies, is obvious from their frequent and repeated complaints concerning the lack of a
circulating medium, and by the fact that at one time or
another almost every colony passed a law which was disallowed because it conflicted with the established rates.[3]
Pennsylvania and South Carolina made ingenious but vain
attempts to obtain their own pleasure by indirection. The
former passed an act providing that the prices of all goods
should be computed at three-forths the sum which the

[1] Report of the Lord High Treasurer, *CO*/5-323, G, 1; 10 May, 1704.

[2] *B. T. J.*, vol. xx, p. 138; 14 May, 1708.

[3] Such were: an act of New York " Regulating Current Coin," which
was passed in October, 1708, and disallowed March 3, 1709; *N. Y. Col.
Docs.*, vol. v, p. 67; an act of South Carolina, which was open to other
objections, as well, was disallowed in 1754, *A. P. C.*, vol. iv, p. 211; an
act of Jamaica for " Ascertaining the Value of Spanish Milled Money"
was disallowed May 20, 1760, *A. P. C.*, vol. iv, p. 450. An act of New
Hampshire, " Ascertaining the Value of Coined Silver and Gold," was
disallowed August 12, 1768, *A. P. C.*, vol. v, p. 159; and a law of
North Carolina " To Encourage the Importation of British Copper
Half Pence" on June 7, 1771, *A. P. C.*, vol. v, p. 308. An act of Pennsylvania was annulled just prior to the promulgation of the royal
proclamation, *A. P. C.*, vol. ii, p. 441. *CO*/5-1262, L, 46.
A Massachusetts act upon the subject had been confirmed, and in
accordance with an opinion from the attorney general, remained in
force despite the royal proclamation. But after the passing of the act
by Parliament, the provincial courts, at least, appear to have followed
the values prescribed therein. *CO*/5-323, F, 14. *CO*/5-913, p. 285; 29
January, 1711.

vender would have taken for them had no change been made in the currency by act of Parliament; while the latter allowed a rebate of ten per cent upon all duties paid in gold or silver.[1]

[1] *CO*/5-1264, Q, 39, Q, 42; 20 February, 1714. *A. P. C.*, vol. iii, p. 553.

CHAPTER V

THE POLICY OF THE BRITISH GOVERNMENT IN LEGISLATIVE REVIEW: INSISTENCE UPON CONFORMITY TO THE LAW OF ENGLAND

IN addition to the requirement that colonial legislation conform to the economic aims and policies of the Empire, the government insisted, in the language of its grants and charters, that laws be not repugnant, but as nearly as might be conformable to those of England. This wording imposed no particular laws, not even the common law, upon the colonies,[1] while its indefiniteness permitted both the colonists and the mother country a wide discretion in judging what the law of England upon any particular subject might be, and what deviations from strict conformity should be deemed advisable because of social and economic differences. For the government realized the absurdity of forcing the polity of a long-established community upon newly-settled colonies where conditions of life were primitive, and permitted, from the first, the enactment of legislation founded upon local usages and customs which differed from those of England.[2] Indeed, attempts of the assemblies to re-enact English statutes, or to declare the

[1] The charter granted by Charles II to Pennsylvania required that laws of property and crimes should be the same as in England, until altered by the Proprietor. Reinsch, "English Common Law in the Early American Colonies," *Select Essays in Anglo-American Legal History*, vol. i, p. 397. But in no other case was a presumption of identity placed upon the colonists.

[2] Report of the committee upon the laws of New Hampshire, *C. S. P.*, 1681-5, p. 174. Report of Attorney General Harcourt upon acts of Maryland, *CO/5-716*, H, 48; September, 1707.

laws of England wholly or partially in force, were discouraged, lest they operate to diminish the power of the executive in the dominions, or to deprive the crown of its right to veto each individual enactment. Attorney General Trevor objected to a Maryland law which included the *Magna Carta*, upon the ground that it might conflict with the constitution and other laws of the province, or with the royal prerogative.[1]   Against a provision in the bill of rights passed by the first assembly of New York, that the province should be "Governed by and according to the Laws of England," the committee cited the fact that this privilege had not been granted " to any of His Majesty's Plantations, where the act of *habeas corpus* and all such other Bills do not take place." [2]   The attorney general even took exception to an obscure clause empowering justices to "do justice according to the Laws of England and Virginia," lest " all the laws of England be enacted there." [3] A law of New York which declared the extension to the colony of several acts of Parliament was disallowed, although it introduced nothing in itself objectionable, because it did not seem fitting that laws should " be adopted *in Cumulo*, and that, too, without stating more of the acts than the titles and sections adopted.   [This] deprives both the Crown and the Governor of that distinct approbation or disapprobation that is essential to the constitution of the Province, . . . and would occasion great difficulties in Construction, . . . such as ought not to be left to Courts of Justice." [4]

[1] *C. S. P.*, 1693-6, p. 627 ; 11 December, 1695.

[2] *N. Y. Col. Docs.*, vol. iii, p. 357.

[3] *CO*/5-1314, L, 17 ; 15 August, 1704.

[4] *A. P. C.*, vol. v, p. 285; 9 December, 1770. A similar objection was raised against several acts of Jamaica for " Declaring the Laws of England in force," *C. S. P.*, 1677-80, p. 67. *A. P. C.*, vol. ii, p. 833. *CO*/5-725, p. 436.

In other cases the Council deemed the adoption of English statutes inexpedient. A Pennsylvania law for quartering soldiers was disallowed because, by enacting provisions from an act of Parliament originally passed when the army was maintained without the consent of the legislature, it threatened to obstruct the defence of the province; and New York was forbidden to pass a law for " Preventing Disputes by the Demise of the Crown," because it was " too closely modelled on English laws inapplicable to conditions in the Colonies." [1]

Although generally tolerant of mere difference, the law officers and the Board of Trade almost invariably condemned acts whose provisions they deemed inconsistent with the law of England. In the interests of conformity they demanded, (1) a certain technical perfection, insisting that legislation be passed in a regular manner by a competent law-making body, and that it be clearly worded and of reasonable intent. Furthermore they required, (2) that acts be not inconsistent with the mandates of a higher authority or with a more fundamental law, such as the governor's instructions, the charter of the colony, or an act of Parliament; and that there be no falling short from such standards of justice and equity as were embodied in the jurisprudence of England.

It will be well, perhaps, to consider at some length objections offered to what may be styled the technic of colonial laws. Not until the early part of the eighteenth century was there any considerable number of trained lawyers in the plantations. Moreover, the prejudice against them was so strong that some of the colonies for a time forbade their acting as members of the assemblies. The settlers, comparatively few of whom were from the professional

---

[1] *A. P. C.*, vol. iv, p. 338; 7 July, 1756. *A. P. C.*, vol. iii, Intro., xvi.

class, possessed the English deference to custom and desire for fair play rather than any extensive legal knowledge. Thus isolated and confronted with new conditions and problems, they based their first codes, in the Quaker and Puritan colonies, upon the word of God, or elsewhere, upon local custom and their own conception of justice and equity. It was inevitable, therefore, that when trained English lawyers began a systematic perusal of colonial enactments during the latter part of the seventeenth century, they should note many lapses from legal perfection.

The most common complaint, especially during this early period, was that laws were vaguely and loosely worded. The Board objected, for example, to the use, without further specification, of the phrases " enumerated commodities " and " infectious sickness " in laws of Massachusetts, and to a provision that a certain act of Parliament should be enforced in Pennsylvania " as far as circumstances permit." [1] This fault was, if possible, even more objectionable in criminal legislation, where exception was taken to such phrases as " Devilish Practice," and " playing at cards, dice, lotteries or such like." [2] An act of New Jersey imposed capital punishment upon counterfeiters of foreign coin which was " by common consent " passed as full satisfaction for debts.[3] The Board complained that definitions of crime were too general, that they often contained no clause making premeditation or intent essential to conviction, and that they afforded judges an undue discretion, which was liable to arbitrary extension and abuse.[4] Laws renewing or amending other laws, or adopting acts of Par-

[1] *C. S. P.*, 1700, pp. 475, 555. *Pa. Stats.*, vol. iii, p. 465.
[2] *B. T. J.*, vol. viii, p. 16. *CO/5-1263*, N, 40.
[3] *N. Y. Col. Docs.*, vol. v, p. 46.
[4] *A. P. C.*, vol. iv, p. 73. *CO/5-1263*, N, 40.

liament in the colonies, sometimes failed to cite in an exact manner the precise enactments, or parts thereof, to which they had reference. A law of North Carolina altered two former acts and repealed another only as to matters "within the perview" of itself.[1] Even more objectionable was an act of Maryland which vaguely secured the rights and liberties of the inhabitants according to the laws and statutes of England, in all matters concerning which the legislation of the province was silent.[2] In some cases acts were so carelessly framed that they were in parts inconsistent or unintelligible. The king's counsel reported, for example, that a Massachusetts law which made lands and tenements liable for the payment of debts, was so unhappily worded that he could not see how, "by any construction whatever, it could effect the end proposed by it."[3]

In other instances the Board condemned laws because they appeared to be unnecessary and trivial, or absurd and unreasonable. To a Pennsylvania act for regulating the names of days and months, it was objected that "every man may call [them] as he pleases."[4] Another law of Pennsylvania made persons guilty of bearing false witness liable to the same penalty which persons against whom they testified would have suffered, if convicted.[5] Massachusetts attempted to award, in certain cases, the full penalty prescribed by a bond, without recourse to chancery—an exclu-

---

[1] *CO*/5-299, E, 50.

[2] Act for "The Service of God." *CO*/5-725, p. 179.

[3] *Acts and Resolves,* vol. ii, 67, ch. 3. A similar criticism was made against an act of South Carolina for issuing bills of credit, *CO*/5-402, p. 158; December, 1748. Board to the Governor of the Leeward Islands, *C. S. P.,* 1700, p. 736. Comment of Bellomont upon laws transmitted, *C. S. P.,* 1700, p. 529.

[4] *Pa. Stats.,* vol. i, p. 464.

[5] *CO*/5-1263, N, 40.

sion of equity in express words which the Board characterized as absurd;[1] while Maryland required masters of vessels importing convicts to bring a transcript of their conviction under seal of the court, something which, in England, they had no authority to obtain.[2]

Penalties imposed by criminal legislation were in many cases excessively severe. This was particularly true of early legislation in the Puritan colonies and in Pennsylvania, where offences were made capital in accordance with the word of God. " If by the word is ment the Mosaical law," says an early report upon Massachusetts laws, " the patent will not in many instances be fit to be followed by Christians, for example, to make it death to gather sticks on the Sabbath and many others." [3] In a report upon acts of Pennsylvania, Attorney General Northey objected to castration as a penalty " never inflicted by any law in His Majesty's dominions," and to making fraudulent taking a felony, when it was not regarded as such in England.[4] A New York act for " Regulating Fees " was disallowed because of several objectionable features, one of which was the perpetual disbarment of lawyers violating its provisions, although the duration of the act itself was but three years.[5]

Acts whose provisions were in any way retrospective were condemned as bad law. Within this category fall an act of Antigua, passed after a crime had been committed in order that slaves might testify against the supposed offenders;[6] a law of Georgia which rendered void deeds,

---

[1] *Acts and Resolves,* vol. ii, p. 129; 20 May, 1725. Antigua, *A. P. C.,* vol. v, p. 364; 1773.

[2] *CO/5-1278,* Z, 8; June, 1771.

[3] *C. S. P.,* 1677-80, p. 139; 2 August, 1677.

[4] *CO/5-1263,* N, 40; 13 October, 1704.

[5] *CO/5-1121,* p. 455; November, 1709.

[6] *A. P. C.,* vol. iii, p. 612; 30 November, 1738.

conveyances and wills already operative, unless they were again registered within three months;[1] an attempt to levy back taxes upon lands of the proprietors in Pennsylvania, although such lands had not been liable under former tax acts;[2] and, finally, a law disqualifying one John Adams for membership in the Barbadoes assembly because he had been convicted and punished for a crime.[3]

The law officers objected in numerous instances to the practice of joining two or more acts under the same title, or to the blending under one title of provisions upon unrelated subjects. Such defects resulted from ignorance or carelessness, or occasionally from a deliberate attempt to secure questionable ends by means of "riders." But in any case, they rendered the task of review more difficult, and shocked the legal sensibilities of men trained in the English law.

Numerous acts, many of which were otherwise unexceptionable, were disallowed because their operation was contingent upon a previous law already annulled. Such, for example, was the fate of a Pennsylvania act appointing collectors for a duty on convicts which had already met with the royal veto.[4]

Laws were considered defective, also, because of irregularity in the manner of their enactment. Fourteen acts of Maryland, for instance, were condemned because, having been passed in the absence both of a governor and a lieutenant governor, they were signed by the entire council instead of the president of the council, who in accordance with the governor's instructions should have assumed the

---

[1] *A. P. C.*, vol. iv, p. 405; 3 March, 1759.

[2] *CO/5-1275*, W, 45; March, 1760.

[3] *A. P. C.*, vol. iv, p. 686; 20 July, 1764.

[4] *A. P. C.*, vol. iv, p .72; 29 October, 1748.

government during the interval.[1] An act of South Carolina, passed during a time of civil confusion, by an assembly which had been dissolved and a governor who had
usurped authority, was held by the Board not to be a law
in force.[2] In other cases unseemly haste in enactment was
the determining factor against a law. An act of Pennsylvania which granted to an individual a ten-year exemption
from suits for debt was disallowed because, after having
been introduced upon the application of only part of the
creditors, it was passed through all the readings in a single
day.[3] An ordinance of South Carolina concerning the Indian trade was declared to have been passed " in an illegal
and precipitate manner " because the assembly was summoned upon only eight days' notice, and the ordinance
passed in two days.[4]

Many acts were declared void upon the ground that the
assemblies in passing them had exceeded their proper jurisdiction. A majority of these laws were concerned with
alleged crimes or disputes regarding private property which
were properly cognizable by courts of law. This excess of
legislative zeal was due partly to the dominant position of
the assemblies in the provincial governments, more particularly that of the "General Courts" in the charter colonies,
and to a common lack of satisfactory equity courts. One
of the most conspicuous acts of usurpation was that of the
Massachusetts general court, which passed several acts fin-
ing Vetch and his associates for carrying on an illegal
trade with the enemy. As this crime was not one "cogniz-

[1] *CO*/5-727, p. 188; 2 November, 1710.

[2] *CO*/5-372, I, 65. *B. T. J.*, vol. lvii, unpaged, 26 October, 1750.

[3] *A. P. C.*, vol. iv, p. 341; 16 June, 1758.

[4] *A. P. C.*, vol. iii, p. 514. *B. T. J.*, vol. xlvii, p. 56; 25 May, 1738.
The law officer made a similar criticism against an act of North Carolina, *CO*/5-296, B. 77.

able before the General Assembly," the Privy Council
ordered that the accused give security and abide by the result of " a fresh trial in the ordinary course of law." [1]　An
attempt of Jamaica to regulate the exportation of prize
goods brought to the Island, was declared " an arrogant
assumption of power," the matter being one of general
policy " to which the jurisdiction of the British legislature
alone can extend." [2]

In the great majority of cases, however, laws disallowed
upon grounds of non-conformity, or " repugnance to the
law of England," were deemed contrary to the dictates of
some higher authority, or to the provisions of a more fundamental law.　Governors frequently violated their instructions by passing laws upon forbidden subjects, or by neglecting to insist upon the inclusion of a suspending clause.
Because such legislation was always objectionable in itself,
the breach of royal instructions, although often mentioned,
usually assumed a minor place among the reasons given for
disallowance.　An appropriation act of South Carolina,
however, was ordered to lie by, and the governor was instructed to secure the passage of a new law altering so much
of the old as was inconsistent with the twentieth article of
his instructions. [3]　An act passed in Jamaica which increased
the membership of the assembly and, despite standing instructions, contained no suspending clause, was disallowed
solely upon that account; although, in view of the evident
necessity of the act, the governor was allowed to approve
a new law identical with that repealed. [4]

In numerous instances the Council declared laws incon-

---

[1] *A. P. C.*, vol. ii, p. 516; 20 February, 1707.

[2] *A. P. C.*, vol. iv, p. 511; 15 February, 1762.

[3] *CO/5-365*, F, 8; October, 1735.

[4] *A. P. C.*, vol. v, p. 352; 5 March, 1773.

sistent with the terms of a provincial charter, and therefore void. Several objectionable acts passed by the proprietary governments of the Carolinas were annulled upon the broad ground that being repugnant to the law of England, they constituted a violation of the law-making power conferred by the charter. Thus, with much show of logic, an act of North Carolina which gave a preference to executions upon judgments for local debts, was declared "contrary to reason, inconsistent with the Laws, [and] greatly prejudicial to the Interests of this Kingdom, and therefore not warranted by the Charter, and consequently void." [1] A Connecticut law against " Hereticks," against which the Quakers complained, was characterized as "contrary to the Liberty of Conscience Indulged by Dissenters by the Law of England, as likewise to the Charter granted to the Colony." [2] Massachusetts lost several laws which were deemed inconsistent with her charter. In these cases, however, disallowance was based upon more specific grounds. Quakers and members of the Church of England contended with success that their taxation for the support of Puritan ministers was a violation of the charter provision allowing liberty of conscience to all Christians except Catholics. [3] An early act for " Regulating Chancery " was held to violate the charter in that by implication it prohibited appeals to his majesty in real actions; while a law " Impowering the Inhabitants of Rochester to Regulate the taking of Fish " was held to conflict with a provision that no subject of England should be debarred from fishing on the sea coast. [4]

[1] *A. P. C.*, vol. iv, p. 43; 7 August, 1747.

[2] *A. P. C.*, vol. ii, p. 832; 11 October, 1705.

[3] *CO/5-915*, p. 400. *B. T. J.*, vol. xxxvi, p. 254. *Acts and Resolves*, vol. ii, pp. 477, 635. *A. P. C.*, vol. iii, p. 491.

[4] *CO/5-895*, p. 213. *A. P. C.*, vol. v, p. 395; 1 June, 1774. *CO/5-907*, p. 75.

Repugnance to such acts of Parliament as extended to the plantations proved fatal to a considerable number of colonial laws. These included acts imposing obnoxious duties upon British goods, interfering with the admiralty courts or with the royal customs officers, regulating the exchange upon foreign coins, or taxing the importation of convicts. In several instances laws annulled were not in direct conflict at the time of their enactment with any act of Parliament which extended to the colonies. A law of New York, passed at the behest of the Board, was disallowed because a subsequent act of Parliament covered the subject and rendered its further operation unnecessary.[1] The crown disallowed a Pennsylvania act for " Regulating the Value of Coins " in order to clear the way for the royal proclamation and the act of Parliament upon that subject; and a law of New Jersey for the salvage of ships was disallowed because it extended to the province in their entirety two acts of Parliament which by their own provisions already had partial application there.[2]

Because of variance with the common law, the Privy Council annulled numerous acts in regard to the division of intestate's estates, the control of married women over their own property, the granting of divorce, the issuing of attachments for debt, and various other subjects. An act of South Carolina which granted new-comers a five years' exemption from arrest for previous debts, was declared " in its own nature repugnant to the Common Law." [3] As a rule, however, the law officers stated that acts offending in this respect were " repugnant to the law of England," and did not specifically mention the common law. Jackson,

[1] " Restraining Pirates," *N. Y. Col. Docs.,* vol. v, p. 47; 3 March, 1708.

[2] *A. P. C.,* vol. v, p. 111; 26 February, 1768.

[3] *CO/5-362,* D, 64. *A. P. C.,* vol. iii, p. 396.

who, as king's counsel, loved to play with large abstractions, frequently based his criticisms upon the broad ground that a law constituted a violation of the British constitution, or, in other words, that it failed to maintain the English standard of legal justice. Provisions empowering magistrates to commit or to exempt alleged offenders upon their own oaths were held to establish " a kind of inquisitorial authority" which was "contrary to the spirit of the laws of this country," and "little conformable to the British principles of Justice." [1] Upon Jackson's suggestion, the Council disallowed with similar comment two acts from the Island colonies which permitted attachments upon the goods of absent persons,[2] and a law of Pennsylvania which fixed a penalty for an offence committed outside the limits of the province.[3]

In view of the importance which English law accorded to the preservation of personal security and freedom, it was natural that the law officers should be critical of unseemly infringements upon the domain of individual liberty. Upon this ground they made numerous objections to excessively severe penalties imposed by criminal laws. They insisted that no man should be outlawed or attainted except by judicial proceedings and upon failure to surrender himself within ample time after being summoned to do so.[4] They

---

[1] An act of West Florida, impowering magistrates to prohibit the sale of rum to the Indians, *A. P. C.*, vol. v, p. 312; 7 June, 1771. A similar criticism was made against an act of New York, *A. P. C.*, vol. v, p. 399; 6 July, 1774.

[2] *A. P. C.*, vol. v, p. 390; 7 June, 1771. *A. P. C.*, vol. v, p. 390; 2 February, 1774.

[3] *A. P. C.*, vol. v, p. 398; 6 July, 1774. *A. P. C.*, vol. v, p. 38; North Carolina, 26 June, 1767.

[4] A North Carolina act for "Preventing Tumults and Riotous Assemblies" provided that when judges or justices should post proclamations commanding an offender to surrender within sixty days and stand trial, he should, upon failure to comply, be deemed guilty, and that it

objected both to the conviction of a person accused, upon
his mere refusal or failure to clear himself by an oath—a
provision which could not but " prove an irresistable temp-
tation to perjury," [1] and to conviction upon an information
in writing unsupported by the oath of the accuser.[2] The
Board regarded with disfavor acts which conferred arbitrary or excessive powers upon commissioners, or upon
justices of the peace. Upon a law of Massachusetts regarding the care of the poor, the king's counsel reported:
It " vests unaccountable power in parish officers. At their
pleasure they may disturb the profitable living of any person
whatsoever by Informing for the strangest misdemeanors
ever Invented. No single person of either sex must live at
their own hand, but under some orderly family government; in other words, not keep house for themselves—a
most unreasonable restraint." [3] In the interests of personal
security the Council disallowed an act of Virginia, passed
in order to preserve the peace by preventing assaults, which
exposed citizens to corporal punishment upon a hasty verdict, and allowed any person whatever to prosecute in his

should be lawful for any person to kill him, and that his property
should be confiscated. Although Jackson conceded that the disor-
dered state of the province afforded some excuse for this act, he declared it " altogether unfit for any part of the British Empire " and
" irreconcilable to the principles of the constitution." *A. P. C.*, vol. v,
p. 336; 22 April, 1772.

A law of New York which declared two men outlaws after ten days,
without further proceedings against them, the Board considered " unjust and contrary to the laws of England, which allow a much longer
time in case of Outlawry." *CO*/5-1119, p. 273. *CO*/5-1048, V, 8; 31
December, 1702. Opinion of Attorney General Northey upon an act
of Virginia, " Apprehending an Outlying Negro," Chalmers, *Opinions*,
p. 405.

[1] *A. P. C.*, vol. v, p. 399; 6 July, 1774. *CO*/5-942, p. 271; 10 July,
1764. *CO*/5-1055, Dd, 99; 11 December, 1729.

[2] *A. P. C.*, vol. iv, p. 73; Antigua, 28 November, 1748.

[3] Opinion of West, *CO*/5-878, Bb, 133; 15 May, 1725. *CO*/5-885, 15.

own name for an injury to another, provided the person
wounded neglected to bring action within three months.[1]
A like fate befell a law of South Carolina whereby the
assembly declared a virtual suspension of *habeas corpus*,
and sought to indemnify certain judges who were charged
with arbitrary and illegal conduct.[2]

The great importance accorded by English jurisprudence
to the protection and security of rights in private property
is also strongly reflected in the attitude of the law officers
and the Board of Trade toward colonial enactments.
Hence arose the additional restrictions and elaborate safeguards placed upon the passage and review of " private "
laws, most of which affected the property of particular
persons. Moreover, general laws which contained provisions, even though obscure and relatively unimportant, look-
ing towards the confiscation of private property without
compensation or trial at law, were sure to be challenged in
England. The Board refused, for example, to sanction the
pulling down of certain houses in Kingston, Jamaica, until
provision should be made for indemnifying the owners.[3]
Lamb objected to a Virginia act for dividing two counties,
because without legal process it compelled a man to pull down
a mill and a mill-house, thus depriving him of property upon
a mere " suggestion of inconvenience arising therefrom." [4]
An attempt to lower the rate of interest upon existing loans,
and another to set a price upon lands taken over by the

[1] *A. P. C.*, vol. v, p. 362; 7 April, 1773.

[2] *CO*/5-363, E, 5. *A. P. C.*, vol. iii, p. 396; 11 April, 1734. The act
for " Preventing Suits and Disturbances to Judges according to the
Habeas Corpus Act," grew out of a quarrel in the assembly over the
granting of unsettled lands. Several deputies were restrained illegally
in the custody of messengers of the house for " running out patent
lands contrary to the Quit Rent Act."

[3] *A. P. C.*, vol. ii, p. 684; 25 October, 1714.

[4] *CO*/5-1330, p. 239; 22 May, 1762.

colony without affording the owner an opportunity of opposing the act, were held to be confiscatory.[1] In its solicitude for the security of private property, the Board defeated attempts to dispose of the property of minor heirs
without the consent of a legal guardian.[2] It insisted that
acts empowering vestries to sell glebes should specify the
future application of the money thus obtained, and not
leave its disposal wholly to the discretion of the vestry, lest
the interest of the parish be injured.[3] It objected also to
the delegation of final or extensive jurisdiction in regard
to the disposal of private property to commissioners or
justices of the peace. Jackson, for example, criticized an
act of New York for defraying the expenses incurred in
settling the boundaries of certain lands, because the sums
due were to be fixed by commissioners from whose decision
there was no appeal, while the lands of claimants, some of
whom were absent, some of whom were infants and some
femmes couvertes, were to be sold in default of prompt
payment.[4] Any attempt to dispense with the statute of
limitations was sure to meet with disapproval, because, in
the language of the king's counsel, no law was " more
essential to the security of private property." [5]

The numerous colonial acts regarding the conveyance of

[1] *A. P. C.*, vol. v, p. 160; New Hampshire, 12 August, 1768. *A. P.
C.*, vol. v, p. 363; Antigua, 7 April, 1773.

[2] *CO*/5-300, F, 5; North Carolina, 30 June, 1766. Report of West
upon an act of Pennsylvania for "Vesting the House and Lands of
the Clark estate in Philadelphia in trustees to be sold," *CO*/5-1265, O,
191; 12 November, 1719. A concise summary of this law and the facts
relevant to it, appears in Dickerson, *American Colonial Government*,
p. 259.

[3] *A. P. C.*, vol. iv, p. 684; Virginia, 20 July, 1764. *CO*/5-1369, p. 237

[4] *CO*/5-1077, p. 293; 13 January, 1774. *CO*/5-972, E, 46; 24 December, 1723. *CO*/5-855, p. 289; 21 July, 1774.

[5] *CO*/5-301, G, 48. *A. P. C.*, vol. v, p. 308; North Carolina, 7 June,
1771. *A. P. C.*, vol. iii, p. 226; Virginia, 26 March, 1729.

lands were practically all of a private nature. They fall, for the most part, into three classes: those (1) confirming doubtful titles, those (2) authorizing sale or partition, and (3) those for barring or docking entails. In reviewing these laws the Board insisted with special firmness upon adherence to the formalities prescribed for private bill procedure, and the absence of the required saving or suspending clause was almost certain to cause disallowance. An adverse report upon three laws of Virginia observes: " these acts affect the Rights and properties of your Majesty's subjects. Yet they were passed without the observance of any of the [prescribed] regulations. . . . [There is] no certificate of any previous Notification in the Parish Church of the intention of the parties to apply for such an act, . . . nor any proof of the consent of the several persons interested, . . . nor saving of the right of Your Majesty, or of any Body Politic or Corporate, nor of any private persons not mentioned, nor any clause suspending the effect until royal approval. These regulations [are] essential to the security of the right of property of Your Majesty's subjects [and] are coeval with the Constitution of the British Colonies. [They] cannot be set aside without subverting a fundamental principle." [1]

In considering laws which confirmed titles, care was taken to safeguard the possible rights of any prior claimants; while in passing upon acts authorizing sale or partition, the Board was especially solicitous for the interests of minor or future heirs. It was objected that an act of Maryland which directed the sale of real estate for the payment of debts, left the personal property wholly exempt, to the manifest prejudice of the heirs. [2] A public act of

[1] *A. P. C.,* vol. iv, p. 449; 20 May, 1760.

[2] *CO/5-716*, H, 48; 17 September, 1707. In connection with an act of New Hampshire the Board refused to accept the consent of a minor to the exchange of his land. *A. P. C.,* vol. iv, p. 679; 20 July, 1764.

New York for the partitioning of lands held in joint tenacy was disallowed because it gave lands to all tenants in common and their heirs, thus favoring the heirs of tenants for life at the expense of those inheriting from owners in fee simple.[1]

In several instances the Board refused to consider the merits of a controversy regarding property, upon the ground that its settlement should have been intrusted to a court of law, rather than to a private act of the legislature. It was held unreasonable for a legislature to pass a law setting aside a conveyance of land as fraudulently obtained, without even hearing the parties concerned, some of whom were infants residing in England.[2] An act of Georgia which was aimed to confer upon certain persons a clear title to lands near Savannah, was disallowed because " the determining upon a question of this nature by a partial act of Legislature without any hearing of the parties or any of those Regulations and Exceptions which Justice and Policy have prescribed in all general laws for quieting possessions, is arbitrary, irregular and unjust, and subversive to those principles of the Constitution by which disputes

---

[1] *CO/5*-1124, p. 107. *B. T. J.,* vol. xxviii, p. 380; 9 July, 1719.

[2] An act of New York for "Annulling a fraudulent Conveyance of Mary Davenport." The facts were as follows: One John Miseral willed part of his estate to his children and the remainder, a farm, to his wife Mary, with power to sell or dispose of the same during her life. If she retained it, the property was to be equally divided among the children. Miseral died, and the widow assigned the estate to one Brown in trust for one Price, whom she soon married, and Brown made over the estate to Price. He willed it to his wife during her life, and after death to his cousins and their heirs. After Price's death the wife, unknown to the cousins and their minor heirs, obtained from the legislature an act vesting in her the fee simple. This was done upon the suggestion that she was illiterate, and did not know the purport of the document by which she relinquished her right to the land. The matter was the subject of a long hearing before the Board of Trade. *B. T. J.,* vol. xliii, pp. 52-56.

. . . in all matters of private property . . . are referred to the decision of the Court of Law." [1]

Laws for cutting off the entail, or, in other words, doing away with the limitation of an estate to certain heirs, were common in the colonies, because the king's writs for executing a fine and recovery—the method observed in England—were held not to run there.[2] No objection was made to these acts provided the tenant in tail could have obtained the same result by fine and recovery had he been in England, and provided that all the parties interested gave their free consent.[3] Attempts to make entails perpetual, an object in conformity with the earlier intent of English law, though contrary to its later practice, were discountenanced because they tended to "create a perpetuity" which the law did not allow.[4] The legislature of Virginia passed many acts authorizing the exchange of exhausted lands held in tail, for fresh lands which might be either entailed or in fee simple. In behalf of the persons in whom rested the prospect of remainder or reversion, the Board insisted, not only that these laws have the consent of all persons whose interests were affected, but also that lands taken in

---

[1] *A. P. C.*, vol. iv, p. 492; 2 July, 1761. *A. P. C.*, vol. iv, p. 678; New Hampshire, 20 July, 1764.

[2] Blackstone, Book II, p. 111 (Ed. Geo. Sharswood, Pa, 1870), explains the origin of the custom of leaving estates in tail, and of the ways in which, upon grounds of policy, lands were gradually freed from the encumberance, until in England, an estate tail differed but little from a fee simple.

[3] *CO/5-1054*, Dd, 19; 7 January, 1727. *CO/5-1326*, V, 70; 6 May, 1745. Pennsylvania alone passed a general law for barring entails, modeled upon the English custom of fine and recovery. Lamb pronounced it conformable to the law of England, but thought that the methods observed in other colonies were preferable. It was confirmed May 13, 1751, *A. P. C.*, vol. iv, p. 116. *CO/5-1273*, V, 78.

[4] *CO/5-1330*, Y, 112; Virginia, 12 November, 1763. *CO/5-1330*, Y, 128.

exchange for those entailed be of as great a yearly value, and, except for the possible barring of the entail, subject to exactly the same uses and legal limitations as had been the original property.[1]

Colonial laws governing the proof of wills, and the powers and duties of executors appear to have followed closely the English precedents upon these subjects. South Carolina attempted to make the process of proving wills regarding real estate less tedious and expensive; but Lamb, while conceding that the change might make for convenience, recommended, in the interests of conformity, that the law be disallowed, and that the province continue to use the method observed in England and in the other colonies.[2] Various attempts of the legislatures to order, upon considerations of equity, the disposal of estates otherwise than as directed by will, were held to constitute an encroachment upon the proper domain of the courts, and an undue limitation upon the inalienable right of every man to dispose of property acquired by himself. It was enacted by New Hampshire, for example, that if any child born during the life of a parent testator was not mentioned in the will, he should receive the same proportion as though the parent had died intestate.[3] Even more objectionable was a private act of Massachusetts by which part of an estate entailed to one of two brothers was directed to be sold, two-thirds of the proceeds being devoted to the education of both brothers, and the remainder being allotted to the mother.[4] An act of South Carolina for " Settling the Estate of

---

[1] *CO*/5-1320, R, 29. *CO*/5-1323, S, 18. *CO*/5-1366, p. 394. *CO*/5-1366, p. 468.

[2] *A. P. C.,* vol. iv, p. 486; 25 June, 1761.

[3] *CO*/5-915, p. 174. *CO*/5-867, W, 40; 27 August, 1718.

[4] *Acts and Resolves,* vol. vi, appendix, p. 161.

Richard Beresford" made several alterations in a will, taking part of the estate from one son and giving it to another, and altering certain limitations and bequests. Before recommending the disallowance of this law, however, the Board obtained, in the interests of equity, a promise from the favored brother to maintain and educate his half-brother who had been neglected.[1] The legislature of New Hampshire attempted to change an estate entailed to fee simple upon a suggestion, unsupported by proof, that it had been entailed by mistake in writing the will; and Maryland ventured, upon grounds of equity, to validate a document made in the form of a will in the deceased's handwriting, but neither witnessed nor published by him as such.[2]

Under the English common law the wife of an intestate received one-third of the real property for life, while the eldest son inherited the remainder to the exclusion of the other children. In 1692 the assembly of Massachusetts sanctioned a custom which prevailed throughout New England by enacting that the wife should have one-third of the intestate's realty for life, and that the remainder should be divided in equal portions among the children, with a double allotment to the eldest son. This law appears to have passed the committee without special notice, and it was confirmed, together with thirty-four others, in 1695. Toward acts of similar intent passed by other colonies during this period, however, the Board was less lenient. Laws of Pennsylvania and New Hampshire, the essential provisions of which were identical with those of the Massachusetts act, were disallowed in 1706 upon the ground that they were unreasonable, inexpedient, and would affect many

[1] *CO/5-401*, p. 95. *B. T. J.*, vol. xlii, p. 39. *A. P. C.*, vol. iii, p. 412; 8 August, 1734.

[2] *A. P. C.*, vol. iv, p. 256; New Hampshire, 21 June, 1754. *CO/5-1271*, V, 13; Maryland, 1 November, 1703.

owners of land who were resident in England.[1] The attorney general also took exception to a proposed law of similar tenor which had been submitted by Virginia because it "varied in several particulars from the laws in force here," and provided that in case the intestate died without issue, the wife should receive one-half the estate, and the next of kin to the husband the other, whereas under English law she was entitled to the whole.[2]

Within the next few years, however, the Board abandoned its attempts to exact a strict conformity to the English law regarding intestates' estates, and conceded, by its tolerance, the inadvisability of forcing the agrarian rules of a long-established feudal régime upon a sparsely-settled frontier. An act of Pennsylvania which was considered at the Board in October, 1709, and allowed to remain in force, provided, as did the Massachusetts law, that one-third of the realty should go to the wife for life, and the remainder be divided among the children with a double share to the eldest son. The act contained as well the provision previously refused to Virginia, that in the absence of children the estate should be equally divided between the wife and the husband's next of kin.[3] In like manner no objection was offered to an act of New Hampshire, passed in 1718, by which " the course of Descent and Distribution " was "greatly altered from that of England." [4] The judicial

[1] *CO/5-1263*, N, 40. *CO/5-912*, pp. 156 and 159. A supplementary law of Pennsylvania which permitted the sale of an intestate's realty for the purpose of paying his debts, educating the children or improving the remainder of the estate was disallowed at the same time because it contained no exclusion of lands which had been conveyed by any marriage settlement.

[2] *CO/5-1314*, L, 17; 15 August, 1704.

[3] *Pa. Stats.*, vol. ii, p. 199; passed 12 January, 1705-6.

[4] Report of Lamb upon a supplementary law, *CO/5-926*, B, 4; 17 March, 1747. *CO/5-926*, B, 17. *CO/5-941*, p. 226.

committee of the Privy Council, without consulting the Board of Trade, annulled the Connecticut intestate law of 1699 by deciding for the appellant in the case of Winthrop *vs.* Lechmere in 1728.[1]   But this decision was reversed in 1745 after a second hearing, and the validity of the Connecticut act which was similar to that of Massachusetts, was finally established.   An intestate act of Virginia was disallowed in 1751 because it had been passed in consequence of an objectionable law which declared slaves personal property; and an act of North Carolina in 1764 because it allowed one-third of the realty to the wife and the remainder in equal portions to the children without making any provision for the legal representatives of children deceased.[2]   Despite these exceptional cases, the Board of Trade conceded, after the first decade of the eighteenth century, practically all that the colonists desired in regard to the settlement of intestates' estates, a course which constitutes a rather marked digression from its usual insistence upon a close conformity to English law.

Upon grounds of repugnancy the government consistently rejected deviations from English law in regard to the property rights of married women.   Against an act of Pennsylvania, it upheld their right to inherit a life interest in one-third of the husband's real estate.[3]   An act of

[1] *Cf. supra*, p. 105.

[2] *CO/5-1327*, W, 55. *A. P. C.*, vol. iv, p. 139; 31 October, 1751. *CO/5-299*, E, 83. *A. P. C.*, vol. iv, p. 683; 20 July, 1764.

[3] This law for "Acknowledging and Recording Deeds," provided that no woman should recover her dower of one-third upon any lands or tenements which had been sold by her husband during his coverture, although she had been no party to the deed, and had in no way consented to the sale. *CO/5-1292*, p. 148. *CO/5-1264*, P, 79; disallowed 24 October, 1709. Another act of Pennsylvania provided, upon the other hand, that if any absent husband should alienate or mortgage lands, except in certain cases of necessity, without making an

Georgia was annulled simply because it allowed a married woman, consenting to part with her right of dower by becoming a party with her husband to the sale of lands, to sign and seal an acknowledgment of consent before a justice of the peace, whereas in England she could do this only after a private examination before one of the king's judges.[1] Upon the other hand, the crown uniformly disallowed acts in which the legislatures took a position somewhat in advance of contemporary English law, by enlarging the control of married women over their own property. Numerous private laws allowing women long deserted by their husbands to sue and be sued, or to dispose of their own property as though single, rested upon strong and undisputed grounds of equity. But they were held to constitute too wide a deviation from the settled law of England, and too great an encroachment upon the property rights of absent husbands. However great the hardship upon the wife, it was insisted that the husband's right to her property, both real and personal, should not be taken away by an act of the legislature without his consent.[2]

In the interests of justice and conformity the English government desired that the rules and methods of procedure observed in colonial courts of law and equity should differ as little as possible from the corresponding rules and methods in Great Britain. The Quaker colonies, New Jer-

---

equivalent provision for his wife and children, the alienation should be void. The king's counsel objected that this act would render titles uncertain, but it appears to have been confirmed by lapse of time. Chalmers, *Opinions,* p. 495. $CO/5$-1269, T, 22; 5 February, 1740.

[1] *A. P. C.,* vol. iv, p. 489; 25 June, 1761.

[2] $CO/5$-1326, V, 42; Virginia, 1746. *A. P. C.,* vol. v, p. 150; Massachusetts, 29 June, 1768. $CO/5$-1328, W, 152; Virginia, 3 February, 1754. *A. P. C.,* vol. iv, p. 558; Massachusetts, 16 March, 1763. *B. T. J.,* vol. lxviii, pp. 273, 310; Georgia, 2 July, 1761. *A. P. C.,* vol. iv, p. 674. New Hampshire, 20 July, 1764.

sey and Pennsylvania, passed various laws allowing witnesses, jurors and office-holders to qualify themselves by taking a " solemn affirmation " in place of the customary oath. The earlier acts of Pennsylvania were disallowed because, contrary to the practice in England, they permitted the taking of affirmations in criminal as well as civil cases, and because the form prescribed did not contain the name of Almighty God.[1] But after the accession of the Whigs to power, the Board became more liberal in matters of religion. Upon the plea of absolute necessity in administering justice, both Pennsylvania and New Jersey were allowed, after 1719, not only to sanction the use of the affirmation in criminal cases and as a qualification for office-holders, but also to omit from it the obnoxious phrase naming the Deity.[2] This concession, somewhat grudgingly made to communities where Quakers were in the majority, the Board regarded as a great indulgence. In other colonies the use of the affirmation was allowed only under the same restrictions which prevailed in England, where persons refusing to take the oath were disqualified from giving evidence in criminal cases, serving as jurors, or holding any office or place of profit.[3]

With a like solicitude for the virtue of all legal proceedings, the Board refused to sanction a general use of affi-

[1] A law for " Giving Evidence and Qualifying Magistrates " was disallowed in January, 1708. *CO*/5-1263, O, 78. *B. T. J.,* vol. xviii, p. 345; vol. xx, p. 21. A second act was annulled in December, 1711. *CO*/5-1292, p. 330.

[2] *CO*/5-995, p. 426; 27 January, 1718. *B. T. J.,* vol. xxvii, pp. 87, 126. *CO*/5-1293, pp. 172, 204. *Pa. Stats.,* vol. iii, pp. 437-739. The words " in the presence of Almighty God " were omitted from the English affirmation in 1721. As a safeguard it was insisted that persons refusing the oath in Pennsylvania and New Jersey should declare that they did so because of conscientious scruples, and that for making a false affirmation they should be liable for perjury.

[3] *A. P. C.,* vol. iv, p. 407; Georgia, 3 March, 1759.

davits as evidence in court. Their employment was con-
doned only in cases of utmost necessity in civil actions, and
after notice of their taking had been given to the other
side. The admission of depositions, said the Board in connection with an act of Pennsylvania, is " seldom allowed
in this Kingdom even in Civil matters, nor even then without observing a more solemn and safe method of allowing
the same than what is [here] laid down, [and is always]
disallowed in criminal proceedings, because of the known
benefit of cross examining a witness, . . . which often by
an unexpected question discovers the truth, . . . and sometimes from the manner of delivering his testimony a jury
has not believed a witness." [1] Objectionable, also, were
methods of drawing juries which might permit bribery or
intimidation,[2] and regulations in regard to the form of
writs, or the manner of their serving, which were contrary
to the practice of England. South Carolina, because of
abuses committed by the provost marshals, changed the
first process at law from a summons to a capias. The
Board urged that the act be amended in this respect, " as
in our law processes a summons is always supposed to be
made in the first instance, . . . and the rather as it will be
the least expensive way of proceeding and ye most speedy
to obtain justice." [3]

[1] Report upon an act for " Giving Evidence and directing the Qualification of Magistrates." It admitted as evidence in any case the deposition of a person sick or leaving the Province. *Pa. Stats.*, vol. i, p. 523.
CO/5-1264, P, 19; disallowed 8 January, 1707-8. *CO*/5-912, pp. 169,
186, 210; New Hampshire, 19 November, 1706. *CO*/5-1263, O, 78.

[2] *C. S. P.*, 1693-6, p. 84; Carolina, 12 April, 1693. *A. P. C.*, vol. iv,
p. 405; Georgia, 3 March, 1759. *CO*/5-648, E, 25; Georgia, 19 May,
1761.

[3] Board to Governor Johnson, *CO*/5-401, p. 17; 2 April, 1731. *CO*/
5-362, D, 25. Mass., *Acts and Resolves*, vol. i, p. 362. Note on ch. 5.
A. P. C., vol. iv, p. 676; New Hampshire, 20 July, 1764.

The governors' commissions empowered them to establish courts of equity; and the crown imposed no restrictions upon the rules of procedure to be observed therein,
except the usual stipulation that they be as nearly as possible conformable to those of similar tribunals in England.
The lack of equity courts, frequently complained of in the
colonies, seems to have resulted from the jealousy of the
assemblies respecting the powers exercised by the governor,
as chancellor, rather than from any objection to their establishment upon the part of the home government. Comments upon laws made by the Board of Trade frequently
assume the existence of courts of chancery in the colonies;
while any express exclusion of equity in a colonial act was
sure to meet with objection.[1]

In some instances the government complained that newly
established courts and their mode of procedure made for
unnecessary delay and a needless multiplication of suits.
An act of Massachusetts provided that either after or before judgment was rendered by the supreme court, the
court of original jurisdiction could review the case again,
and that the third verdict obtained by either party should
be final, save for the right of appeal to the crown. This
" so oft renewing of trials in the same case," with long
suspense in obtaining a final issue, the Board condemned
as too dilatory and vexatious.[2] Upon similar grounds the
crown based its refusal of a supreme court for Pennsylvania which, although limited as to original jurisdiction,
could draw from inferior tribunals " what business they
thought proper " by writs of error. Moreover, a provision
that the court of equity should neither try anything deter-
minable at common law, nor decide any question of fact

---

[1] *A. P. C.*, vol. v, p. 364; Antigua, 7 April, 1773.

[2] *CO/5-909*, pp. 186, 239. *CO/5-862*, A, 59; 22 October, 1700.

without sending it to an issue at law, threatened to " make proceedings in equity unsufferably dilatory, and to multiply trials . . . in the plainest cases to no purpose." [1]

As a rule, however, the complaint was that the colonists had missed the happy mean of English judicial procedure and rendered justice uncertain, not by encouraging litigation, but rather by limiting appeals and intrusting summary and final jurisdiction to incompetent courts. To colonists in the back country justice necessarily became an attribute of the local community rather than of the crown or even of the province. The general lack of trained lawyers, the expense and difficulties of travel, and the distrust of distant courts, all contributed to enhance the functions of the local justice. This fact English officials, accustomed as they were to a settled and centralized system of jurisprudence, viewed with apprehensive disapproval. They begrudged justices of the peace the power to perform marriages, and insisted that under no circumstances should they decide as to the validity of a title to real estate. [2] In England the local magistrate, sitting without a jury, could decide cases involving not more than forty shillings. Although the Board seems not consciously to have formulated any rule in the matter, this limitation was extended to the colonies where its enforcement contributed to the disallowance of many laws. In a moment of weakness the Board heeded the urgence of the governor of New York and permitted, not without misgivings, the confirmation of an act conferring upon mayors, justices of the peace and recorders, jurisdiction in cases to the value of five pounds in local money. But later, when the amount permitted was raised

[1] *CO*/5-1264, Q, 37. *CO*/5-1264, Q, 42; 13 January, 1714.

[2] *CO*/5-912, pp. 156-168, 210; New Hampshire, 19 November, 1706. *CO*/5-1278, Z, 6. *A. P. C.*, vol. v, p. 301; Pennsylvania, 26 May, 1771.

to ten pounds, the act was disallowed.[1] Besides cherishing an instinctive dislike for arbitrary and partial determinations at law, the Board was, in some cases, not unmindful that the increased prestige of the justices would detract from the usefulness and importance of the local courts of common pleas, whose officials were appointed by the crown.[2]

With perverse and persistent fondness for " summary and despotic justice," some of the colonies empowered judges of the local courts to decide without jury cases involving considerable sums. But here again the law officers cited the English limit of forty shillings sterling and objected to larger amounts unless either of the parties could upon request obtain a jury. An act of South Carolina which empowered judges of the circuit courts to determine in a summary way all disputes cognizable in their courts for any sum not exceeding twenty pounds sterling, was disallowed notwithstanding a provision that cases involving land titles should be excepted, and that both parties, or either party at his own expense, could secure a jury.[3] North Carolina conferred upon the judges of county courts,

---

[1] *CO*/5-1070, Oo, 13, Oo, 18. *CO*/5-1129, p. 149; 14 November, 1759. *A. P. C.*, vol. v, p. 285; 9 December, 1770. In like manner New Jersey enjoyed for some years a five-pound limit, and attempted in vai.1 to raise the amount to ten pounds. *CO*/5-999, p. 232. *A. P. C.*, vol. v, p. 309; 7 June, 1771. After considering a law of Massachusetts entitled " Fence for Cattle," the committee decided in 1683 that controversies under the value of forty shillings could be decided by a justice of the peace. *C. S. P.*, 1681-5, p. 415. *A. P. C.*, vol. v, p. 329; Bahamas, 15 January, 1772.

[2] *A. P. C.*, vol. iv, p. 407. *B. T. J.*, vol. lxv; Georgia, 22 November, 1758. This act gave an exclusive jurisdiction over cases of less than ten pounds sterling to justices of the peace. *CO*/5-372, I, 66; South Carolina, 13 February, 1750.

[3] *CO*/5-404, p. 383. *A. P. C.*, vol. v, p. 166; 7 October, 1768. *CO*/5-979, p. 37; New Jersey, disallowed 7 June, 1771. *CO*/5-304, K, 63; North Carolina, 3 February, 1775.

whom the Board characterized as ignorant and unfit, a power over the settlement of estates and the care of orphans —an encroachment upon chancery " not warranted by any law or similar practice in this Kingdom." [1]

In like manner the government regarded with disfavor attempts to discourage litigation in appellate courts. To the general features of a judicial system in North Carolina which included county and district courts, the latter having jurisdiction over civil cases involving more than ten pounds current money, the Board gave its approval.[2] But when Virginia raised the limitation upon the original jurisdiction of her superior court from ten pounds to twenty, and imposed a new prohibition upon appeals in cases under ten pounds, the act was disallowed, upon the ground that it would cause great inconvenience and detriment to his majesty's trading subjects.[3] A law of New York which limited the jurisdiction of the supreme court to sums exceeding fifty pounds, was annulled with the comment that it was "directly counter to the judicial policy of this country." [4] The home government was no doubt guiltless of any desire to encourage needless litigation. The law officers well realized that only through able courts of review could the errors and eccentricities of untrained judges and justices be corrected, and a fair conformity with decisions of other colonies and the mother country be secured. As Jackson observed, where probably more than one hundred judges

---

[1] *CO/5-324*, pp. 299, 304, 306; 14 April, 1759.

[2] *A. P. C.*, vol. iv, p. 502. This was disallowed upon other grounds, December 14, 1761.

[3] *A. P. C.*, vol. iv, p. 139; 31 October, 1751.

[4] *A. P. C.*, vol. v, p. 284; 9 December, 1770. A like fate befel an act of New York which prescribed a minimum of twenty pounds current money and costs. But this law was also objectionable in that it gave the court no power to extend a limited time allowed the parties for pleading. *CO/5-1124*, pp. 57, 109; 26 May, 1719.

were to determine, each according to his own notions of justice, the laws of a country could be neither uniform nor certain.[1]

Eighteenth century England was at best suspiciously tolerant of foreigners. The benefits of naturalization were limited to Protestants, and could be obtained only by virtue of a special act of Parliament.[2]   Nor could any unnaturalized alien, unless he received letters of denization from the crown, acquire or give title to real estate.   Similar restrictions, it was assumed, ran against foreigners in the colonies.   Moreover, the government by enacting in the navigation laws that no alien not naturalized or made a free denizen should exercise the trade of a merchant or factor in the plantations, sought to discourage unnaturalized foreigners from settling there.   Despite these restrictions, many aliens not only migrated to the colonies, but also engaged in trade and acquired an equitable title to lands. Under these circumstances the necessity for some settled and inexpensive method of naturalization was patent.   The colonists assumed that a power of granting naturalization corresponding to that exercised by Parliament in England, was vested in the assemblies, and enacted laws prescribing the conditions under which the privilege would, upon application, be granted to individuals by a special act of the assembly.   A Virginia law passed in 1671 provided that " any stranger desiring to make this country the place of their constant residence," could, upon petitioning the grand assembly and taking the oaths of allegience and supremacy, be admitted to naturalization, which was to confer all the privileges of which a natural-born Englishman was cap-

[1] *A. P. C.,* vol. v, p. 309. *CO/*5-979, p. 185. *CO/*5-304, p. 59.

[2] Except, during the period from 1709 to 1712, when a general act for naturalizing foreign Protestants upon their taking the oaths and receiving the Sacrament in any Protestant church, was in force.

able.[1]   But the act which was drafted in England, sent over by Culpeper and accepted by the assembly in 1680, took this power from the legislature and vested it in the governor, and, with a view to the enforcement of the acts of trade, provided that nothing therein should be construed to extend any privileges contrary to the laws of England.[2] This arrangement was continued by an act passed in 1707, notwithstanding an objection from Attorney General Montague that it was " too great a power to be lodged in any one person . . . though he be governor, to make aliens and foreigners to be upon the same foot, as the natural-born subjects are." [3]   In the other colonies the assemblies passed acts from time to time for naturalizing foreigners, or foreign Protestants, then resident.   Although these laws were generally allowed to remain in force, the Board several times expressed doubts concerning their propriety, and upon the basis of a ruling by the attorney and solicitor, it assumed that they conferred no benefit outside the limits of the province.[4]   To settle doubts and define the powers of the assemblies in the matter, Parliament passed an act in 1740 which authorized the naturalization of foreign Protestants in the colonies.   As the requisites for eligibility, it imposed a residence of seven years without an absence of more than two months at a time, taking the oaths of allegiance and supremacy, making the declaration and, with the exception of Quakers and Jews, receiving the sacrament

[1] Hening, vol. ii, p. 289.

[2] Hening, vol. ii, p. 464.

[3] *CO*/5-1363, p. 226; 20 August, 1707.

[4] Report of the Board upon letters of denization granted by Governor Fletcher, *CO*/5-725, p. 391 ; 27 October, 1698.   This was based upon a former opinion by Chief Justice North.   Opinion of the attorney general upon an act of New Jersey, *CO*/5-995, p. 450; 10 December, 1718.   *B. T. J.,,* vol. xlv, p. 29; 2 March, 1736.

of the Lord's Supper in some Protestant and reformed congregation.[1]

The uncertain validity of land titles derived from aliens who had acquired possession without being naturalized, caused much complaint in some colonies. New York, Pennsylvania, North Carolina and New Jersey all made one or more attempts to confirm such titles by blanket laws. Although the Board conceded the inherent justice of these acts, it could hardly condone so sweeping a dispensation from the consequences of a settled point of law. Moreover, they deprived the crown of a right to escheat lands held by deceased aliens. Several acts for this purpose appear to have remained in force despite objections from the law officers, and one such, a law of New Jersey which secured persons holding real estate under purchase of aliens from any possible defect of title, was confirmed in 1772, " His Majesty waiving his right of escheat for the sake of quieting possessions." [2] Soon after, however, the government took this troublesome subject from the discretion of the assemblies by issuing a general instruction to the governors against assenting to any act for the naturalization of aliens, or for establishing a title to real estate originally granted to, or purchased by, aliens antecedent to naturalization.[3]

[1] Pickering, *Statutes,* vol. xvii, p. 370, ch. vii, 1740. Quakers were allowed to subscribe to a declaration of fidelity, and an act of Pennsylvania which extended this privilege to all Protestants having conscientious scruples against taking oaths, in other words to the Moravians, was confirmed. *A. P. C.,* vol. iv, p. 21 ; 17 December, 1746.

[2] *A. P. C.,* vol. v, p. 379; 1 September, 1772. Report of the attorney general upon an act of New York, *CO/5*-1123, p. 499; 27 January, 1718. *B. T. J.,* vol. xxii; 19 February, 1718. Lamb upon an act of North Carolina, *CO/5*-300, F, 5; 28 October, 1764. Lamb upon an act of Pennsylvania, which was disallowed September 2, 1760, *CO/5*-1275, W, 45. *CO/5*-1076, p. 419; New York, 1771. *CO/5*-1074, p. 457.

[3] *A. P. C.,* vol. v, p. 552; 19 November, 1773. *B. T. J.,* vol. lxxx, p. 141.

In like manner the assemblies assumed and lost a jurisdiction in regard to questions of divorce. The common
law, although it recognized as valid an agreement of separation between a husband and wife, afforded no facili-
ties for divorce. Gradually, however, there had grown
up in England a regular procedure by virtue of which
those who could afford the expense were able to secure
divorces by act of Parliament. Such bills were introduced in the Lords and heard by them practically as a
judicial matter. The petitioner was obliged to produce
upon oath a definitive sentence of divorce " *a mensa et
thoro* " obtained at his suit in the ecclesiastical courts,
while at the second reading he must attend and, if the house
saw fit, be examined at the bar.[1]

The first colonial act of divorce was passed by Jamaica
in 1739. When, after careful examination, the Board
found that no previous action had been commenced, nor
had any verdict for adultery been obtained at common law,
as was the custom in England, and that the fact of adultery had not been positively proved, it concluded that the
legislature had not "conformed itself to the usual practice
in acts of this nature in Great Britain," and urged that the
law be disallowed.[2] The colonies enacted in all at least a
dozen acts of divorce. In the four years preceding 1760
Massachusetts alone sent seven. The majority of these
were granted to women because of adultery committed by
the husband, a concession as yet unknown in England,
where no wife obtained a divorce by act of Parliament
until 1801. None were accompanied by adequate proof of

[1] Blackstone, bk. i, p. 441, note 26. Bryce, " Marriage and Divorce "
in *Essays in Anglo-American Legal History,* vol. iii, p. 823.

[2] *A. P. C.,* vol. iii, p. 681. This act " To Dissolve the Marriage of
Edward Manning and Elizabeth Moore, and enable him to marry
again " was disallowed July 16, 1741.

wrong-doing, while all were defective in that they dissolved the marriage and conferred the privilege of re-marrying with reference to only one of the parties to the original contract.[1] These acts were not disallowed because it was presumed that the parties released might have re-married. But the Board was strongly of the opinion that no colonial legislature had a power of passing laws of this nature, and that they were consequently "of themselves null and void." The whole question was referred to the attorney and solicitor general, with the suggestion that proper instructions be formulated for regulating the conduct of the governors in like cases. But the law officers failed to report, and there, for the time being, the matter rested.[2]

In 1770 the Board received the first of several acts from New Hampshire, New Jersey and Pennsylvania. Jackson, who had recently become king's counsel, pronounced these laws to be, in proper cases, " as agreeable to those of England as might be, the circumstances considered." He took advanced ground by urging the reasonableness and expediency of allowing the dissolution of marriage by a sanction equivalent to that which had given it validity, at the same time suggesting that the matter be referred to the attorney and solicitor general.[3] The Privy Council, however, regarded recent encroachments upon the part of the assemblies with marked disfavor. Failing to receive any report from the law officers, it disallowed an act of Pennsylvania to the end that it should be thought " that acts of Divorce in the Colonies, more especially when there does not appear to have been any suit instituted in any ecclesiastical court nor any verdict in any court of Common Law,

[1] *CO*/5-888, Ii, 3 and 4. *CO*/5-919, p. 11; 31 July, 1759. *CO*/5-918, pp. 486-490. Dickerson, *Am. Col. Govt.*, p. 260, note 606.

[2] Board report, *CO*/5-918, p. 489; 1758.

[3] *CO*/5-1278, Z, 1; 10 August, 1770. *A. P. C.*, vol. v, p. 365.

are either improper or unconstitutional." [1]   This was followed by general instructions forbidding the governors' assent to any acts for divorce, as well as for naturalization, or the confirmation of land titles derived from unnaturalized aliens.

[1] *A. P. C.*, vol. v, p. 366.   *Pa. Stats.*, vol. viii, p. 599; 7 April, 1773.

CHAPTER VI

THE POLICY OF THE BRITISH GOVERNMENT IN LEGISLATIVE REVIEW: ATTITUDE TOWARD ENCROACHMENTS UPON THE PREROGATIVE

THE third major objection which the government frequently made to colonial laws was that they "encroached upon the prerogative." Like the phrase "repugnant to the laws of England," this also was loosely applied to cover a multitude of irregularities; an inclusiveness due in part to a largeness and vagueness of concept. For the term "prerogative" was made to convey not only the sum of legal rights and privileges inherent in the British executive, but also by implication, a sense of the dignity and divine aloofness of the sovereign. It was invoked against laws which threatened to impair the necessary and proper supremacy of the crown in the colonies, and to decrease the due sense of subordination and dependence upon their part, which was consequent to it. The prerogative served as a convenient barrier against the increeping of liberal ideas, and could always be used to justify the refusal of measures which in any way threatened to alter the settled order of government or to change the political *status quo*.

The government objected consistently to legislation which was detrimental to the material interests or property of the crown. It insisted that the proceeds from all fines and forfeitures be reserved to his majesty, although the legislature could specify the manner and purpose of their expenditure.[1] In the settlement of estates, debts due the crown must be given a priority to all others; and any disregard for his majesty's right of escheat was deemed an infringement upon the royal prerogative.[2]

Enactments regarding the collection of quit rents most frequently brought the assemblies into conflict with the pecuniary interests of the crown. Indeed, so jealous was the home government of encroachment in this direction, that it allowed comparatively few of the numerous quit-rent laws submitted to go into operation. Against these acts it was commonly objected that under color of regulating quit rents they confirmed large grants of land to favored persons, that the collection of rents was ill provided for, to the encouragement of default and evasion, and that the values of subsisting rents were needlessly diminished.[3] Several acts placed the crown under difficulties in the recovery of forfeitures and arrears. A law of Maryland, for example, provided that no orphan should be sued in action of debt for arrears until five years after attaining his majority.[4] An act of Virginia did away with a provision for forfeiture after three years of non-payment, and allowed the crown a double rent and one moiety to the discoverer. Walpole, the auditor general, thought the former penalty perhaps too severe, but the latter certainly too lenient.[5] New York required

[1] *CO*/5-915, p. 278. *A. P. C.*, vol. iii, p. 125.

[2] *CO*/5-300, F, 5; 28 October 1764. *CO*/5-1074, p. 457; 5 June 1770.

[3] *CO*/5-401, p. 57; South Carolina, 1 November 1732. *CO*/5-362, D, 18. *B. T. J.*, vol. xlvii, p. 53. *CO*/5-402, p. 94; Georgia, 28 February 1744.

[4] *CO*/5-727, p. 96. *B. T. J.*, vol. xx, p. 402. Disallowed 25 November 1708.

[5] *CO*/5-1319, O, 35; 13 June 1723.

all actions for recovery to be prosecuted in the superior court, thereby depriving the crown of its right to sue in chancery.[1] Other laws permitted payment in paper money or rated commodities, although the rents were reserved in sterling or proclamation money.[2] The attitude of the government toward quit rent acts was well summarized by the lords commissioners of the treasury when they reported that a law of South Carolina was prejudicial to revenue, and " not proper for approbation, the whole tenor thereof Encroaching upon the Royal Prerogative."[3]

Second only to the crown's apprehension for the security of its revenue, was the solicitude displayed regarding encroachments upon its dignity or privilege. Thus, a law of recognition passed as an act of fidelity after the accession of a sovereign was considered presumptuous and unnecessary.[4] For similar reasons the Board disliked to have the assemblies enact as law clauses from his majesty's commission to the governor. An attempt of Virginia to explain and amend a royal charter was declared " unwarrantable, and highly prejudicial to His Majesty's authority."[5] And because of his majesty's

---

[1] *CO*/5-1126, p. 279; 23 May 1745. *CO*/5-371, H, 75.

[2] *CO*/5-1519, O, 35; Virginia, 15 June 1723. An act of South Carolina made the rents payable in produce at a rate to be fixed by three persons appointed by the governor and council, and three to be appointed by the assembly. *CO*/5-400, p. 285. *CO*/5-323, p. 285; 14 November 1731. *CO*/5-323, p. 273; North Carolina, 26 June 1740. *B. T. J.*, vol. lxix, p. 312; Virginia, 16 December 1762.

[3] *CO*/5-401, p. 57; 1 November 1732.

[4] Attorney General Harcourt upon an act of Maryland, Chalmers, *Opinions*, p. 332; 17 December 1707.

[5] *CO*/5-1328, W, 150. *A. P. C.*, vol. iv, p. 257; 21 January 1754. But a later act, enlarging the jurisdiction of a court beyond the limitations established by a borough charter, was confirmed. *CO*/5-1331, Z, 88. *CO*/5-1332, Aa, 5; 26 June 1767.

undoubted right of "giving motion to his own royal bounty," the king's counsel went so far as to suggest that no laws affecting the rights of the crown should be passed by a colonial assembly without the royal assent having been first obtained.[1]

Many laws encroached upon the prerogative in that the colonists presumed to regulate in acts of the legislature matters which, by virtue of English precedent or the governor's commissions belonged to the sole discretion of the executive. Upon this ground the government objected when acts establishing schools or colleges failed to give the crown, through its governor, a customary right of visitation;[2] and as well, when South Carolina intrusted the oversight of her fortifications, a task imposed upon the governor by his commission, to commissioners of their own choosing.[3] Despite the insertion of clauses saving his majesty's right, Virginia lost several laws which authorized local communities to initiate fairs or markets, the power to do this being "undoubtedly a branch of the Royal Prerogative," by "commission vested in the governor."[4]

[1] Jackson upon laws validating the titles of aliens to real estate, *CO*/5-1074, p. 457. *CO*/5-979, p. 49.

[2] Two acts for incorporating Harvard College were disallowed for this reason, and also a Maryland law which was additional to an act for erecting free schools. *Acts and Resolves*, vol. i, p. 39, ch. x. *B. T. J.*, vol. viii, p. 11. *CO*/5-908, pp 53, 124; 3 February 1699. *C. S. P.*, 1693-6, p. 636; 4 January 1696.

[3] *CO*/5-233, p. 70; 15 November 1750.

[4] *A. P. C.*, vol. iv, p. 138; 31 October 1751. *CO*/5-1327, W, 56. *CO*/5-1326, V, 93. *CO*/5-1329, X, 24. *A. P. C.*, vol v, pp. 163; 12 August 1768. The laws disallowed were also objectionable in that they granted to persons attending such fairs an exemption from arrests, attachments and executions, except for capital offences or breach of the peace. The conferring of so sweeping an immunity was considered repugnant to the laws of England.

The power to grant letters of incorporation lay well within the disputed zone between the domain of the legislature and the executive. The Board declared that "Incorporations should arise from the bounty of the Crown by letters patent, rather than by act of Assembly." But notwithstanding this opinion they recommended for confirmation acts granting incorporation to various projects of a pious, charitable or educational nature, among which was a law of Pennsylvania which made the overseers of the poor in every township a body corporate to take real or personal estates by deed or will.[1] Acts of South Carolina and Massachusetts, incorporating in the one case, the city of Charlestown, and in the other, establishing a society for the propagation of Christian knowledge among the Indians, were disallowed. But in both cases the crown based its refusal upon the inexpediency of the project, rather than upon any undue presumption on the part of the legislature.[2] Governor Bernard and Governor Hutchinson both warned the Board that their yielding to the assembly in this matter was tending to a prescription against the king's right of granting incorporation. But Jackson was of the opinion that the power to incorporate had been vested in the general court by the Massachusetts charter.[3]

An act of New Hampshire which gave absolute con-

---

[1] *A. P. C.*, vol. v, p. 103; 2 August 1750. *A. P. C.*, vol. iv, p. 173; South Carolina, 20 December 1752. *CO*/5-403, p. 218; South Carolina, 20 December 1757. *CO*/5-380, p. 161; 15 June 1770. *CO*/5-380, p. 187; 15 January 1772.

By extending the Bubble act of 1720 to the Plantations, Parliament in 1741 forbade the granting of corporate privileges for business purposes.

[2] *CO*/5-400, p. 164; 19 June 1723. Chalmers, *Opinions*, p. 395. *A. P. C.*, vol. v, p. 559; 20 May 1763.

[3] *CO*/5-891, Ll, 33; 12 April 1762. *CO*/5-894, p. 365; 8 May 1772.

trol over the person and property of lunatics to local overseers of the poor and select men was disallowed because, without notice or care of the royal prerogative, it deprived the crown of privileges enjoyed under English law. There custody was obtained by a commission issued upon application to his majesty from a court of chancery; and the yearly value of lands owned by subjects born in lunacy was reserved to the crown. But the repeal of the New Hampshire act miscarried, and the law remained in force until amended many years later. The Privy Council not only disallowed the amendatory act, but also ordered the Board of Trade to insert in the commissions of all governors a clause giving them power, as chancellors, to issue commissions for the custody of lunatics.[1] Another act of New Hampshire, for regulating the manufacture of potash, was disallowed because it tended to establish a monopoly—a privilege conferred only by letters patent; while a law of Jamaica providing for the stamping and issuing of money, and making the counterfeiting thereof high treason, was held to have established a mint—a power which had never been delegated to any of the American colonies.[2]

The crown was particularly jealous of encroachments upon its power to reprieve or pardon. In laws objectionable upon this score, New Jersey twice extended amnesty to persons concerned in disorders, without even excepting any who might be guilty of high treason, the pardoning of which was reserved to his majesty by instruction.[3] And in an act granting compensation to the

---

[1] *CO*/5-915, pp. 163, 172; 27 August 1718. *A. P. C.*, vol. v, p. 189; 26 May 1769.

[2] *A. P. C.*, vol. v, p. 159; 12 August 1768. *A. P. C.*, vol. iv, p. 455; 20 May 1760.

[3] *N. Y. Col. Docs.*, vol. v, p. 46; 28 June 1708. *CO*/5-997, pp. 208-344; June 1750.

sufferers from the riots in Boston incident to the stamp act, Massachusetts unwarrantably incorporated a pardon to all concerned.[1] Equally objectionable were acts in which the assembly without exercising the power themselves, nevertheless limited the crown's opportunity for doing so. This they did by enacting that a penalty should be exacted without benefit of pardon, or that offenders who failed after proclamation to surrender themselves might be killed by any person at sight.[2]

In many cases laws were considered inimical to the prerogative in that they injured the standing and interests of patent officers by regulating and prescribing their duties, or by depriving them of power or income. Officers of the customs were frequent sufferers from legislative aggression. Massachusetts created a provincial naval office with a general supervision over local shipping.[3] Massachusetts and Pennsylvania both attempted to establish ports of entry, a power vested in the lord high treasurer and his subordinates by act of Parliament;[4] while Virginia sought to impose three years residence as a qualification for appointment to local customs offices.[5] An act of Pennsylvania laid a penalty upon any customs officer who should clear a vessel without a required certificate for the payment of lighthouse dues, a provision, said the Board of Trade, which "would operate to control a Constitutional officer of the Crown in the exercise of those duties which the laws of trade and navigation

[1] *A. P. C.*, vol. v, p. 86; 13 May 1767.

[2] Board to Cornbury, *CO*/5-1120, p. 384; 4 February 1706. *A. P. C.*, vol. v, p. 317; West Florida, 15 January 1772. *A. P. C.*, vol. v, p. 336; North Carolina, 22 April 1772.

[3] *B. T. J.*, vol. viii, p. 11. *CO*/5-906, p. 200; August 1695.

[4] *C. S. P.*, 1700, pp. 475, 555.

[5] *CO*/5-1364, pp. 224, 253; 31 August 1715.

require of him."[1] The Privy Council disallowed a law
of North Carolina which vested the power of appointing
to benefices in the local vestries, notwithstanding the
fact that by the charter the right of patronage was given
to the crown and the king's governor.[2] An act of Massachusetts was annulled because it was prejudicial to the
office of the postmaster general, and to the rights of
Thomas Neale, who had been granted a patent to establish a post office in America.[3] At the request of the
admiralty the Board complained to the proprietors of
South Carolina regarding an act which subjected officers
and judges of the admiralty courts there to unseemly
suits and penalties;[4] and it assented only with evident
reluctance to acts limiting the governors' right of appointment by conferring the power to nominate candi-
dates for sheriff upon the county courts, and as well to a
limitation of the sheriff's term of office, although its
duration in England had been fixed by an act of Parliament.[5] Claiming that the inhabitants had been needlessly prosecuted for trivial offences, the assembly of
New York passed a law which forbade the attorney-
general to institute proceedings save upon the present-
ment of a grand jury or an order from the governor.
For each violation of the act he became liable to a penalty of one hundred pounds current money, which could
be recovered by an action of debt. The king's counsel
declared this "a very violent and extraordinary attack

[1] *A. P. C.*, vol. iv, p. 763; 18 June 1766. *CO/5*-1057, Ee, p. 54; New
York, December 1734.

[2] *A. P. C.*, vol. iv, p. 408; 3 March 1759.

[3] *Acts and Resolves*, vol. i, p. 117, ch. iii; November 1696.

[4] *CO/5*-1289, p. 344. *C. S. P.*, 1702, p. 61; 3 February 1702.

[5] *CO/5*-975, G, 36; New Jersey, 30 September 1749. *A. P. C.*, vol. v,
p. 166, South Carolina, 7 October 1768.

upon the prerogative of the Crown, the right of the Attorney General to file information having been delegated from the King, and ever thought an essential and necessary power."[1]

The governors's instructions impowered them, together with their councils, to regulate fees, and bade them give all possible encouragement to patent officers in the enjoyment of their legal and accustomed privileges and emoluments. But frequent and widespread complaints that local officials made exorbitant charges, an evil for which there was no satisfactory remedy at common law, were followed by a strong popular demand for the regulation of fees by acts of the assemblies. The Board conceded that the royal instruction did not prevent this, and almost all of the colonies passed laws for the purpose. Patent officers in turn complained that the fees prescribed were below those sanctioned by custom. But, as a rule, they secured the disallowance of offending laws only when they suffered obvious and continued injustice, for the Board of Trade regarded any reasonable regulation of fees as a matter of domestic concern, and interfered only when a lessening of income threatened to defeat his majesty's intention in making appointments.[2] In several instances laws were disallowed because the amounts prescribed were so inconsiderable that they rendered it difficult or impossible for patentees to live

[1] Chalmers, *Opinions*, p. 493. *CO*/5-1054, Dd, 76. *CO*/5-1125, p. 120; 6 November 1728. Many years later a less extreme act for the same purpose was permitted to lie by. *CO*/5-1066, Kk, p. 40. *B. T. J.*, vol. lxvi, p. 63; 14 February 1759. Attorney General Harcourt delivered an unfavorable opinion upon a similar law of Maryland, " Rectifying the Powers of Attorneys," *CO*/5-716, H, 48; 17 September 1707.

[2] *CO*/5-672, p. 370; Georgia, 12 November 1755. *A. P. C.*, vol. iv, p. 311. *CO*/5-324, p. 241; North Carolina, 10 March 1757. *CO*/5-652, p. 9; Georgia, 30 December 1773.

on their places, and served to discourage persons of character and reputation from accepting office.[1]

By dint of many complaints and representations, Lawrence, the Secretary of Maryland, secured an order from the Board which commanded the assembly to restore to his office the revenue from ordinary licenses, a perquisite which it had enjoyed under Lord Baltimore.[2]   The privy council prevented the assembly of South Carolina from abolishing the office of provost marshal by transferring its duties to the sheriffs, until the patentee had received security for the full value of his interest in the patent; and as the result of an attempt by Massachusetts to levy an income tax upon the salaries of customs officers, the governor was instructed to withold his consent in the future from acts taxing incomes received from the crown.[3]

At no point did the crown more firmly insist upon the integrity of the prerogative than in maintaining its control over the assemblies.   By their commissions and instructions the governors were impowered in the king's name to issue writs for the election of members, to designate the time and place of sitting, and to prorogue and dissolve the sessions as they saw fit.   But the colonists, who were ever disposed to regard their assemblies as local parliaments, sought for them a freedom from executive control equal to that enjoyed by Parliament in England.   To this end they passed laws which prescribed

[1] *CO*/5-1121, p. 455. *B. T. J.*, vol. xxi, p. 319; New York, disallowed, 15 December 1709. *CO*/5-996, p. 369. *A. P. C.*, vol. iii, p. 454; New Jersey, disallowed, 3 April 1735. *CO*/5-365, F, 54, F, 49. *CO*/5-401, p. 202; South Carolina, disallowed, 21 April 1737. *A. P. C.*, vol. iv, p. 9; New Jersey, disallowed, 28 June 1749.

[2] *CO*/5-716, H, 44, 56, 75, 100. *CO*/5-726, p. 487.

[3] *A. P. C.*, vol. iv, p. 59; 4 August 1748. *A. P. C.*, vol. v, p. 167; 7 October 1768. *B. T. J.*, vol. lxxvi, p. 158. *CO*/5-893, p. 329. *B. T. J.*, lxxviii, p. 17; 30 January 1771.

the maximum period which should elapse between elections and fixed definite times of meeting, irrespective of the governor's writ of summons. Without exception these acts met with disallowance, or if they contained suspending clauses, with refusal, upon the ground that the right of calling and continuing an assembly at such times and as long as seemed necessary for the public service was the sole prerogative of the crown.[1] By an amendment to a revenue law, Jamaica attempted to obtain the crown's acquiesence to an annual sitting; while North and South Carolina each ventured a biennial act.[2] Far more numerous were the laws modeled upon the contemporary rule in regard to Parliament, which required that a session be held at least once in three years. New York, New Hampshire, New Jersey, Jamaica, Virginia and Georgia all made one or more vain attempts to assure themselves of a triennial assembly.[3] Although the assemblies were usually summoned and dissolved more frequently than these laws required, the Board insisted that no pretence of right could be deduced from the usage.

The government required that members of the assembly should be freeholders, duly elected by the major

[1] Chalmers, *Opinions*, p. 343. *CO*/5-323, p. 257. *A. P. C.*, vol. iii, p. 568; North Carolina, 21 July 1737. *CO*/5-1059, Gg, 19. *A. P. C.*, vol. iii, p. 617; New York, 30 November 1738. *CO*/5-1330, Y, 83; Virginia, 17 May 1763. *A. P. C.*, vol. v, p. 286; Virginia, 9 December 1770.

[2] *B. T. J.*, vol. iv, p. 74; 1 November 1682. *A. P. C.*, vol. iii, p. 568. *A. P. C.*, vol. iv, p 141.

[3] *N. Y. Col. Docs.*, vol. iii, p. 358; March 1685. *B. T. J.*, vol. xxxvii, p. 1631 New Hampshire, May 1728. *CO*/5-941, p. 279; New Hampshire, 9 July 1752. *A. P. C.*, vol. iii, p. 343; New Jersey, 25 November 1731. *B. T. J.*, vol. lxvi, p. 108; Jamaica, 1741. *CO*/5-1330, Y, 83; Virginia, 17 May 1763. *CO*/5-674, p. 347; Georgia, 23 November 1770.

part of the freeholders or men of assured yearly income in the respective townships or parishes.[1] Within these bounds the colonists appear to have exercised a rather limited discretion.[2] Nor were they allowed to exclude office holders. An act of South Carolina, which provided that no person holding any other office should serve as a member of the assembly, was disallowed, partly for other reasons.[3] New York attempted to disqualify judges upon the ground that executive and legislative powers ought not to be vested in the same persons. Judges, it was urged, could not sit in the House of Commons, and in the assembly they had often become leaders of factions. The act was disallowed, nevertheless, because it affected the prerogative, and did upon "reasons not applicable to the state of the colony, make a very essential alteration in its constitution."[4] In 1773 the Board conceded to Virginia the right to disqualify sheriffs and inspectors of tobacco during their continuance in office. But it objected to a clause which continued their disability for two years thereafter.[5]

Questions propounded to the law officers indicate that the Board of Trade was not certain whether the enactment of a law conferring upon a local community the right of representation in the assembly conflicted with the governor's power to summon members by writs

[1] *A. P. C.*, vol. iv, p. 217. This rule did not obtain in South Carolina, where a law enacted during the proprietary regime was allowed to continue in force.

[2] *C. S. P.*, 1693-6, p. 84; South Carolina, 12 April 1693. *CO*/5-994, p. 204; New Jersey, 4 February 1706. *A. P. C.*, vol. iv, p. 49; Jamaica, 30 June 1748.

[3] *A. P. C.*, vol. iv, p. 49; 30 June 1748.

[4] *A. P. C.*, vol. v, p. 244; 6 June 1770.

[5] *CO*/5-1369, p. 324.

issued in the king's name; and, as well, whether by virtue of that power, the governor alone could authorize the sending of representatives.[1] Notwithstanding this uncertainty, the Board seems to have conceded that the assemblies could pass such laws provided they did not so word them as to preclude the governors from issuing writs, or to convey thereby any other power than that of demanding a writ upon proof of qualification.[2] But, as a matter of fact, the home government early became alarmed at the continual growth of membership in the lower houses and forbade the governors to assent to further increase without the insertion of a suspending clause.[3]

In 1742 Governor Shirley of Massachusetts complained that the enlarged membership of the house, due to the continual division of townships and the settlement of new territory, rendered it unwieldy and caused it to overshadow the council, thereby destroying the proper balance between the two bodies established by the charter. The Board concurred in these views and instructed him not to pass any further act erecting a new township or dividing an old without insisting upon a suspending clause. Inasmuch as Massachusetts claimed under its charter an exemption from suspending clauses and refused to insert them, this command amounted to a prohibition, and the membership of the house remained without further increase for several years.[4] In 1761 the

---

[1] *B. T. J.*, vol. xxxviii, p. 152; 30 May 1729. *CO*/5-323, p. 370; 7 May 1753.

[2] *CO*/5-941, p. 212; 3 February 1749. *A. P. C.*, vol. v, p. 29. *B. T. J.*, lxix, p. 169.

[3] *CO*/5-973, F, 34; New Jersey, 26 May 1739.

[4] *CO*/5-883, Ee, 70. *CO*/5-918, pp. 90-94, 109. An act "Errecting the Township of Lincoln" escaped disallowance in 1756 because it had

Board admitted that this restriction was in conflict both with the charter and with an act of the assembly which had been confirmed, by virtue of which every township was entitled to send either one or two representatives, according to the number of its freeholders. The Board accordingly withdrew its instruction and advised the governor to obtain, whenever possible, acts conferring upon newly-organized districts all the privileges of townships except that of sending representatives.[1]

Meanwhile the Board twice interfered to end local disputes between a governor and an assembly regarding laws for the erection of towns or counties. New Hampshire passed several acts which so regulated the sending of representatives as to preclude the governor from issuing writs. The assembly having refused to modify them, the Board recommended five laws for disallowance, with the expectation that in their place the governor would issue charters of incorporation. But the assembly yielded the principal points of contention, and the affair gave place to more important concerns of French and Indian warfare.[2] In 1754 an act of North Carolina for "Ascertaining the number of Members of the Assembly" caused the Board to take cognizance of a dispute between the northern and southern counties as to their respective representations. Thirteen laws for erecting counties were disallowed, and Governor Dobbs was instructed to pass only such acts for this purpose as did not impower

already been carried into operation. But a similar law "Errecting the Township of Danvers" was declared void. *CO*/5-913, p. 330. *CO*/5-919, p. 11.

[1] *A. P. C.*, vol. iv, p. 475. *CO*/5-920, pp. 130, 140, 174-183. *CO*/5-891, p. 349.

[2] *CO*/5-941, pp. 212, 226, 364. Board report, *CO*/5-941, p. 267; 9 July 1752.

the sending of representatives. He proceeded to grant charters of incorporation; but the inhabitants insisted upon their right to representation, and in some cases held elections without writs. There followed a long period of contention during which neither side appears to have scored decisively; but the plan of incorporation proved by no means a success.[1]

In 1767 the Board made a strong representation in regard to the enactment of laws operating " to the augmentation and Encrease of the Representative Body [and] leading to . . Inconveniences . . . found to arise from the Encreasing Greatness and Disproportion of the number of that Branch of the legislature." The Privy Council, perforce, allowed eighteen acts of Massachusetts for erecting townships, to lie by; but three laws from New Hampshire, Nova Scotia and South Carolina it disallowed. Furthermore an instruction strengthening the control of the executive over the legislature, already issued to some colonies, was made general. Henceforth governors were not upon any pretence to assent to a law by which the number of the assembly was enlarged or diminished, the duration of it ascertained, or the qualification of the electors or the elected, fixed or altered.[2] Nothing could reveal more plainly the distrust and apprehension with which the government viewed the " leveling tendencies " at work in the colonies, and the alarm with which it noted the continual encroachments made upon the prerogative by the only branch of the provincial governments which was responsive to popular sentiment.

[1] *CO*/5-323; 14 March 1754. *B. T. J.*, vol. lxii; 11 April 1755. *CO*/5-297, C, 91. *CO*/5-298, D, 60. *CO*/5-325, C, 74. *CO*/5-297, E, 52. *B. T. J.*, vol. lxix, p. 169.

[2] *B. T. J.*, vol. lxxv, p. 16. *A. P. C.*, vol. v, 25-34. *N. Y. Col. Docs.*, vol. vii, p. 946.

In theory the king, as the fountain of justice, was the source of authority for both courts and judges, and accordingly the governors' commissions impowered them to erect the one and to appoint the other. But in obtaining appropriations requisite for the payment of salaries and the maintenance of judicial systems, the crown was dependent, for the most part, upon the assemblies. This fact goes far to explain why the provincial courts were established and regulated by law, despite the Board's repeated assertions that the power to do this was the unalterable prerogative of the crown.[1] It was assumed, nevertheless, that this privilege was delegated from the king and exercised only by his forbearance. Nor could the assemblies in any way restrain him from constituting courts other than those authorized by provincial law if he saw fit.[2] The government did insist that the appointment of judges and justices should be vested without restraint in the king, and not in the assembly, or in the governor with the advice of the council and assembly.[3] With the alleged purpose of obtaining appointments for particular individuals, the legislature of North Carolina enacted that no person should become a judge or justice save barristers of five years standing in one of the Inns of Court in England, who had practiced in the courts of that or some other colony. But this was deemed " an unconstitutional restraint upon the power of appointing judges."[4]

[1] CO/5-1314, L, 17. CO/5-912, p. 169. *Acts and Resolves*, vol. ii, p. 34, note on ch. xx. *A. P. C.*, vol. iv, p. 218; Jamaica, 28 February 1754.

[2] CO/5-1362, p. 111; Virginia, 26 March 1707.

[3] *Acts and Resolves*, vol. i, p 418, note on ch. ii. CO/5-1326, p. 111. CO/5-324, p. 300. CO/5-305, p. 89. *B. T. J.*, vol. xliv, pp. 177-187; South Carolina. CO/5-401, p. 150; 11 August 1735.

[4] *A. P. C.*, vol. iv, p. 504; 14 December 1761.

In several colonies the assemblies, following the English act of Settlement, sought, while granting judges permanent salaries, to change the tenure of their commissions from during "His Majesty's Pleasure" to during "good behavior." When Jamaica led the way in 1751 the Privy Council condemned the change as one affecting the royal prerogative in a point of great moment. Even assuming that there had occurred any abuse of power to justify such an innovation, the report continues, it were "more suitable to Your Majesty's Honor and dignity to reform it by Your own authority, which is fully sufficient for the purpose."[1] Acts of similar intent from Pennsylvania, New York, North Carolina and South Carolina met with no better success. In reporting upon the New York law, the Board of Trade observed: "The granting of Judges' Commissions during good behavior ought to be discountenanced, .. as subversive of the Interest of the Crown and people, and tending to lessen that just Dependence which the Colonies ought to have upon the government of the Mother Country." Following the disallowance of this act in 1761, instructions were sent to all governors forbidding their assent to laws of like nature.[2]

In some instances laws in regard to courts were held to trench upon the prerogative in that they hindered the exercise of his majesty's right of allowing appeals from colonial courts to the King in Council. Massachusetts was bidden to correct a law which prevented appeals in real actions.[3] New Hampshire and Maryland

[1] *A. P. C.*, vol. iv, p. 216; 28 February 1754.

[2] *B. T. J.*, vol. lxviii, pp. 348, 384. *CO/5-1275*, W, 45. *A. P. C.*, vol. iv, p. 502; North Carolina, 14 December 1761. *A. P. C.*, vol. v, p. 166; South Carolina, 7 October 1768.

[3] *CO/5-907*, p. 75; 10 December 1696.

each prohibited appeals in cases involving less than three hundred pounds sterling; and without objecting to the sum named, the Board nevertheless insisted that no obstruction should be placed upon the royal privilege to hear cases of less value if the crown pleased.[1] From a special court established in the Bahamas any appeal to the Privy Council was expressly prohibited, a provision deemed "altogether inconsistent with the constitution of the Colony."[2]

Many laws were disallowed because in passing them the colonial legislatures had usurped functions properly belonging to the king's courts of justice. Such were the acts by which Massachusetts passed sentence upon several of her citizens for engaging in illegal trade with the hostile French.[3] Jamaica, upon the other hand, reversed the decision of a court of law and declared the prisoner free.[4] The assembly of New Hampshire persisted in passing upon the validity of contested land titles, a practice "so unconstitutional and unjust" that in 1764 the Privy Council disallowed sixteen laws at one time, "in order to deter the legislatures . . . from assuming powers and taking cognisance of matters that do constitutionally belong to courts of justice alone."[5] The assemblies also attempted to redress injuries inflicted upon private persons by fraudulent lotteries, and to compel performance

[1] *CO*/5-912, pp. 169, 186, 210; New Hampshire, 19 November 1706. *CO*/5-716, H, 48. *CO*/5-727, p. 251. *A. P. C.*, vol. ii, p. 633; Maryland, 14 June 1711.

[2] *A. P. C.*, vol. v, p. 329; 1772. *C. S. P.*, 1681-5, p. 185; Virginia 1682. *CO*/5-1362, p. 111.

[3] *CO*/5-912, p. 354.

[4] *A. P. C.*, vol. iv, p. 412; 29 March 1759.

[5] *A. P. C.*, vol. iv, p. 674; 20 July 1764. *CO*/5-942, p. 266. *A. P. C.*, vol. v, p. 160. *A. P. C.*, vol. iv, p. 490; Georgia, 2 July 1761.

in cases of alleged breach of contract.[1]   They lost no
opportunity of enlarging their control over the granting
and expending of provincial appropriations, thereby ham-
pering the executive in its appointment of officials and
conduct of the government.   Massachusetts, Barbadoes
and South Carolina all attempted to supply the revenue
by means which deprived the governor of power to sign
warrants for issuing money.[2]   In 1751 the Board complained of the power wielded by the assembly of New
York by virtue of its practice in granting supplies for
one year only, and of making salaries payable only to the
present incumbent of offices.[3]   South Carolina passed an
act whereby all civil officers who received any salary from
the provincial treasury were to be nominated, appointed
and removed only by the general assembly—a provision,
said the king's counsel, which "cuts up at the roots all
the king's prerogative, and bars the Crown from ever
intermeddling with any of the civil employments."[4]   The
attitude of the Board of Trade in regard to this whole
matter received its strongest statement in a representation of July 24, 1760, upon several acts of Pennsylvania.
In passing these laws the assembly had encroached not
only upon the power of the executive, but also upon the
material interests and charter rights of the proprietors.
After rebuking them for lack of firmness in maintaining
their rights, the Board urged them to be mindful in the
future of their duty to restore the constitution of the

[1] *A. P. C.*, vol. iv, p. 684; New Jersey, 20 July 1764. *CO/5*-1296, p. 201;
Pennsylvania, 29 April 1768. *A. P. C.*, vol. v, p. 31; Massachusetts,
26 June 1767.

[2] *Acts and Resolves*, vol. ii, p. 574. *A. P. C.*, vol. iii, p. 203, Barbadoes, 1728. *A. P. C.*, vol. v, p. 229; South Carolina, 1770.

[3] *CO/5*-1127, pp. 48, 216; 2 April 1751.

[4] *CO/5*-371, H, 57.

colony to its proper principles, " to check the growing influence of the assembly, and to distinguish what they are perpetually confounding, the executive from the legislative parts of the government." " Nothing," said their Lordships, " is so likely to preserve the tranquility of the Province or its dependence on the mother country as maintaining with a strict and steady hand the necessary powers and just prerogatives of the Crown. . . . . It is in vain to negotiate away His Majesty's prerogative, every new concession become[s] the foundation of some new demand and that [demand] of some new dispute." [1]

[1] *CO*/5-1295, pp. 295-385 ; 24 June 1760. *B. T. J.*, vol. lxvii, p. 141.

CHAPTER VII

The Policy of the British Government in Legislative Review : Attitude Toward Laws Deemed Inexpedient

ASIDE from considerations of trade, conformity and prerogative, the Board of Trade weighed laws, and sometimes recommended their disallowance, upon grounds of mere expediency. If an act was considered objectionable upon other grounds the question of its expediency received, as a rule, scant mention. The opinion of the Board that an excessive issue of paper money injured the British merchants, for instance, was paramount to the belief that it was inimical as well to the economic interests of the colonists themselves.

In reviewing laws upon certain subjects which did not involve questions of imperial policy, however, the Board appears to have acted with a single eye to the well-being of the colonial inhabitants. Upon this ground, for example, was based the consistent disapproval accorded after 1760 to acts authorizing lotteries. After having accepted these ventures as a matter of course, the Board came gradually to discourage their organization for purposes of private gain, or for the accomplishment of unimportant public undertakings. And by a general instruction of 1769 their establishment without previous consent from the crown was prohibited altogether.[1]

[1] CO/5-1068, Mm, 61. CO/5-921, 44. CO/5-325, C, 195. CO/5-999, p. 185. B. T. J., vol. lxxvi, p. 48.

The raising of money by lottery, said the Board in one of its representations, "ought by no means to be Encouraged, as obviously tending to disengage and mislead Adventurers therein from Industry and Attention to their proper callings and Occupations, and introducing a spirit of Dissipation prejudicial to the fortunes of Individuals and the Interests of the Public." [1]

Upon grounds of local welfare the Board discouraged, also, acts for lowering the current rate of interest. The price of money being of necessity high in a new country, it was feared that a low return would prohibit lending and retard the economic development of the colony. [2] And in passing upon laws in regard to the granting of lands the crown, apart from its solicitude for the security of quit rents, sought to prevent conditions which might injure the colonies by retarding their settlement. To this end it confirmed an act of New York for vacating several exorbitant grants of land, notwithstanding a most careful and elaborate presentation of their case made by the grantees. [3] Lest all lands ungranted should "fall into a few rich mens' hands and be a discouragement to settlement" it disallowed acts of Virginia which, by allowing an unlimited number of patents to the same person and neglecting to oblige reasonable cultivation,

---

[1] *A. P. C.*, vol. v, p. 186. This representation of March 7, 1769 was upon an act of Pennsylvania for "Raising by Lottery 5,250 pounds for purchasing a Public Landing and paving the streets of Philadelphia." The act was allowed to remain in force because it had been carried into effect; but its consideration led to the general instruction forbidding the future enactment of similar laws.

[2] *A. P. C.*, vol. v, p. 405; New Jersey, 20 February 1775. *A. P. C.*, vol. v, p. 159; New Hampshire, 12 August 1768. *A. P. C.*, vol. v, p. 282; New Hampshire, 9 December 1770.

[3] *CO/5-1044*, p. 130. *CO/5-1121*, p. 83. *B. T. J.*, vol. xx, p. 232; 26 June 1708.

would have entitled the owner of one hundred slaves to take nineteen thousand acres.[1] It was objected also against quit rent acts of North Carolina, South Carolina and Georgia that in addition to weakening the security of the rents, they would discourage settlement.

As the patron of religion, the government encouraged the enactment of laws enforcing the humane treatment of slaves, the suppression of vice and immorality and the erection and maintenance of schools.[2] At the instance of the Bishop of London, the Board even objected to an act of Virginia which relieved youths of from fifteen to twenty-one years from punishment for absenting themselves from church and for immorality.[3] In colonies which established the Church of England, it insisted that the general supervision of the clergy be vested in the Bishop of London rather than in the local vestry, and that a more or less adequate provision be made for ministers.[4] In no colony, on the other hand, did the government attempt to compel the establishment of the English Church, or to impose tests which would exclude dissenters from office. Because of local conditions it permitted Quakers a somewhat more extensive use of the affirmation than in England, and, when they were called to its attention, it consistently disapproved of laws by which the dominant sect in any colony ventured to oppress the others.

---

[1] *CO*/5-1362, p. 117. *B. T. J.*, vol. xix, p. 153. This act for " Granting, Seating and Planting " was disallowed April 17, 1707. *CO*/5-1363, pp. 249, 266. *B. T. J.*, vol. xxv, p. 436. *CO*/5-1364, p. 375; 30 May 1716.

[2] *B. T J.*, vol. iv, p. 213. *CO*/5-403, p. 76. *CO*/5-996, p. 147. *A. P. C.*, vol. iii, p. 153.

[3] *B. T. J.*, vol. xix, p. 187; 26 May 1707. *CO*/5-1362, p. 232.

[4] *CO*/5-299, E, 51. *CO*/5-325, p. 201; North Carolina, 3 June 1762. *CO*/5-305, p. 45. *A. P. C.*, vol. v, p. 100; 26 June 1767.

Noteworthy among acts of this type was that for the " Service of God, and the Establishment of the Protestant Religion " which was thrice disallowed and was thrice re-enacted by Maryland. By declaring that the acts passed for this purpose in 1692 and 1695 enacted in too sweeping and unwarranted a fashion the laws of England, the government avoided taking cognizance of the religious controversy in the colony.[1]   A third law, passed " without any material alteration in anything for which the former had been disallowed," compelled the use of the prayer book and the administration of the Sacraments according to the Church of England, in all places of worship.[2]   Catholics and Quakers protested strongly against being deprived of liberty of conscience and taxed for the maintenance of the English Church.   Mindful of previous failures, the Board drafted a bill " agreeable to the toleration allowed here " which contained a clause repealing the law then in force.   This they transmitted to the colony for enactment, together with instructions that meanwhile the present law " be not too rigorously executed." [3]   Shortly after the colony passed two acts, aimed " to check the insolent extravagences of priests." The first forbade all ministrations by Catholic priests, while the second suspended for the period of eighteen months as much of the former as applied to private families.   But the Privy Council, remarking that the rigorous execution of such acts would tend " to depopulate that profitable Colony," disallowed the first and

[1] *C. S. P.*, 1693-6, p. 636.   *CO*/5-725, p. 441.

[2] *C. S. P.*, 1700, p. 11.   *C. S. P.*, 1701, pp. 26, 78.   Moreover the vestries were made closed corporations and possessed with excessive powers.

[3] *B. T. J.*, vol. xiii, p. 441.   *C. S. P.*, 1701, pp. 211, 300.   The new law, duly enacted and found agreeable to the draft sent over, was confirmed. *CO*/5-726, p. 170.   *CO*/5-715, p. 71, E, 53; 18 January 1703.

ordered the governor to secure from the assembly an indefinite continuation of the second.[1]

In 1718 an act of Virginia containing severe discriminations against Quakers was disallowed with the similar remark, that "if put in execution it would prove very injurious to the Colony by banishing a great number of industrious inhabitants."[2]   With a like solicitude for the rights and welfare of the minority, the crown ordered the Carolina proprietors to repeal an act which decreed that members of the assembly should conform to the Church of England.[3]   And it several times intervened in the interests of Quakers, Baptists or member of the Church of England who were being taxed for the support of "orthodox" ministers in Massachusetts.[4]   In this case interference was based upon the ground that inasmuch as the charter granted liberty of conscience to all Christians except Catholics, taxes levied by act of the legislature for the support of Congregational ministers in townships where that sect constituted a minority were unwarranted and illegal.

---

[1] *CO*/5-715, G, 12. *B. T. J.*, vol. xviii, p. 149. *CO*/5-726, p. 354. *A. P. C.*, vol. ii, p. 497; 3 January 1706.

[2] This act for "Prohibiting Unlawful assemblings of Quakers" was passed in 1663 and escaped observation until 1718. It prohibited shipmasters from importing any Quaker more than fourteen years of age, and forbade Quakers assembling for religious worship, under penalty of heavy fines, and upon the third offense, of banishment. *CO*/5-1365, p. 36. *CO*/5-1316, p. 44. *B. T. J.*, vol. xxvii, p. 121; 13 February 1718.

[3] *CO*/5-1263, O, 63. *A. P. C.*, vol. ii, p. 506; 10 June 1706.

[4] Two acts taxing the Quakers of Dartmouth and Tiverton were disallowed in 1724, while several laws prejudicial to the Church of England were allowed to stand only because they had been confirmed by the charter. *CO*/5-915, p. 400. *CO*/5-878, Bb, 157. *A. P. C.*, vol. iii, p. 491; 2 February 1736. One law was disallowed upon the petition of Anabaptist settlers. *A. P. C.*, vol. v, p. 323; 31 July 1771.

In two instances, however, the crown acted otherwise than as a champion of tolerance. A law of West Florida was disallowed because it permitted the free exercise of religion to Catholics, "a sect proscribed by several acts of Parliament in all Dominions of the Crown." And the Privy Council annulled the founding of a college under Presbyterian auspices in North Carolina upon the recommendation of the Board, who, while sensible of the "tolerating spirit" generally prevailing throughout the dominions, doubted whether it was advisable "to add encouragement to toleration" by assenting to an establishment which promised advantages to Dissenters.[1]

The power of veto rendered the Crown a virtual arbiter in frequent disputes arising from the conflicting interests of neighboring colonies. New York and New Jersey sought to adjust a boundary controversy, first by an informal agreement embodied in an act of New Jersey, and, failing in this, by a law of New York which submitted the matter to his majesty for final determination. But the Crown, solicitous both for the security of private property and for its own interests in the escheats and quit rents of New York, rejected both laws and insisted upon the appointment of a royal commission from the decision of which parties aggrieved could appeal to the King in Council.[2] Of less importance was a controversy

---

[1] *CO*/5-577, C, 29. *A. P. C.*, vol. v, p. 286; West Florida, 9 December 1770. *CO*/5-326, pp. 188-199. *A. P. C.*, vol. v, p. 338; North Carolina, 22 April 1772. The latter act was also objectionable in that it laid a tax upon one particular county.

[2] *CO*/5-997, pp. 386-8. *A. P. C.*, vol. iv, p. 214. *CO*/5-1129, p. 12. *A. P. C.*, vol. iv, p. 301; 24 June 1755. *A. P. C.*, vol. iv, p. 686; 20 July 1764. The matter was finally settled by the confirmation of acts from both colonies, accepting the commission's decision and withdrawing the appeals which had been entered from its findings. *A. P. C.*, vol. v, p. 45; 1 September 1773.

which arose between Georgia and certain citizens of South Carolina. Georgia imposed requirements of settlement and cultivation upon the owners of land within her borders, some of whom derived their titles from previous grants of doubtful validity made by the government of Carolina. The grantees, who were citizens of the latter province, objected that the Georgia act prescribed terms other than those upon which the lands had been granted, that the determination of titles rested wholly with the governor and council of Georgia, and that owners were allowed but six months in which to establish their claims. The Privy Council adjusted the matter by disallowing the offensive act of Georgia, and by ordering that the governor of South Carolina transmit to Georgia copies of the patents in question, together with all the proceedings thereon. Georgia, in turn, was instructed to pass a new law for the cultivation of lands, and to establish a court for the substantiation of claims.[1]

The great majority of inter colonial differences which found their way into law were caused by an attempt of one colony to tax or limit the trade of a neighbor. Maryland imposed a levy of ten per cent. upon English goods passing through her territory to Pennsylvania,[2] New Hampshire offended Massachusetts by an export duty upon timber and boards, and the latter retaliated by imposing duties both upon goods imported from New Hampshire and those exported thither.[3] A New York duty upon tonnage proved injurious to the trade of Ber-

---

[1] *CO*/5-649, p. 147. *CO*/5-674, p. 311. *A. P. C.*, vol. v, p. 113; 26 August 1767.

[2] *C. S. P.*, 1696-7, p. 243. *CO*/5-725, p. 165. *B. T. J.*, vol. x, p. 352.

[3] *CO*/5-911, p. 209. *CO*/5-913, p. 503. *CO*/5-915, p. 148; 7 May 1715. *Acts and Resolves*, vol. ii, p. 235, ch. v.

muda,[1] and the Province of North Carolina which had no good ports within its own bounds, complained of an act of South Carolina which laid an impost upon its naval stores, and of an effort by Virginia to prohibit the importation and sale of its tobacco.[2]   It did in fact appear, as West observed, that the colonies considered themselves alien to each other and able to " act as independent Kingdoms in point of trade."[3]   Although deprecating the evils which arose from this general freedom of taxation, the home government realized its absolute necessity for raising adequate provincial revenues, and sought, not to prohibit the levying of duties upon inter-colonial trade, but rather to prevent excesses and consequent reprisals which would appreciably injure any one colony, the colonies as a whole, or the trade and interest of Great Britain.[4]

The crown interfered to prevent the taxation by Carolina of goods transported across her frontier by Indian traders from Virginia and again several years later to free the Indian traders of South Carolina from burdensome restrictions imposed by Georgia.   The need for concerted

---

[1] *CO*/5-1059, Gg, 13. *B. T. J.,* vol. xlvi, pt. ii, pp. 2, 149; 1739.

[2] *N. Car. Col. Records,* vol. v, pp. 786-7; Cited by Dickerson, p. 250. *CO*/5-1366, p. 76. *A. P. C.,* vol. iii, p. 345; Disallowed, 25 November 1731.

[3] In spite of urgent need, Virginia was unable to lay duties upon ships entering and leaving Chesapeake Bay for the erection and support of a light house, because Maryland was exempt from such levies by a provision of its charter. Attempts of Virginia to erect such a beacon failed because of the opposition of Maryland in 1728 and 1759; but she finally succeeded in 1772, when Governor Dunmore violated his instructions by assenting to an act for the purpose without a suspending clause. *B. T. J.,* vol. xxxvii, pp. 270, 281. *A. P. C.,* vol. iv, p. 401. *CO*/5-1333, p. 513. *CO*/5-1369, p. 309. *CO*/5-1334, Cc, 40.

[4] *CO*/5-894, Oo, 5. Report of Jackson on a Massachusetts " tonnage bill."

action upon this subject was frankly admitted by the Board of Trade in a letter to the governor of South Carolina, endorsing his proposal for a conference among the governors of the southern colonies.   An intercolonial agreement, they hoped, "might stop those mischiefs and inconveniences which have followed from different Provinces connected with the same Indians passing partial acts, not only differing from, but frequently obstructing and counteracting each other. [This] has been one . . . source of that jealousy and discontent among the Indians, which of late years has been attended with such terrible consequences."[1]   Nevertheless, a law of Virginia passed for this very purpose ten years later, was regarded as an act of usurpation and was disallowed, ostensibly because it contained no suspending clause.[2]

[1] Board to Gov. Boone, *CO*/5-404, p. 171; 3 June 1762.
[2] *CO*/5-1369, p. 235. *CO*/5-1334, Cc, p. 15; 14 June 1771.

CHAPTER VIII

THE RESULTS OF LEGISLATIVE REVIEW

THE English experiment of endowing over-sea dominions with a power to make laws which should be as nearly as possible conformable to those of the mother country, committed the home government to a second venture,— that of reviewing and checking the enactments of the colonial legislatures. We have seen how the necessity of such a supervision came gradually to be realized in England; and how, piece by piece, the administrative machinery for its accomplishment was assembled. We have seen that in the exercise of this power the government aimed to further the economic interests of the Empire as a whole, to enforce a rather close conformity both to the spirit and the letter of English law, to preserve the supremacy of the crown in the dominions, and to protect the colonists from the consequences of their own legislative indiscretions. These conclusions naturally provoke inquiry as to how far the government succeeded in the accomplishment of its ends, as to the approximate causes of such success or failure, and furthermore, as to whether the system of review was in its operation such a hardship upon the colonists as to constitute a just grievance against the mother country.

In its review of legislation the government found much with which to contend. The great distance of the colonies from England, the slowness and uncertainty of communication, the ignorance, indifference and procrastination of many local officials, all militated against success. An obstacle even more formidable was the particularist temper of the colonists, a people always jealous of precedent and ever suspicious of the slightest infringement upon their alleged rights. Nevertheless, the government by its control over the colonial legislatures did achieve the main objects of its desire. In such policies as the crown chose to maintain consistently and without compromise the colonies learned to acquiesce; for against a disallowance, followed by an instruction to the governor forbidding his assent to any future act of like purpose, the popular party, as a rule, could make little or no headway.

In this manner the assemblies were restrained from placing imposts upon goods of English manufacture, from regulating the value of foreign coins, and from encouraging the establishment of manufactures which would compete with those of Great Britain. For the most part, they were prevented from enacting provisions unduly favorable to the local inhabitants; although exemptions from dues upon shipping were sometimes inserted in necessary supply acts. In its efforts to restrict the issue of paper currency the crown was less uniformly successful. The government would fain have forbidden its use altogether. But the dearth of any proper medium of exchange in the colonies rendered some concession to local sentiment unavoidable. Nor could bills once issued be summarily recalled or declared void without injury both to private holders and to trade. Until the last intercolonial war the government succeeded fairly well in limiting amounts outstanding, in obtaining adequate provisions for refunding and in preventing the bills from being made legal tender. The urgent necessity for obtaining supplies for the war, however, caused a relaxation of instructions, and an increased volume of currency, especially in New York, New Jersey and Pennsylvania.[1]

In the larger sense the government succeeded in keeping the colonial laws in conformity with those of England. Differences in minor technicalities were common, and not all of them were excusable because of local conditions or long-established usage. But by reason of many annulments the colonists learned to respect the personal rights and private property of individuals, and to abide by the forms and larger precedents of English law. When the Board of Trade began its work at the close of the seventeenth century the acts of every colony were ill-kept, loosely worded, and burdened by contradictory amendments. The Puritan colonies in basing their legislation upon the Mosaic code had enacted many absurd prohibitions and excessive penalties. Left to their own initiative, no doubt the colonists, with the gradual development of a trained bench and bar, would have remedied these defects. But the marked improvement in the technic of law-making displayed during the early part of the eighteenth century by all the colonies whose acts were subject to review at home, was due primarily to persistent tutelage from the Board of Trade and the law officers. Their guidance constituted the most potent factor in the gradual moulding of a colonial jurisprudence similar in broad lines and essential features to that of England.

In attempting to defend the prerogative from legislative encroachment the government was less successful. The assemblies learned to acquiesce in the proper forms of loyalty, to make no grants save to the king, and to

[1] Hardy to the Bd, *CO/5*-1067, D, 30; 23 February 1756. *A. P. C.*, vol. iv, p. 346; 8 July 1757. *A. P. C.*, vol. iv, pp. 362, 372; 1 April 1758. *A. P. C.*, vol. iv, p. 341.

forbear from interfering with the property of the crown. But the popular support accorded the lower houses, together with their control over supplies, frequently enabled them to override the king's governors in matters which were properly within the latter's sole discretion or had originally been placed there.

An effective review of legislation in England was often hampered by irregularities upon the part of colonial legislatures and officials. Failures of the governors to transmit promptly acts and other official papers was a constant source of inconvenience and annoyance. The Board complained in 1754 that they had received no word from New Hampshire for two and a half years; and in 1742 that during almost a decade only six acts had been submitted from New Jersey.[1] Despite the renewal of instructions reminding the governors of their duty in this respect, complaints regarding the ill effects of legislation frequently reached the Board in advance of the acts to which they had reference.[2] In many cases delay in transmission was caused by irregular and uncertain communication between the colonies and the mother country. This was especially true of the more isolated colonies like New Hampshire and the Carolinas, although Governor Fauquier of Virginia excuses himself by the fact that "no ships for London went out of these ports for a long

---

[1] Board to Wentworth, *CO*/5-941, p. 354; 5 July, 1754. Board to Morris, *CO*/5-997, p. 25; 3 August, 1742.

[2] Hillsborough to the Gov. of N. Y., *Col. Docs.*, vol. viii, p. 82; 11 July 1768. John Penn protested to Hillsborough that this fact did not necessarily imply official neglect. For "merchantile people have more frequent opportunities of writing to their correspondents, having a wider knowledge of conveyances from other Provinces. Also they transmit intelligence when it would be improper for Governors to transmit accounts before they are fully ascertained."

time." [1] Far more often, however, tardy submission appears to have been caused by negligence and procrastination upon the part of governors or the colonial secretaries. The latter who were usually ill paid and sometimes incompetent, were apt to slight the transcribing of laws, while the governors sometimes neglected the matter of transmission entirely or left it to subordinate officials. [2] The charter of Pennsylvania allowed that colony five years in which to submit laws to the Privy Council, and there can be no doubt that she sometimes took advantage of this unnecessarily long interval to prolong the operation of acts which she well knew would be disallowed.   In 1718 and again in 1766 there was a delay of over three years between the enactment of laws and their consideration at the Board.[3]

The review of legislation was sometimes hampered also by the inclusion of provisions upon unrelated subjects within the same enactment.   In the majority of cases this also was due to ignorance or carelessness. Maryland, for example, submitted an entire code under a single enacting clause.   In 1695 the committee complained that diverse acts of Massachusetts were "joined together under ye same title, whereby it has been necessary for the repealing of such of them as have not been thought fit to be confirmed to vacate such others as have

---

[1] *CO*/1329, X, 65; 10 April 1759.   Hillsborough urged the Governors to avail themselves of any private ship and not to wait for packets. *N. Y. Col. Docs.,* vol. viii, p. 82.

[2] Board to Dudley, *CO*/5-911, p. 18; 29 April 1703.   *CO*/5-913, p. 504. *CO*/5-869, Y, 38.   *CO*/5-942, p. 260; 10 July 1764.   *CO*/6-907, p. 359. *CO*/5-911, p. 422.   *N. Y. Col. Docs.,* vol. viii, p. 277.   *C. S. P.,* 1677-80, p. 388; Barbadoes.   *C. S. P.,* 1699, p. 165; Antigua.

[3] *Pa. Stats.,* vol. iv, p. 467; 21 April 1739.   *A. P. C.,* vol. ii, p. 614. *CO*/5-1293, p. 160.   *Pa. Sts.,* vol. vi, p. 608; 9 June 1766.   Root, *Relations of Pa. with the Br. Govt.,* pp. 138, 141.

been comprehended under such titles.''[1]   The Privy
Council forbade this practice by a standing instruction
to the governors.   Yet apparently without ill design the
colonies passed many such inclusive laws as that of
Jamaica, "for better regulating slaves and rendering
free negroes and mulattoes more useful, and preventing
hawking and peddling, and enlarging the time for Commissioners collecting outstanding debts;" or that of
South Carolina "in addition to an act preventing the
spread of contagious distempers, and renewing an act for
establishing a market in Charleston."[2]   When, in rare
instances, this expedient was used to circumvent the
Board of Trade, the objectionable provision was usually
inserted as a rider to a supply act.   Thus, in 1760, the
Board complained that a Pennsylvania law issuing bills of
credit included a loan to Col. Hunter with which it had
not the least necessary relation.[3]

The enactment, and sometimes the re-enactment of
objectionable laws of brief duration was another source
of annoyance to the Board of Trade.   This practice, if
unrestricted, would have enabled the colonists to defeat
the object of review altogether.   Accordingly the governors were instructed that all laws save those for a
temporary end should be indefinite and without limitation,
and that no law once enacted should be re-enacted except
upon very urgent occasions, and in no case more than
once without the king's express permission.[4]   It was

[1] *CO*/5-906, p. 205; August 1695.

[2] *A. P. C.*, vol. iii, p. 344.   *A. P. C.*, vol. iv, p. 141.   Both were disallowed upon other grounds.

[3] *Pa. Stats.*, vol. v, p. 715.   *C. S. P.*, 1681-5, p. 316; Jamaica.   *B. T. J.*,
vol. lxix, p. 40; South Carolina.

[4] *B. T. J.*, vol. x, p. 206.   *C. S. P.*, 1696-7, p. 589; 26 August 1697.
Board to Bellomont, *Acts and Resolves*, vol. i, p. 308.

scarcely practical or feasible to make the prohibition of temporary acts absolute. Yet the qualification left a loophole for evasion, in that the governor must decide what constituted a temporary end. The interpretation both of the governors and the Board of Trade was liberal, for many tempo ary laws were enacted in all the colonies and the great majority met with no objection upon that account. Approximately four per cent. of the laws of Pennsylvania, eight per cent. of New York acts and seventeen per cent. of those enacted by Massachusetts expired within two years, and a large part of these had already ceased to have effect when examined by the Board of Trade. They included revenue acts, laws providing for defence, regulating the militia, maintaining highways, establishing fees and bounties, and governing various matters of domestic concern.

Temporary acts which incurred the particular displeasure of the Board were for the most part revenue measures upon which the assembly had grafted some obnoxious provision. A Pennsylvania law of 1710 laid a duty of nine pence per ton upon all ships except those owned by inhabitants of the province.[1] A Massachusetts act of 1718 contained a double impost upon goods imported from Great Britain, together with an exemption in favor of local vessels. This was an annual law, and the Board, presuming its re-enactment, went so far as to recommend that the governor be ordered to declare his majesty's disapprobation of the new act, and to prevent its being put into execution.[2] A Jamaica law which levied an

---

[1] *Pa. Stats.*, vol. i, p. 555; 15 January 1714. This law was of three years duration; but because of delay in submission it had only two months to run when considered at the Board. It was re-enacted with the exception of the tonnage duty and again disallowed, but only after it had expired. Root, *Relations of Pa. with the Br. Govt.*, p. 148.

[2] *Acts and Resolves*, vol. ii, p. 127. *A. P. C.*, vol. ii, p. 760.

annual tax was disallowed because in attempting to regulate the number of white men upon estates, it discriminated against absentee owners.[1]   The clergy of Virginia asserted that some of the laws regulating the payment of their salaries were made temporary to prevent royal consideration.   Yet in view of the unsettled price of tobacco it is difficult to see how they could have been of long duration.[2]   In some comparatively unimportant instances temporary laws other than supply acts were doubtless used to secure objectionable legislation.   But their enactment, except possibly in Pennsylvania, was not an effective means of thwarting the home government.   If the attempted evasion were incorporated in a revenue act, properly of limited duration, there was small chance of its escaping observation and achieving re-enactment.   Moreover, the governors feared to commit such an obvious breach of instructions as the passing of temporary acts for the accomplishment of permanent ends, such as the disposal of private property, the regulation of assemblies or the erection of courts.

A more common and, upon the whole, a more effectual mode of evasion was the re-enactment of laws disallowed. This practice also was forbidden by instructions.   But there was scarcely a colony which did not offend at one time or another.   A Pennsylvania act of 1700 granting a jury to freemen in all cases whatsoever was disallowed because it interfered with the jurisdiction of the admiralty courts, where juries were not permitted.   It was re-enacted with a clause saving the admiralty jurisdiction. Because the crown still feared that the law would be

---

[1] *A. P. C.*, vol. iv, p. 39; 30 June 1748. Another Jamaica revenue law, which the Board found to have expired, laid an additional duty of 40 shillings upon slaves. *A. P. C.*, vol. v, p. 407; 27 February 1775.

[2] *CO*/5-1329, vol. x, p. 57; 23 May 1759.

used to hinder the enforcement of the acts of trade, it was disallowed, only to be again re-enacted and again disallowed.[1] A Pennsylvania law of 1700 which gave a preference to colonial debtors was re-enacted after disallowance, and acts for establishing courts were several times repeated with modifications.[2] Aroused by the fact that acts, tardily submitted in 1718, contained several re-enactments of laws previously vetoed, the Board sent the Pennsylvania charter to West, and inquired whether it did not prohibit the practice. He replied that it contained nothing to forbid the re-enactment in substance of laws disallowed.[3] Inasmuch as the governors of Pennsylvania, unlike those of other colonies submitting their laws to the Privy Council, were subject only to the general instructions regarding the enforcement of the acts of trade, the assembly of Pennsylvania by repeated re-enactments could have nullified the effect of the royal veto. The fact that they did not pursue such a course was due largely, no doubt, to the realization that it would have provoked an annulment of the charter.

Bermuda offended the Board by enacting a four per cent impost on goods after the Crown had disallowed a similar law levying five per cent.[4] New Jersey twice re-enacted under different titles laws reducing the fees of the secretary's office, and North Carolina repeated an ill-advised attempt to facilitate the proving of wills.[5] By re-

[1] *Pa. Stats.,* vol. ii, pp. 18, 359, 451, 467, 543, 550. *Pa. Stats.,* vol. iii, pp. 31, 439, 463. Root, *op. cit.,* p. 147.

[2] *Stats.,* vol. ii, pp. 63, 364, 494, 550. Root, *op. cit.,* pp. 147, 159-174.

[3] *B. T. J.,* vol. xxviii, p. 167. Chalmers, *Opinions,* p. 336; 24 March 1719. *CO/5-1265, O,* 171.

[4] *A. P. C.,* vol. iii, p. 70; 4 July 1724. The second act was the more offensive in that it reduced the amount to 2% for inhabitants of Bermuda.

[5] *CO/5-972, E,* 56. *A. P. C.,* vol. iii, p. 343; New Jersey, 25 November

enactment the colonists could secure the operation of a
law between the time of its passage and the arrival of
an order of disallowance in the colony. But there was
little chance of eluding the vigilance of the law officers
and the Board of Trade, even though the objectionable
provisions were disguised in form and title. Usually the
assemblies made concessions, sometimes insufficient, it is
true, towards eliminating objections made to the former
act, and in many cases these were so effectually remedied
that the second law passed the Board without objection.[1]

In some instances a disallowance was rendered of no
effect by the failure of an order in council to reach the
province, or by the neglect of colonial officials to enter
it upon the law books. In this manner a provision in a
Virginia revenue law, disallowed in 1680, continued in
force until the fact was brought to the attention of the
Board in 1707.[2] The repeal of a Massachusetts act
" Establishing the Township of Danvers " was never
observed in the colony, and a law of New Hampshire
regarding the care of idiots, which was disallowed in
1718, remained in force until it was re-enacted and again
annulled fifty years later.[3] In 1761 Lieutenant Governor
Colden wrote to the Board—" I am told that several acts
in Basket's edition of the acts of New York in 1718 are

1731. CO/5-973, F, 3. A. P. C., vol. iii, p. 454; 9 January 1735.
CO/5-325, C, 189. A. P. C., vol. iv, pp. 502, 503; 14 December 1761.

[1] For example, an act of New Hampshire "Restraining Excessive
Usury," CO/5-943, p. 16; 20 July 1770. Such laws were supposed to
contain a suspending clause, but this requirement was not always
complied with.

[2] B. T. J., vol. xix, p. 399. In like manner the Board sent a second
order in council repealing a Virginia law " Granting, Seating and
Planting Lands " in 1710. CO/5-1263, p. 219.

[3] CO/5-915, pp. 163, 172; 27 August 1718. A. P. C., vol. v, p. 189;
26 May 1769.

noted to be repealed, of which not the least evidence appears anywhere in the Province. . . . I make no doubt the judges continue to proceed upon them as of force.[1]

Experience in reviewing colonial legislation convinced the English officials at an early date that some check upon the assemblies' power of initiative was an absolute necessity. Without it the colonists could enact what manner of laws they pleased, and after disallowance they could defy the royal authority by re-enacting them again. Following an ill-considered and unsuccessful attempt to compel the submission of proposed legislation to the Privy Council prior to its enactment, the government placed an increasing reliance upon instructions which limited the governors' discretion in giving assent to acts of the assemblies. The strictness with which they were observed varies somewhat in different colonies, and from time to time in the same colony, according to the temper of the assembly, or the popularity and political sagacity of the governor. But upon the whole they imparted a necessary continuity to the enforcement of the government's policies, and constituted a fairly effective means of controlling legislation. The prohibitions most emphasized,—those regulating matters of trade, shipping and finance,—were well obeyed, with the exception of restraints upon the issue of paper currency. Mandatory instructions that governors should use their utmost endeavor in securing the amendment or the enactment of legislation were binding upon the governors, but not upon the assemblies; and the latter frequently neglected or refused to comply with the government's requests.[2]

[1] *N. Y. Col. Docs.*, vol. vii, pp. 454-455. Dickerson, *op. cit.*, p. 272.

[2] *CO/5-362*, D, 18; 1731. *B. T. J.*, vol. lxx, p. 360; 1763. And many others.

Least effectual were the several instructions which forbade governors to pass laws without the insertion of a suspending clause. Massachusetts and Pennsylvania consistently refused to make use of this expedient inasmuch as their charters provided that laws should operate from the time of their enactment.[1] Because of the expense and long delay involved in securing a decision from the crown the assemblies consented to suspending clauses only with the greatest reluctance. By repeated disallowances the government schooled most of the royal colonies to their insertion in private laws. But in spite of repeated complaints from the Board of Trade the instruction which required the suspension of acts repealing former acts, whether the law repealed had received royal confirmation or not, was violated repeatedly.[2]

Another instruction which received at best a perfunctory compliance was that requiring the insertion of a suspending clause in laws " of an unusual or extraordi-

[1] Upon several laws, however, the governor of Massachusetts secured a previous permission to give consent and another he so worded that it would have no effect until His Majesty's pleasure could be known,— an expedient which was practically equivalent to the insertion of a suspending clause. Hutchinson to the Board, *CO*/5-894, p. 365; 8 May 1772, "Incorporating the Overseers of the Poor of Boston." Permission was obtained for a bankruptcy act, *CO*/5-919, p. 61; 12 March 1760, a lottery for Harvard College, *CO*/5-891, p. 535; 15 July 1765, and for the repeal of a bounty for killing crows. In the latter case the Board stated that it would have been better pleased had the assembly passed the bill with a suspending clause. *CC*/5-918, p. 129; 9 August 1744.

[2] *A. P. C.*, vol. iv, pp. 131-141, a report upon sixty-seven Virginia laws. The Assemblies of Massachusetts and Virginia complained of the injustice of this prohibition, and asked that it be modified. Parliament, they pointed out, was free to repeal laws of its own making whenever they proved inexpedient. The Board replied that the instruction was " founded on such good and solid reason " that they could not advise any alteration therein. *CO*/5-875, p. 306; 12 January 1733. *A. P. C.*, vol. iv, p. 174; 20 December 1752.

nary nature, wherein His Majesty's prerogative or the property of his subjects might be prejudiced." This vague phraseology enabled governors when pressed by the assemblies to give questionable legislation the benefit of a supposedly honest doubt. The Board, upon the other hand, found no difficulty in applying it to almost any legislative indiscretion which failed to fall under some other head.

In a few instances the colonists ventured to put laws into immediate operation, notwithstanding the fact that they contained a suspending clause. In this manner the assembly of New Jersey disregarded the protests of the governor, and ordered an act for regulating fees printed " as a rule for the government of the people." Georgia also inserted a suspending clause and then issued bills of credit without waiting to learn the royal pleasure.[1]

In many cases the governor's failure to obey instructions was due to a necessity of obtaining supplies from a recalcitrant assembly. This was particularly true of acts authorizing bills of credit, although the assemblies used their control of appropriations to good effect in securing laws for other purposes as well. The assembly of Jamaica, for example, forced the governor to pass a law limiting the duration of future assemblies, by holding back an annual supply bill.[2] Again, the governors failed because of carelessness, or because of inability to grasp the imperial idea and the necessary implications thereof, or because they feared to incur unpopularity by resisting public sentiment.

[1] Morris to the Board, *CO/5-974*, F, 57; 3 March 1744. *A. P. C.*, vol. iv, p. 9; 28 June 1749. Ellis to the Board, *CO/5-673*, p. 264; 21 April 1758. A similar complaint was made against a Virginia act regarding the export of hides. *CO/5-1331*, Z, 88; 29 October 1766.

[2] *A. P. C.*, vol. iv, p. 91; 30 June 1752.

In addition to the neglect and evasion of colonial officials, the government's review of legislation suffered in effectiveness both from the nature of the machinery evolved for the task in England and from the laxity which frequently pervaded the colonial administration there. The work could have been accomplished in a comparatively simple and expeditious fashion had the Privy Council delegated its discretion in regard to legislation to a small body of colonial experts, at least one of whom was competent to decide questions of law. Instead there was built up, precedent upon precedent, a system under which the Council followed the recommendations of a committee of its own members, who in turn relied upon reports from a board acting largely upon the advice of other officials. This procedure, involving as it did a series of references from board to board, was at best cumbersome and dilatory. Moreover, there was no particular person charged with the oversight of laws during their entire course from one office to another. Consequently, unless the colonial agents or the merchants, or other parties having interest, visited the various officials and speeded their progress, acts were liable to be delayed for years. In July, 1697, the secretary of the Board informed that body that in getting ready acts to be sent to the attorney and solicitor, he found it necessary to look many years backwards for those that had lain in the plantation office without any report upon them.[1] Several Massachusetts laws sent to the attorney and solicitor in September, 1696, became misplaced and were not found until May, 1698.[2] Indeed, the failure of the attorney and solicitor to render desired

---

[1] *B. T. J.*, vol. x, p. 156.
[2] *Acts and Resolves*, vol. i, p. 231.

reports was a subject of repeated remonstrance at the Board of Trade. The king's counsel, as a rule, was reasonably prompt. But in numerous instances laws returned with his report either were entirely neglected at the Board or remained long without consideration. Eighteen acts of Massachusetts, passed in 1715–16, were referred to the counsel in 1724. He reported in 1725, but the greater part of these laws were not considered at the Board until November, 1735, long after they had been confirmed by lapse of time. In 1739 twenty-six acts of Pennsylvania, passed prior to 1734, were found by the agent "after tedious researches, . . . laid up in a by-corner by the Board of Trade and covered very thick with dust."[1] A Virginia bill for "Settling the Titles and Bounds of Lands" remained in the office of the auditor-general for seven years before the agent secured its return to the Board.[2] Such cases, although numerous, constitute the exception and not the rule.[3] They merely serve to demonstrate that a cumbersome procedure, together with a lax and easy-going administration, permitted much needless uncertainty and delay in the consideration of legislation.

[1] *Pa. Stats.*, vol. iii, p. 493. Cited from the *Penn Papers* in the collection of the Hist. Soc. of Pa.

[2] *CO/5-1367*, p. 321; 2 December 1757. *CO/5-1329*, X, 28.

[3] Laws which the Board of Trade recommended for disallowance sometimes remained unrepealed because the committee of the Council neglected to take action upon them. But almost invariably the committee either found reason for allowing the law to remain in force, or for re-referring the matter to the Board, which failed to render a second report. An act of New Jersey, passed in 1747 for settling its New York boundary, was re-referred by the committee and reconsidered without definite action in February, 1758. A quit rent law of South Carolina was recommended for disallowance in November 1732, and although the committee set a time for a hearing, it took no further action in the matter. The act, or a substitute, however, was con-

The process of review, complex and dilatory as it was, certainly afforded the colonists ample opportunity for presenting their case. Both the Board of Trade and the committee of the Council were essentially fair in their attitude toward colonial affairs, willing to take advice and anxious to gather all available information before pronouncing judgment. The Board was, and repeatedly acknowledged itself to be, hampered by ignorance of the real motives behind the enactment of laws. Indeed, it frequently confessed inability to decide matters at issue with the knowledge of colonial conditions at its disposal and postponed action until the governor could be heard from, or until merchants, former colonial officials or the agents of neighboring colonies could be consulted. It repeatedly urged the governors to give full and explicit reasons for the enactment of legislation. Upon laws involving a disposal of private property it postponed decision for months,—and in some cases for years, in order that any person aggrieved might seek redress. Moreover, those failing to secure a hearing at the Board or dissatisfied with its report, could obtain a judicial review of its findings from the committee of the Council.

Without doubt, however, the negotiations and hearings requisite for securing the repeal or confirmation of legislation involved considerable expense to the colonists.

sidered at the Board in 1739. Three laws of New Hampshire, for establishing parishes and townships were condemned by the Board in 1752, but nothing came of it because the governor wrote that the assembly had yielded the principal points in dispute. *CO*/5-941, p. 364; 6 August 1755. The committee may have failed to take any notice of a Massachusetts law passed in 1735 for preventing the circulation of paper money issued by private parties in New Hampshire. *Acts and Resolves*, vol. i, p. 147, ch. xxi. Dickerson, *op. cit.*, pp. 270-271. In 1709 the Board warned the Privy Council that it must shortly declare the royal pleasure upon the Pennsylvania laws passed in 1705, or they would be confirmed by lapse of time. *B. T. J.*, vol. xxi, p. 232.

Fees must be paid to secretaries and under officials, and in case of formal hearings, counsels and solicitors must be retained. The distribution of fees was especially necessary for securing the progress of laws containing a suspending clause,—a fact which goes far to explain the continued reluctance displayed by the assemblies in consenting to their use. Moreover the expense of private acts, in which the insertion of a suspending clause was obligatory, fell not upon the colonies, but upon individuals interested in securing their confirmation. Consequently such acts sometimes lay by for years, or failed in their object altogether because no person appeared to secure their reference to the law office or consideration at the Board.

In numerous instances the Board, in urging upon the colonies the necessity of maintaining accredited agents in England, frankly stated that fees must be paid to secure the confirmation of private acts.[1] Other sources show that a judicious use of money frequently hastened favorable action upon public laws as well. In 1732 the agent of Rhode Island warned his constituents that the passage by Parliament of a pending bill obliging the colony to submit its laws to the Privy Council would entail a great expenditure of money yearly "at the Council Office, and the Board of Trade to get the acts through here, in fees for Petitions, Reports, References and Royal Orders, besides the tedi-

---

[1] Board to Hunter, *CO/5-1123*, p. 441; 16 April 1716: "Several New Jersey acts, particularly private ones, * require to be sent to the Attorney and Solicitor General for opinion before the Board can present them to His Majesty. But as there is no Agent here * enabled to disburse what may be necessary from time to time, those acts will lye by forever in their hands." Also *CO/5-915*, p. 20. Board to Blakiston, *CO/5-726*, p. 99.

ous delays that may happen."[1]   Penn asked the government of Pennsylvania for "fifty guineas, if not one hundred, to get a favorable report" upon a large collection of laws, and later he wrote that the report of the Attorney-General was held up for want of a large fee to him.[2]   Bellomont wrote the Board in 1698 that twenty-eight merchants of New York had contributed one hundred pounds for use in obtaining the royal approval of an indemnity bill.   Later he reported that on the third reading of a bill at the council a member declared there would be forty thousand pounds available "to stop the King's approbation in England."   This Bellomont considered "so abominable a reflection on the Government of England, but so common a one here," that he ventured to suggest that their lordships should "put all imaginable discountenance upon it."[3]   The ministry and vestry of St. Paul's, Philadelphia, represented to the Board that an assembly of Quakers there had made a law, and raised money "on us as well as themselves, part [of which] goes towards interest to get ye said Law approved."[4]   In 1723 Governor Nicholson of South Carolina wrote the Board that by common report there, those dissatisfied with his majesty's government had raised twenty-five hundred pounds current money to secure the confirmation of a paper money act.[5]   The fee system pervaded all branches of English administration

---

[1] Kimball, *Correspondence of the Govs. of R. I.*, vol. i, pp. 55-6, Cited by Root, p. 133.

[2] Penn-Logan, Corresp., vol. i, pp. 297, 342. *Pa. Col. Recs.*, vol. ii, p. 193, Cited by Root, p. 133.

[3] *CO/5-1041*, p. 260; 27 October 1698. *CO/5-1042*, p. 207; 15 May 1699.

[4] *CO/5-1263*, O, 77; 25 March 1706.

[5] *CO/5-359*, B, 30; 12 November 1723.

and it could hardly be expected that colonial affairs would be favored by special exemption. But it is safe to say that the expense involved irritated the colonists and contributed materially to their dislike for the English control over legislation.[1]

Of 8,563 acts submitted by the continental colonies, 469 or 5.5 per cent. were disallowed by orders in council. By colonies the percentages of laws disallowed are: New Hampshire, 7.2 per cent.; Massachusetts, 2.8 per cent.; New York, 3.4 per cent.; New Jersey, 4.5 per cent.; Pennsylvania, 15.5 per cent.; Virginia, 4.3 per cent.; North Carolina, 8.8 per cent.; South Carolina, 4.9 per cent., and Georgia, 9.4 per cent.[2] Letters from the governors and occasional protests from the assemblies reveal the existence of restiveness and resentment resulting from the loss of popular acts. Governor Dudley speaks of a "riot of about twenty young persons in Hampton," New Hampshire, which was occasioned by the disallowance of two laws regarding land grants.[3] St.

---

[1] Chalmers, *Opinions*, states, on p. 8, that "the Law Officers were each allowed a standing fee of 100 guineas, with 10 guineas to each of the Clerks." This statement, of course, applied to the attorney and solicitor, not to the king's counsel. Even by the former such fees could hardly have been obtained except upon large collections of laws.

[2] This count begins with the New Hampshire laws enacted in 1699, with those passed by Massachusetts in 1692, under the new charter, those of New York enacted in 1691, of New Jersey in 1703, of Virginia in 1676, of North Carolina in 1734, of South Carolina in 1721, and of Georgia in 1755. Because of confusion and frequent re-enactments it does not include laws passed in Pennsylvania prior to 1700. Neither does it include the laws submitted by Maryland between 1691 and 1715, while it was a royal province. The result was obtained by checking laws enacted and noted as repealed in various editions of colonial laws, against those mentioned in the Board of Trade papers as submitted and annulled in England. Numerous discrepancies preclude perfect exactitude, and the figures are only approximately correct.

[3] *CO*/5-911, p. 434; 10 October 1704.

John, a surveyor, was imprisoned by the assembly of South Carolina, the Board found reason to believe, solely because of the part he had taken in securing the repeal of a quit rent bill.[1]   In Pennsylvania much confusion resulted from the repeated annulment, for reasons which seem scarcely adequate, of laws establishing courts.   The disallowance of a Massachusetts bankruptcy law which left numerous insolvents without relief for some years, and the repeal of a scheme for establishing a land bank in the same colony, appear to have caused considerable inconvenience and suffering.   Because of the Board's forbearance there were, however, very few cases in which disallowance brought loss of property to individuals. Rather than inflict undeserved hardship upon taxpayers, subscribers to lotteries, or holders of paper currency, the Board left many objectionable acts in force and contented itself by instructing the governors to procure their amendment or repeal from the assembly.

In addition to injury entailed by actual disallowance, the colonists suffered from the uncertainty and delay involved in the submission of legislation to the Privy Council.   The average time between the enactment of four hundred and thirty-seven laws and their repeal in England was approximately three years and five months. Of these, ten per cent. were disallowed during the first year after their enactment, thirty-one per cent. during the second year, twelve per cent. during the third year, and twelve per cent. during the fourth year, while thirty-five per cent. had been in force more than four years.[2]

---

[1] *CO*/5-401, p. 63; 7 June 1733.

[2] From one to three additional months were required for the orders in council to reach the colony. These laws include nearly all of those repealed from N. H., Mass., N. Y., N. J., Pa., Va., N. Car., S. Car., and Ga. The fact that a few were disallowed many years after enactment

An act of Virginia, which forbade the importation of tobacco from North Carolina was suddenly disallowed in 1731, twenty-six years after its enactment; while a South Carolina law for " Easing Port Charges " was repealed in 1755 after having been in force seventeen years.[1] Governors sometimes, though rarely, complained that they had not been informed of the reasons for disallowance and were consequently at a loss how to proceed when the law was re-enacted by the assembly.[2]

A more common cause of vexatious uncertainty lay in the government's failure to act upon laws containing a suspending clause. New Hampshire submitted a triennial law in 1724, the enforcement of which was suspended until 1731. Failing to obtain either its rejection or confirmation, a second law was passed in 1728, which escaped notice and remained in force until 1752.[3] The assembly of Georgia sought to justify an issue of paper currency under an act containing a suspending clause because of urgent necessity, and the fact that the colony had been in doubt of the law's fate for nearly three years.[4] In 1764 the Virginia assembly refused to pass a suspended law to " Preserve the Breed of Cattle " from a prevailing distemper, upon the ground that the damage would be done before his majesty's pleasure could be known. Fourteen months later the Board gave the gov-

and that others, especially those of Pennsylvania, were sometimes delayed in transmission, renders such an average unsatisfactory as a basis for criticism of the government.

[1] *A. P. C.*, vol. iii, p. 345.

[2] Montgomerie to the Board, *CO*/5-1054, Dd, 83; 30 November 1728. Johnson to Board, *B. T. J.*, vol. xlvii, p. 1, pt. ii. *B. T. J.*, vol. xlix, p. 92; 12 August 1741.

[3] *CO*/5-870, Z, 42, Z, 59. *CO*/5-941, p. 279; 9 July 1752. *CO*/5-926, B, 37.

[4] Ellis to the Board, *CO*/5-676, C, 63; 24 April 1759.

ernor permission to assent, if the necessity for it still existed, complimenting him at the same time upon his firm and proper regard for his majesty's instructions.[1] The fact that the colonists could have obtained reasonably prompt action upon suspended laws, had they always maintained capable agents in England and kept them well supplied with money, did not lessen a sense of irritation and unjust restraint. Perhaps no grievance stated in the Declaration of Independence had greater basis of fact than the assertion that the king had "forbidden his governors to pass Laws of immediate and pressing importance, unless suspended in their operation till his assent should be obtained; and when so suspended he has utterly neglected to attend to them."

The colonists sought half-consciously to possess a field of legislation removed from imperial concerns, within which they might pass laws with a minimum of interference from the British government. The Board of Trade appears to have recognized both the existence and the justice of this desire, and to have been somewhat more lenient towards laws purely of domestic import. Despite defective wording or doubtful expediency many acts were left in force because they related "only to the private economy of the Province" or were "merely of local operation," having reference "to points of internal police and economy."[2] In refusing a request from several Massachusetts towns for the disallowance of an unpopular excise law, the Board stated that "upon the whole the mode of Levying Taxes is a matter of Provincial Oeconomy, of which the Representatives of the People are the

---

[1] *CO*/5-1330, p. 31. *CO*/5-1369, p. 255; 15 February 1765.

[2] *A. P. C.*, vol. iv, p. 104. *A. P. C.*, vol. iv, p. 97. *Pa. Stats.*, vol vii, p. 769.

Competent Judges."[1]   But the forbearance of the government in this respect amounted in truth to little.   As a principle of exemption it was never formulated in general terms.   The requirements that laws be conformable to those of England, and not injurious to the prerogative of the crown, caused the repeal of acts upon all subjects; while the mere fact that they promised to result in injury to the colonists themselves proved fatal to many laws which were purely local in scope.   It was, for example, scarcely a matter of imperial concern that the assembly of Pennsylvania chose to prohibit "stage plays,"[2] that the lawmakers of West Florida made too generous a provision for their own salaries,[3] or that Virginia should repeal without a suspending clause an act which impowered the justices of Norfolk County to establish certain ferries.[4]   It was doubtless for the best interests of Bruton Parish in Virginia that the vestry should be restrained from lending the proceeds of glebe lands upon personal security.[5]   But, upon the whole, the colonists would certainly have preferred a greater freedom to suffer the results of their own mistakes without interference from the English government.

More important than annoying delays and needless interference in domestic affairs was a realm of conflicting interests wherein the natural efforts of the colonies toward economic and political self-development were sacrificed to the dictates of imperial policy.   The charge of the Declaration that the king had "refused his Assent to Laws, the most wholesome and necessary for the pub-

---

[1] *A. P. C.*, vol. iv, p. 295 ; 12 August 1755.   *CO*/5-918, p. 312.

[2] *Stats.*, vol. v, p. 721 ; 24 July, 1760.

[3] *A. P. C.*, vol. v, p. 158; 12 August 1758.

[4] *A. P. C.*, vol. v, p. 164; 12 August 1768.

[5] *A. P. C.*, vol. iv, p. 684; 20 July 1764.

lic good," might well refer to the repeated disallowance
of acts laying prohibitory duties upon the importation of
slaves or the transportation of convicted felons.   The
government did in fact "obstruct laws for the naturalization of foreigners," and with less truth "refuse to pass
others to encourage their migration thither."[1]   It restrained the colonies, not altogether unwisely, it is true,
in their efforts to provide a necessary medium of commercial exchange and to lighten the burdens of debtors.
Its control over legislation acted as a strong, if not an
entirely effective, curb upon the growing power and
influence of the popular branch of the colonial legislatures.   By means of it the government, in defence of the
prerogative, interfered to prevent further increase in the
membership of the assemblies, and to curtail their power
to repeal or amend laws of their own making.   It prevented the assemblies from exercising what they assumed
to be their rightful privilege—a control over appropriations equal to that enjoyed by the Commons in England.
And it defeated a popular desire for local courts of
record whose judges should hold office, as in England,
for good behavior rather than at the pleasure of the
crown.   If we grant the government's premise that the
economic development of the colonies was necessarily
subordinate to the maintenance of a balance of trade in
favor of England, and to the advancement of the commercial interests of a self-sustaining empire; and that
political innovations must in no way impair the power
or prestige of the crown, there is little of which to com-
plain in the policy pursued by the government toward
colonial legislation.   But the colonists, although they

[1] Georgia law for "Encouraging Settlers," *A. P. C.*, vol. v, p. 112;
26 August 1767.

long acquiesced in a rather liberal application of these precepts, never consciously subscribed to them; and ill-considered attempts to secure their enforcement contributed largely to the final breach between the colonies and the mother country.

Strictly speaking, the disallowance of colonial legislation by the Privy Council was not a repeal, because the assemblies took no part in the process of declaring laws invalid. Nor was it a veto, because legislation became effective from the time of its enactment, and acts performed in accordance with its provisions prior to annulment by order in council remained valid. The power of review exercised by the Privy Council was analogous rather to that assumed by the Supreme Court of the United States after the formation of the new government. The Privy Council, it is true, declared acts void upon grounds other than the contravention of a fundamental law; but it frequently did disallow laws because they conflicted with the colonial charters, or with acts of the British Parliament or the common law of England.[1] Under its tutelage the colonists became accustomed to a limitation upon the power of their legislatures. In this sense the work of the Privy Council constituted at once a precedent and a preparation for the power of judicial annulment upon constitutional grounds now exercised by the state and federal courts in the United States.

---

[1] The act of Parliament passed in 1696 for "preventing frauds, and regulating abuses in the plantation trade," asserted the nullity of any colonial law or usage which should be repugnant to acts of Parliament referring to the colonies. *Statutes at Large*, 7 and 8 William III, ch. xxii.

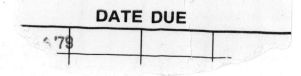